A QUESTION OF COLOUR

MY JOURNEY TO BELONGING

A QUESTION OF COLOUR

MY JOURNEY TO BELONGING

PATRICIA LEES WITH ADAM C LEES

This is a Magabala Book
LEADING PUBLISHER OF ABORIGINAL AND
TORRES STRAIT ISLANDER STORYTELLERS.
CHANGING THE WORLD, ONE STORY AT A TIME.

First published 2020, reprinted 2021
Magabala Books Aboriginal Corporation
1 Bagot Street, Broome, Western Australia
Website: www.magabala.com
Email: sales@magabala.com

Magabala Books receives financial assistance from the Commonwealth Government through the Australia Council, its arts advisory body. The State of Western Australia has made an investment in this project through the Department of Local Government, Sport and Cultural Industries. Magabala Books would like to acknowledge the generous support of the Shire of Broome, Western Australia.

Magabala Books is Australia's only independent Aboriginal and Torres Strait Islander publishing house. Magabala Books acknowledges the Traditional Owners of the Country on which we live and work, the Yawuru people of Broome. We recognise the unbroken connection to traditional lands, waters and cultures. Through what we publish, we honour all our Elders and our stories, past, present and future.

Cover Design Jo Hunt
Typeset by Post Pre-press Group
Printed and bound by Griffin Press, South Australia

ISBN (Print) 978-1-925936-51-3
ISBN (ePUB) 978-1-925936-53-7
ISBN (ePDF) 978-1-925936-52-0

A catalogue record for this book is available from the National Library of Australia

PATRICIA (PATTIE) LEES AM (née Janke) was born in Cairns, North Queensland, but has been a resident of Mount Isa since 1976. Removed from her family at an early age, Pattie was sent initially to an orphanage in Townsville in 1958, before being sent to Palm Island as a Ward of the State under the *State Children Act (1911)*; she was also subject to the *Aboriginals Preservation and Protection Act (1939)* and the *Aborigines and Torres Strait Islander's Affairs Act (1965).* At the age of nineteen, she joined the Women's Royal Australian Navy and served for two years at a number of naval land bases around Australia. She represented Australia as a delegate at several United Nations development forums in New York and Geneva, including the United Nations (UN) Commission of Human Rights (Draft Declaration on the Rights of Indigenous Peoples). She is currently CEO of an Aboriginal and Torres Strait Islander Corporation for Children and Youth Services. Married to husband Terry for 51 years, Pattie is the mother of four children, grandmother to twelve and a great-grandmother.

ADAM C LEES, Pattie's eldest son, has worked in the mining, energy and resources sector as a community relations and sustainability professional since 2000. He is currently a Senior Manager for Woodside based in Perth. Adam commenced his career as a graduate with the Department of Foreign Affairs & Trade (DFAT) in 1994; he was posted to Apia, Samoa, as Third Secretary from 1996–1999. Adam has most recently lived and worked in Angola, Zambia, Gabon, Ethiopia and Tanzania, in addition to supporting exploration projects in Guinea and Liberia for BHP. Raised in Mount Isa, Adam holds tertiary qualifications from Monash University (Melbourne), the Queensland University of Technology and Griffith University (Brisbane). His wanderlust and passion for photography have taken him off the beaten track to more than 65 countries.

In loving memory of my brother Michael (Jumbo)

For Mum and my siblings John, Terry, Johanne and Elin

*For my children, grandchildren, great-grandchildren,
nieces, nephews and future generations*

For Anna Shnukal; thank you for sharing your time and knowledge

CONTENTS

MAPS

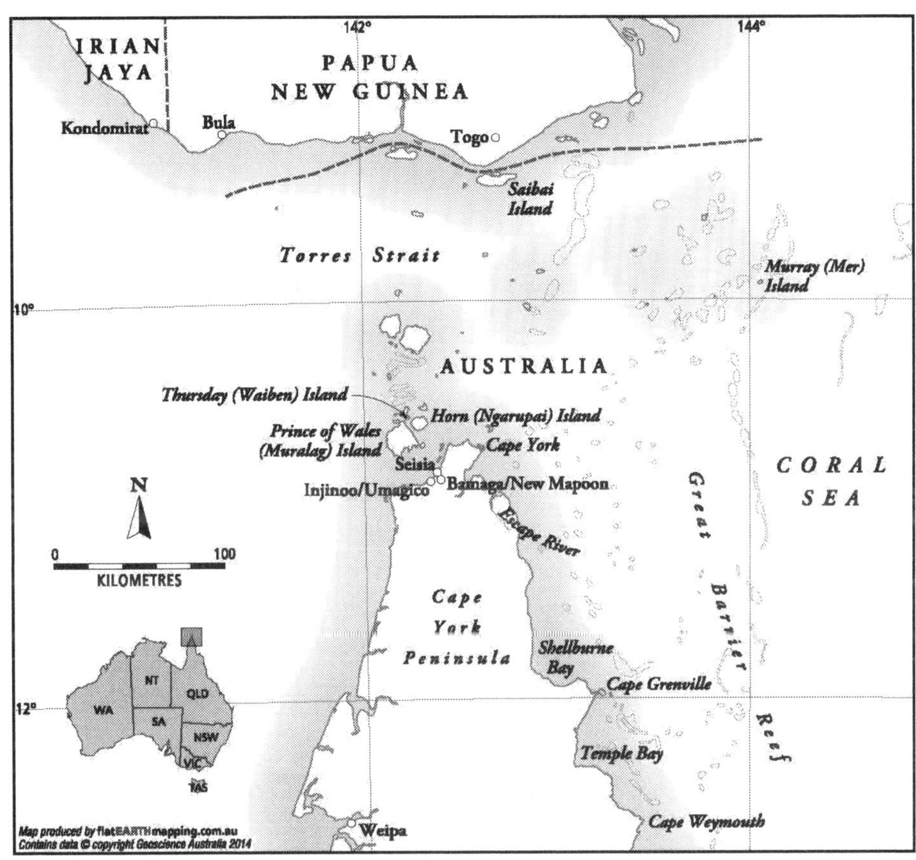

Map of the Torres Strait Islands, including Murray Island (Mer) & Thursday Island (Waiben)

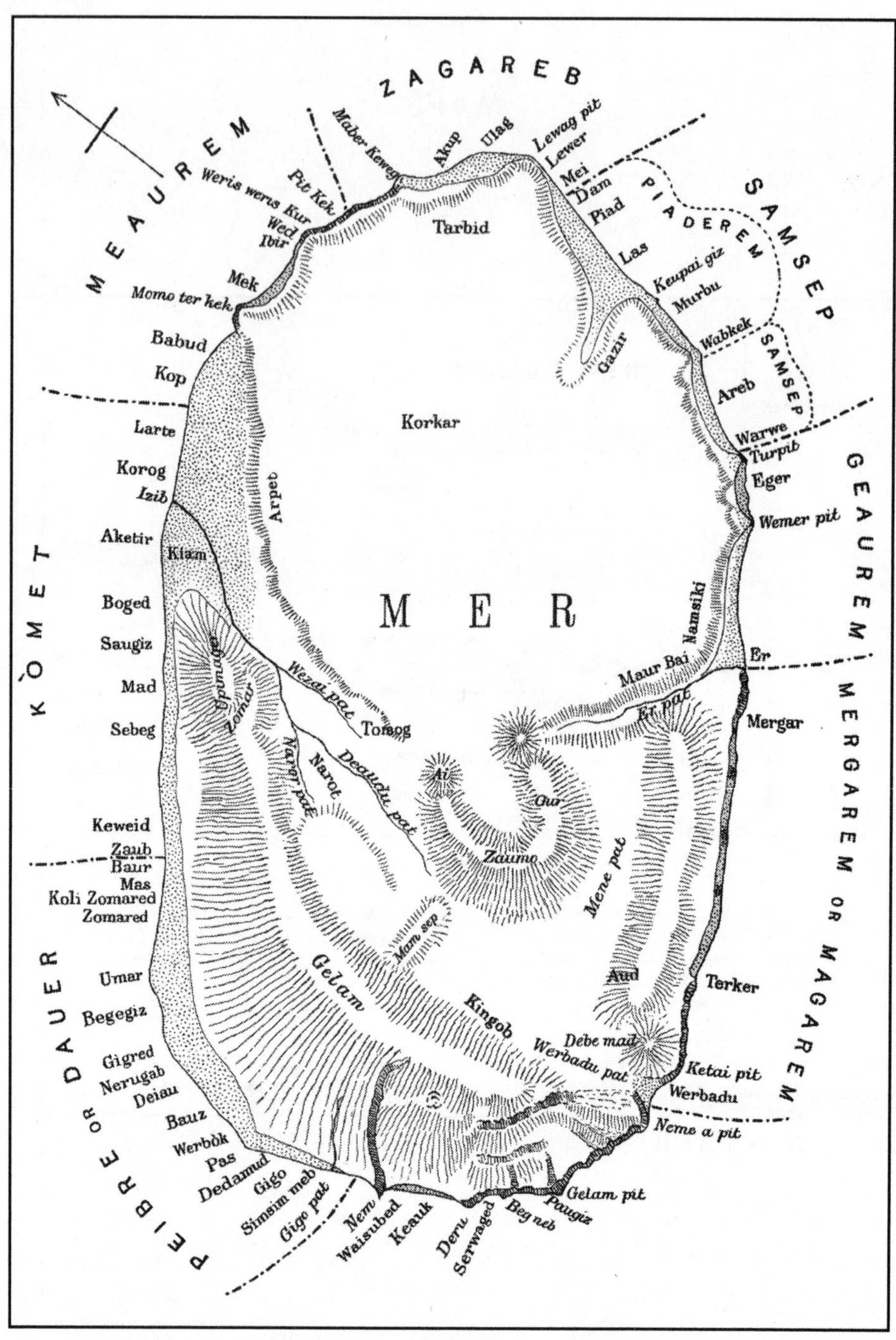

Map of Murray Island: AC Haddon's Reports Vol. VI (1908:170) from the 1898 *The Recordings of the Cambridge Anthropological Expedition to Torres Straits*

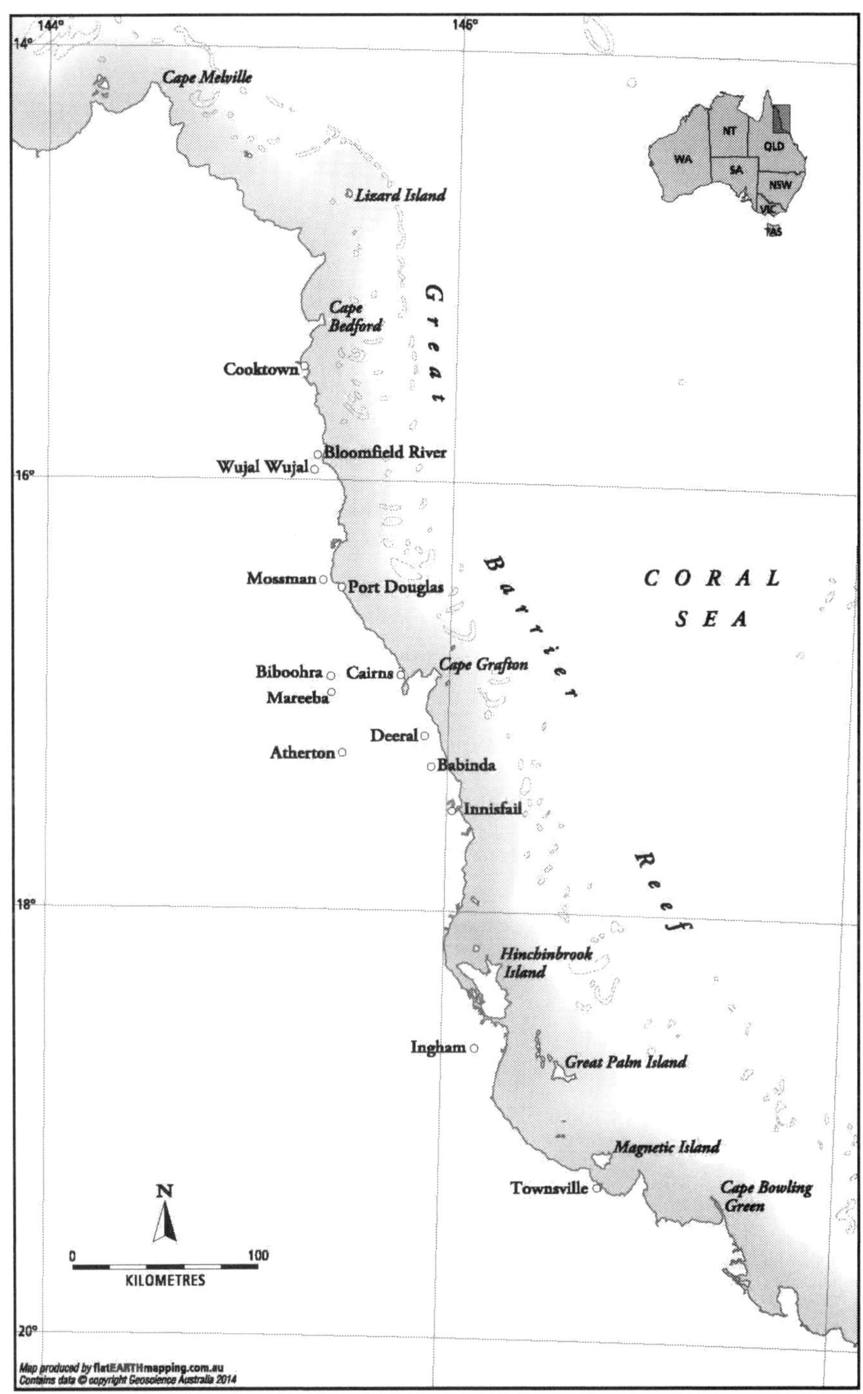

Map of Cairns and surrounding towns

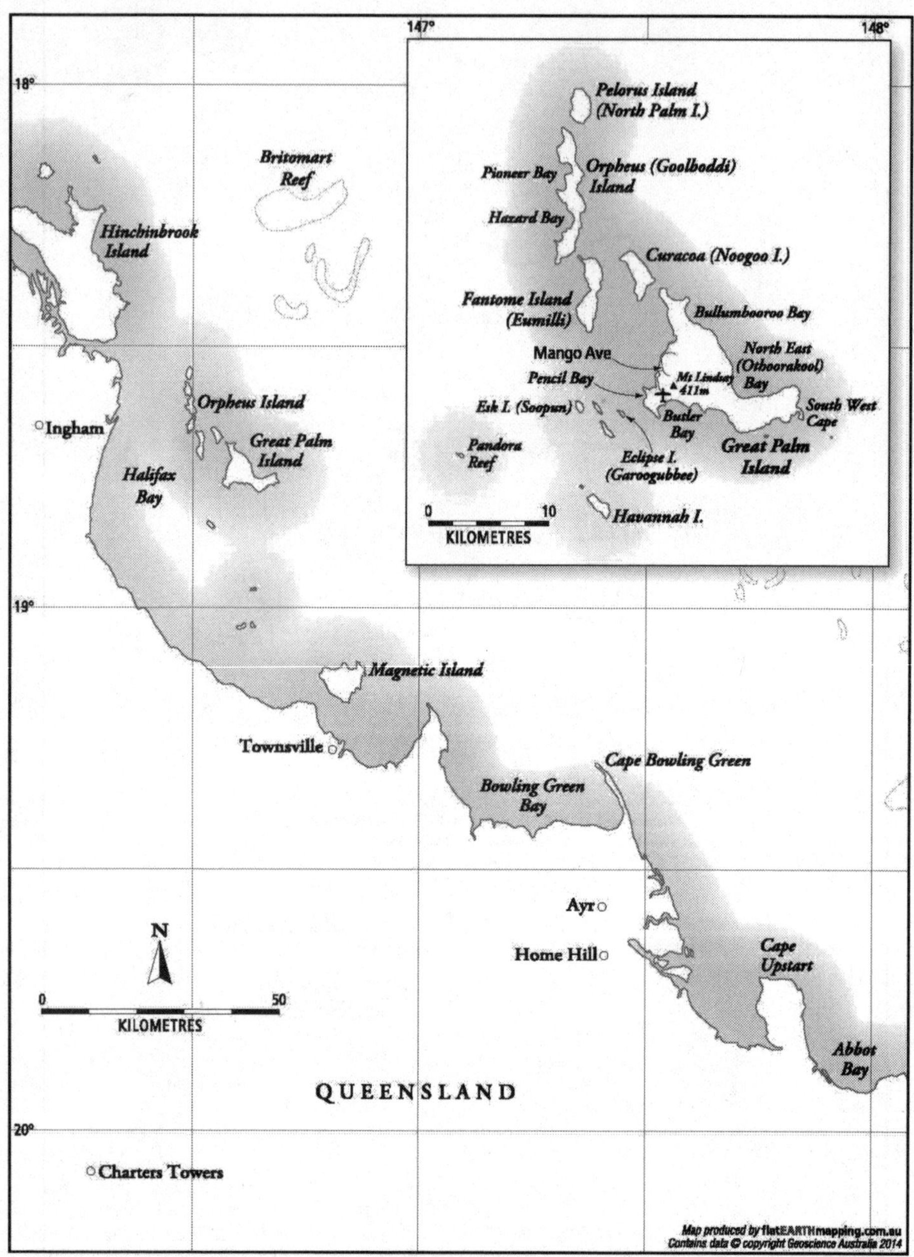

Map of Townsville, Palm Island and Charters Towers

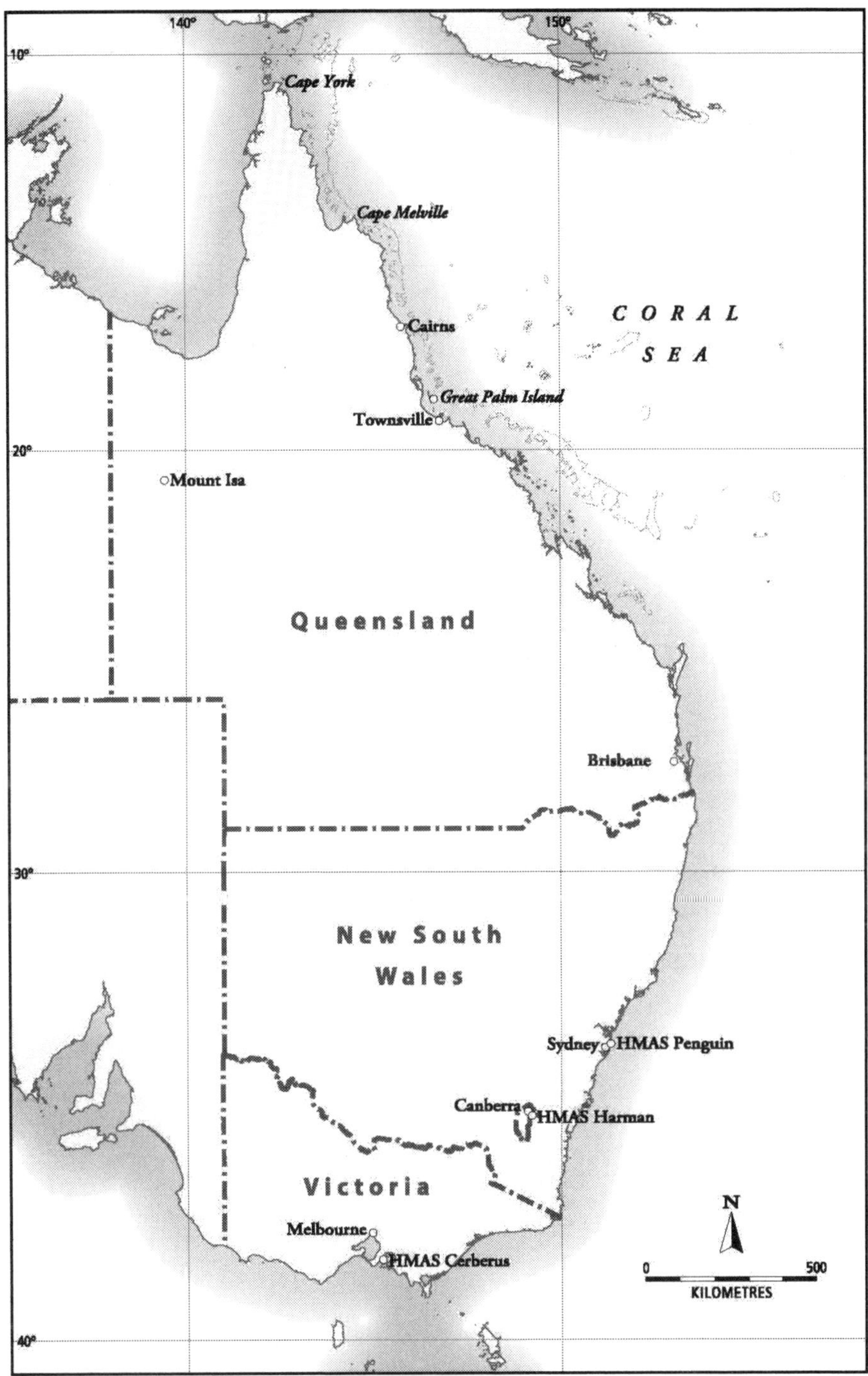

Map of Naval Bases and Eastern Australia

ACKNOWLEDGEMENTS

WITH THANKS TO:

THE CONTRIBUTORS: Alison Bendall (née Bartlam); Irene Doyle (née Simpson); Johanne Holyoake; Theresa Illin (née Anderson); Susie (Elin) Peel; Monica Walton; the Hogbin Family; Joe Glendon; Terry Janke; Judy Nielsen; Olive Bonner; and Terry Lees.

CONTRIBUTORS WHO HAVE GONE BEFORE US (REST IN PEACE): Father Cassian Double (OFM); Mrs Beryl Hogbin; Glenda Hubbard; Kate James; Kieran Michael; Aunty Rita Mills; Marie Saylor; Aunty Ina Titasey.

SPECIAL MENTION: Kevin Rudd AC; Timothy Chia; Jackie Huggins AM; Fleur Foster; Ms Jessie Landsberg.

RESEARCH: Anne Watkins, Anglican Diocese of North Queensland (Townsville); Jean Main, Private Researcher (Canberra); Kathy

Frankland and team at the Queensland Department of Aboriginal, Torres Strait Islander Partnerships (DATSIP); National Archives of Australia (NAA); National Library of Australia (NLA); Ryan Stoker; National War Memorial; Cairns City Library; Queensland Registry of Births, Deaths and Marriages; Queensland Department of Justice & Attorney General (Caroline Boast and Paul Marschke); Queensland Police Museum; Queensland Retired Police Association (Trevor Adcock, Jill Steinkamp, John & Jenny Urquhart, Barbara Zupp); Queensland State Archives (QSA); Royal Historical Society of Queensland (RHSQ); Richmond Tweed Regional Library (Ballina); State Library of Queensland (SLQ); Dr Karl Nuenfeldt; and Henry 'Seaman' Dan; Cambridge University.

CAPE YORK: the Williams family, including Uncle Rusty Williams.

CAIRNS: Ted Wymarra; Ellen Hardaker; the Glendon Family.

THE PHILIPPINES: Marlon Cipriano for your generous support during the search for 'Juan Blanco'; Rose-Marie Mendoza (the Angel of the Archives); the Quimpo Family (Kalibo); Catholic Diocese, Kalibo and Panay; Blanco Families at New Washington, Panay and Laoag City; New Washington Municipalities; FamilySearch Philippines (Elizier Bachian, Kalibo and Quezon City); the National Archives of the Philippines; and University Sto. Thomas, Manila.

MURRAY ISLAND (MER): Alice Kudub (née Blanco); Annie & Burnie Zaro and family; the Blanco and Tabo families; our Mer *pamle*; Mer Gedkem Le (Aven Noah); and the Murray Island Council. Au esoau.

DANISH-ENGLISH TRANSLATION AND SUPPORT: Carsten Ostergaard Pedersen. *Tak* (we thank you very much).

EDITORIAL SUPPORT: With special thanks to Bruce Sims, Janet Hutchinson (Working With Words) & Anna Shnukal.

FAMILY AND FRIENDS: thank you to all our family, our many dear friends and supporters.

AUTHORS' NOTE

In observance of cultural protocols, Aboriginal readers are advised this book contains the names and images of deceased people. This may cause sadness and distress to some. It is our intention to tell this story and to use imagery in good faith and with respect.

Some language and terminology used in the official correspondence reproduced in this book is considered racist and unacceptable by modern standards.

Some names and identifying details have been changed to protect the privacy of individuals and their families.

Copies of original government files and documents have been used wherever possible. Redacted documents have been transcribed for ease of reading.

Written on Bundjalung country in Ballina, New South Wales, Kalkadoon country, Mount Isa, Queensland and Whadjuk Noongar country in Perth, Western Australia.

FOREWORD

A Question of Colour, the autobiography of Patricia Lees and her family, is a truly Australian story. It reflects the history of Australia, a history that we should not always be proud of, but that we must acknowledge. It is a life story the whole nation is not familiar with but should be.

The removal of Pattie from her family at an early age and ultimate placement as a Ward under the *State Children Act 1911* (Qld) on Palm Island is a story too familiar to Aboriginal and Torres Strait Islander Australians. No Aboriginal person, family, or community has been left untouched by the removal of children during the Stolen Generations. The ways in which families and children were treated is something we are only beginning to come to terms with. And the continuing impact of the legacy of the Stolen Generations on our Aboriginal brothers and sisters is a blemish on our nation's history.

In February 2008, as my first parliamentary act as Prime Minister of this nation, I apologised to the Aboriginal and Torres Strait Islander peoples of our land for the pain, suffering and hurt inflicted on the

Stolen Generations, their descendants, and their families. On behalf of the nation, I said 'sorry'.

Pattie was invited to attend the Apology at Parliament House in Canberra. She declined the invitation out of respect for those members of the Stolen Generations who were not invited. Pattie said at the time that she did not need an apology from the government to overcome the pain of being removed from her family, stating:

> *My closure came as a consequence of searching my soul, loving my family, things like that. It's not depending on something external, it's something within yourself. You know, it's like conditional – that somehow I'm going to be well because the government said sorry to me – it's futile.*

Pattie also felt that the Apology would resurrect pain and anger about close family members who have not healed, accepted their loss, and moved on.

I respected her position then, and I continue to respect it today. Saying 'sorry' is only a step on the path to genuine healing and reconciliation that Australians need to travel along together. In isolation, it could never be a meaningful gesture. A future where we are all proud of our Indigenous languages and the achievements of Aboriginal and Torres Strait Islander men and women, children and Elders, requires honesty about the history of treatment of the First Peoples of our land. To do this, we must listen to stories like Pattie's, and we must respect the bravery that it takes for her to share her story with us.

Since the Apology, members of the Stolen Generation and their families have told me that the simple act of hearing a Prime Minister say 'sorry' offered a sense of healing, or the beginning of healing. To this day I get stopped for a cuddle with an Auntie, a moment of reflection with an Uncle, a thank you from a child or grandchild. These meetings are emotional, and always meaningful to both me and those who honour me with their sharing.

After the Apology, Pattie shared that she, like so many millions of people on that day in February 2008, became emotional watching from Townsville. She thought about what this would have meant to her mother and others who did not live to see and hear it for themselves.

Patricia Lees has made many people proud over the course of her life. Despite the difficulties she faced from a young age, she has shown tremendous strength and courage throughout her life. She learnt that closure is a personal experience and relied on herself to travel from being that tiny girl taken from her family, compelled to walk between two conflicting worlds during Queensland's Aboriginal Protection and assimilationist policy eras, to a resilient woman proudly representing her people at the United Nations. Her story is the story of the Stolen Generations; but it is also unique to her. Through this story, we come to understand her search for identity, struggling to belong in either the Aboriginal or White Australian worlds, having the colour of her skin dictate how she was treated.

Pattie's story is as relevant today as it was in 1958 when she was taken from her mother and siblings on the grounds of neglect. Today, the rapidly increasing numbers of Aboriginal and Torres Strait Islander children in the child protection system is disturbing. Since the release of the *Bringing Them Home Report* in 1997, the rate of Indigenous children in out-of-home care has only increased. While child neglect and the safety of all Australian children is paramount, we have to ask ourselves why the numbers of Indigenous children in care are increasing so dramatically. We have to realise that acknowledging the legacy of the Stolen Generations is a necessary part of breaking this cycle and is not something that our nation wishes to repeat. Over a decade after the Apology, progress is slow and there is still a long way to go.

But there are growing numbers of people walking on the path of reconciliation together. Australians from all walks of life are wanting to continue the process of healing, to listen to stories like Pattie's. We still have a way to travel. Aboriginal and Torres Strait Islanders remain unrecognised as the First Australians in our nation's founding document – the *Constitution*. The celebration of Australia Day remains contentious and divisive, with prominent Indigenous leaders calling for the date to be changed. As with the Apology, these actions may only be symbolic, but symbolic acts remain important. They cannot reverse a history of pain and suffering, but they can acknowledge and respect it. As with the Apology, these actions must be underpinned with a commitment from our political leaders to continue work towards closing the gap in opportunities and outcomes for Aboriginal and Torres Strait Islander people.

When Pattie's story and the stories of other members of the Stolen Generations are known and respected as well as those of the Europeans who claimed these lands as their own, we will know that we have reached that point where we can say, yes, we are a reconciled Australia.

Kevin Rudd AC

PREFACE

It is much easier to read someone else's autobiography than to write your own. The book you are holding in your hand, reading on your tablet or other electronic device, has been years, perhaps many lifetimes, in the making.

My story began as a tribute to my mother but morphed into a very personal account of my and my siblings' removal and separation from her in 1958 on the grounds of neglect. This book recounts my journey back to those broken places of my formative years.

My story is as relevant today as it was in 1958. Much has been said and written in Australia in recent years about Aboriginal identity, particularly about 'fair-skinned' Indigenous Australians. Measured by breed, caste, fractions and perceived quantities of white versus black blood, my story takes you back to a time when the Queensland State Children's Department and the Department of Native Affairs adjudged my welfare based on archaic definitions of colour and race. Government bureaucrats decided my 'degree' of Aboriginality based on their perceptions. I did not have the freedom to determine my own identity.

My family's combined experiences as Wards of the State are still meaningful in the context of both current debates and the individual accounts that emerged during the *Royal Commission into Institutional Responses to Child Sexual Abuse*. Aboriginal and Torres Strait Islander children are still being removed in record numbers from their families 20 years after the release of the *Bringing Them Home Report* in 1997. My book is a counter response to both.

This autobiography is infused with memories of family, lifelong friends, mentors and former teachers, some of whom are now deceased. I have included some of their personal recollections, in their own words, to provide a more rounded, richer account of my experiences.

My story has also given voice to others who, for whatever reason, have not been able to tell their own. May this book provide some hope and encouragement to those who have suffered in silence as a result of their own dislocation from family and placement into foster care, orphanages and institutions.

Pattie Lees AM (née Janke)
Mount Isa, August 2020

A book is a version of the world. If you do not like it, ignore it; or offer your own version in return.

Salman Rushdie

1

NO POVERTY OF SPIRIT

The best years of my childhood were spent in an unremarkable two-storey timber house. Our family house at 31 Hartley Street was no different from any other high-set, flood-proof wooden house in 1950s Cairns. The interior was sparsely furnished. Our yard played host to a carnival of animals, including a dozen or so hand-fed chickens. Our ever-faithful dogs, Bjørn and Tige, were enclosed by the ramshackle, flaking picket fence, which surrounded the large block of land. Our three cats, Felix, Tom and Jerry, came and went at their leisure, behaving as though they owned the house, as cats tend to do.

Our family was closely bonded. I was the second of four children who called Hartley Street home. My brother Terry was born in April 1947. I followed in August 1948. Michael, whom we affectionately called Jumbo, was born in January 1951. Our little sister, Johanne, arrived in May 1952. As kids, the four of us shared the same bed. There was always giggling, then discomfort whenever Terry wet the bed – usually while the rest of us were asleep. Disturbed, we would rise as one from our slumber and bounce out of bed, in the process battering Terry about the head with our pillows. Joining forces, we turned the mattress over to the dry side and changed the sheets. When Terry's bed wetting became a habit, we never let him sleep in the middle of the bed again.

Ours was a single-mother household during our formative years. By today's standards, life was tough, both economically and socially, for sole parents in those days. Dad had a limited presence and a minimal interest in our upbringing. He never lived with us nor was he entirely detached. I often wondered how Mum became pregnant because Dad was never around. But our births occurred as a result of his irregular, clandestine visits. Dad provided the roof over our heads and usually stopped by on Friday afternoons to give us small amounts of pocket money. We became accustomed to not having him in our lives any more often.

Our childhoods brimmed with spirited exploits: playing pirates, laughing as the dogs chased Michael around, nipping at his skin and tearing the arse out of his pants as he tried to outrun them. Michael often dressed up in a red cape, which in reality was a red tablecloth. One day he gaily jumped out the window, believing he could fly like Superman. His brilliant adventure ended when he failed to achieve lift-off and required urgent medical treatment after ripping one of his testicles on the clothesline.

I was an inquisitive, circumspect child. Our house backed onto a brothel. Late afternoons, I would climb the tamarind tree, a fixture in the middle of the chicken coop, brush aside the leaves and peer over the fence, hoping to catch a glimpse of the lovely ladies and their activities next door. Usually, the only woman I saw was my rather irate mother bounding down the backyard, clutching her broom or a handful of pebbles and demanding I come down immediately.

When she wasn't shouting at us, Mum was full of comforting

platitudes. It was as if she'd swallowed a dictionary; regurgitating superior words helped soothe her verbal reflux. On most occasions, I never understood what her big words meant, but upon reflection, my life has been dotted with moments of realisation.

As much as Mum banned me from peeking over the back fence, she reminded me to always see the best in people.

'Do not judge other people, Patsy. That should be left to God,' she said. 'We never know the unseen burdens those poor unfortunates are carrying,' she added, nudging me indoors. Circumstances, Mum explained, often conspired to force some women into lifestyles and occupations they would ordinarily reject. In her later years, Mum often bemoaned the fact that some women sold themselves short by opting to remain in loveless marriages just to ensure a roof over their heads or to maintain a highfalutin public image.

'Don't try to keep up with the Joneses. It's much cheaper to bring them down to your level,' was one of Mum's favourite sayings.

And we did.

We wore tattered tops and jeans out of necessity because new clothes and shoes were too expensive. Michael looked like the biggest vagabond. None of us wanted to exchange shorts with him because his had patches sewn onto the back. These days I find it curious that fashion designers command top dollar for ripped, torn and faded clothes. I remember Mum's laughter one afternoon when I got home from school and told her I'd been teased for wearing worn-out shoes and a frayed dress.

'Only poor people wear what you wear!' were the cruel words hissed at me.

Mum always took a keen interest in our response to such situations.

'Well, did you stand up for yourself?' she enquired.

'It's okay, Mum,' I reassured her. 'I hunted them away. I told them that we were not poor. It was that we did not have any money.'

Our family struggled under the weight of poverty. Christmas was rarely celebrated in our home, and birthdays came and went unheralded as just another day on the calendar. We were the epitome of 'Aussie battlers'. Us kids did not have many material possessions growing up, but there was an over-abundance of love, and no shortage of spirit or togetherness. The strength of our family bond enabled us to overcome the gravity of disadvantage. I never felt deprived or that I was missing out in any way, with the exception of skipping an occasional meal.

Terry did most of the cooking in our house. Potato chips with onion gravy was his signature dish; it formed the basis of our monotonous diet. I cannot recall a time when we sat around the table to partake of a family meal. A home-cooked Sunday roast or three square meals a day were non-existent. On special occasions, Mum prepared *sabi sabi* (Miriam Mir sabidsabid) chicken, a popular Torres Strait Islander coconut-based dish. She grated the soft coconut flesh on a hand-made metal *madu* (coconut scraper), wringing it through a cheesecloth or piece of nappy towelling to make creamy coconut milk. Fried scones served with generous dollops of butter and syrup were always an added treat.

In stark testimony to misplaced priorities, the fridge was usually empty, with the exception of cold beers. There were times when extreme hunger forced Terry, Michael and me into scavenging waif-like through the neighbourhood stores in search of cheap or 'five-finger' discounted food. Our need to survive often challenged Terry's ingenuity. He distracted unsuspecting storekeepers by keeping them occupied at the counter while Michael and I quickly made off with a small supply of potatoes and onions, powdered milk, and several apples or oranges.

Confectionery was never among our grocery loot. Terry organised us so that we never took more than what we needed and this practice continued undetected. He told us that a couple of potatoes, onions, apples and oranges would not be missed from a big pile. This was similar to one of the insults Mum hurled at Dad: 'A slice from a cut loaf is never missed!'

A highlight of living in Hartley Street was the day a confectionery truck overturned on the street corner, spilling its colourful load of boiled lollies all over the road. Children, intent on receiving their fair share of the loot, came running from every direction with big smiles on their faces.

Random acts of kindness also helped us to survive the hardships of those humble times. Mrs Harding, our next-door neighbour, had a habit of leaving hot meat pies and sponge cakes to cool on our adjoining fence. To our hungry tummies, these were an irresistible temptation. Cautiously looking about for any sign of Mrs Harding at the window, once certain that the coast was clear, we crouched by the fence and with outstretched hands delivered the goodies into our keep.

I never understood the folly of Mrs Harding continuing to leave her freshly-baked goods on the fence for us to steal week after week. She also regularly changed the selection. I don't think Mum ever cottoned on to our opportunistic thieving; if she did, she chose to ignore it. Being proud, Mum was particular about charity and whom she would accept a helping hand from. In retrospect, I can only speculate that Mrs Harding's furtive generosity was her way of preserving Mum's dignity and helping out at the same time. As for Mrs Harding, I hope she reaped as much pleasure from her generous deeds as we did.

Terry was the ringleader of all our exploits. We scammed our way into the Tropical Picture Theatre under another of his devious schemes;

he carefully wrapped a pile of brown penny and halfpenny coins with aluminium foil that he smoothed to the edges. Our fake silver coins always fooled the box office attendant, who could barely see through her thick, Coke-bottle-style glasses. For years we thought we had conned her. It never occurred to us that she would have felt the difference in the texture or noticed the discrepancy when she reconciled the daily takings. Perhaps the cashier rewarded our creativity by allowing the charade to continue. Otherwise, it too was an act of random kindness bestowed by someone who took pity on our impoverished plight.

Like any responsible parent, Mum worried herself sick when we were not home before dark. Fiercely protective of her brood, there were many standout moments of her motherly concern. In one instance, I almost drowned in a river at Kamerunga, near Cairns, during a family picnic. I was about eight years old at the time. Driven by curiosity, I ventured into the water, swimming from rock to rock, but was swept away by the strong undertow. When Mum jumped into the water to rescue me, with no regard for her own safety, we both got caught in the current. I reached out, wrapping my arms tightly around her throat as she piggybacked me through the water. Midstream, Mum clambered onto a large boulder, but the current was so strong it ripped our clothes off. What a sight to behold! Mum and her beloved daughter stark naked and stranded on a rock. My siblings looked on, helpless, as concerned bystanders broke a large branch from a tree and winched us to safety. Survival made modesty a secondary consideration as we were wrapped in picnic blankets. There was no embarrassment on my part, just an overwhelming sense of gratitude at Mum's selfless act of heroism.

On another occasion, Mum defended me following a complaint by the Hartley Street corner store owner, Mr Ross. He accused me of sticking my finger through a pawpaw and damaging it. He demanded restitution and a heated confrontation ensued. Mum was so angry I thought she was going to slap him. She defiantly stood her ground, refusing to pay Mr Ross one penny. But to this day I have an aversion to pawpaw and refuse to eat it.

Terry's and my schooling in Cairns was intermittent. We were shuffled from one school to another, including Saint Monica's Catholic Primary School, Parramatta Park State School, Balaclava State School and, finally, Hambledon State School.

'Patsy, if you want to get anywhere in life, you need an education,' Mum used to say. 'I never had the chance to finish my schooling so learn from my experience.'

Although Mum extolled the benefits of obtaining an education, her actions were sometimes at odds with her advice. She often kept me at home to assist with the household chores or babysit my younger siblings. Other times, Terry and I chose to skip school to engage in recreational exploits.

In view of our absenteeism, I believe Mum moved us around from one school to another to avoid regular scrutiny and intervention by the education and welfare authorities. She taught me how to read, despite my skipping school. A *bel esprit*, Mum was a prodigious reader, a self-styled 'queen of quotes and quips', often sharing humorous and witty anecdotes. Some of her favourite lines included:

> Vote for the politicians who promise you the least. You will be the least disappointed;

> Entering politics is the cheapest way to have your family tree examined;

> In the country of the blind, the one-eyed man is king; and

> The only exercise some people get is jumping to conclusions, running down their friends, sidestepping responsibility and pushing their luck.

Mum's example influenced my long-held passion for reading. I was literate from a young age and took a great interest in a wide cross-section of children's books: Aesop's Fables, the Little Golden Books and Grimm's Fairy Tales were my favourites. I did not enjoy comics as much as Terry. He struggled with literacy and found it easier to study the illustrations. I was too analytical. The Disney character Donald Duck always mystified me. I never understood why in some scenes Donald Duck hopped out of the bath wrapped in a towel when his bottom half was always bare.

2

AILAN GIRL

Our tight family bond insulated us against the gossip of judgmental neighbours who, because we had a black mother, tagged us as the coloured misfits on the block. Being kids, we were blind to the colour of Mum's skin. We simply accepted her as our mum. She always told us that love was colour blind.

Much of Mum's early history and family life in the Torres Strait has been pieced together in the years since she died and become interwoven with the limited stories and scant accounts she passed down to us. Mum was born in September 1921 on Mer, the largest of the three Murray Islands in the Torres Strait. The first born in her family, Mum was said to have been delivered in Gigrid village on the same ancient parcel of land where our ancestors have been born since time immemorial. It is a beautiful setting in which to enter the world. Gigred sits at the foot of Gelam Hill. The crescent-shaped Waier Island lies one kilometre offshore, with Dauar Island a little further out. According to Meriam mythology, the sandstone patches that can still be seen along the beach between Gigred and Gigo villages were once reef sharks that became stranded and transformed to stone while hunting giant spotted eagle stingrays (*peibri sor*) to the shore.[1]

As a young girl growing up on the mainland of Queensland, Mer was another world away; but to Mum, it was always 'home' and never far from either her mind or her heart. (Mer and Murray Island are used interchangeably.) The fringe of the Great Barrier Reef was her front yard and playground. Mer is a place where dusky, lemon-coloured reef sharks feast casually among the thick, black schools of sardines that resemble a churning oil slick along the water's edge. At the right time of year, wild chilli plants thrive amid the hibiscus and overgrown stalks of bamboo. It is an island where sacred totems, tales, myths, songs and dances are entwined with the land, the sea and the stars.

Mer and Thursday Island (TI) are the best known of the seventeen inhabited islands in Torres Strait. Located between Cape York and Papua New Guinea, the Torres Strait islands became part of Queensland following their annexation in 1879. At that time, all Islanders became British subjects and their islands became Crown lands. At Federation, Torres Strait Islanders became Australian citizens, although until comparatively recently, they were denied the rights and benefits which their fellow Australians took for granted.[2]

Torres Strait Islanders are a distinct Indigenous minority group in Australia. They are often grouped with Aboriginal people but in fact have an entirely different origin, history and way of life. Contrary to what some people think, Torres Strait Islanders are not mainland Aboriginal people who live on islands in North Queensland. Nor are they purely a Papuan people, despite their predominantly Melanesian racial origins and the cultural affinities they have with the people of Papua New Guinea to the north. As much as Aboriginal cultures and customs vary from clan to clan, so each island of the Torres Strait also has its own landscape, stories and histories.[3] Family is at the heart of Torres Strait Islander culture. Clan and kinship are central to all aspects of social, political and religious life. Clans define identity and family groupings with roles and responsibilities according to a complex set of relationships and often along gender lines. Every clan has its own identity defined through totems, patriarchal descent, songs, dances, stories, cosmology and spiritual beliefs.[4]

The first recorded European navigation of Torres Strait took place in 1606 during the expedition of Spanish explorer Luís Vaez de Torres, although islanders had been trading with their Papuan and Aboriginal neighbours for centuries. Thursday Island was established as the commercial hub of the Strait in 1877, although the first formal European settlement was at Somerset, Cape York, in 1863.[5]

Temana Agnes Philomena Blanco, Mum, arrived into the world as a mixed-race child with a striking confluence of Melanesian, Filipino and Aboriginal ancestry. Mum always said 'Temana' (variation, Timena) meant 'pearl of the sea' although the origins of her name remain unknown. It was a befitting title regardless. She was born into a hard-working family of pearl shell divers and a long line of seafarers from all sides of her heritage.

My Miriam grandmother, Azey Leyah Sari, born in 1900, was one of nine children of Charlie and Magina Sari of the Magaram (or Mergarem) clan and the Teg Dauareb sub-clan respectively. Azey's siblings were George (1891–1892), Maria Banuga (1892–1945), Chopa or Sopa (1894), George (1895–1918), Matu or Matutu (1898–1912), War (1906–1907), another child whose name and sex are unknown (1909–1911) and War Kaibo (1909–1958). Via my first known ancestors, Kabur and her husband, Dog, my Miriam ancestry extends to antiquity. Local mythology tells that Kabur was the first person to capture the sacred deity, Malo, when he arrived on Mer in the form of an octopus.

Grandmother Azey was a widow when she met my grandfather, Victoriano (Victor) Blanco; her first husband, Hand, died as a result of bronchitis and malarial complications in August 1917, five months into their marriage. She assumed the name 'Mary Blanco' later in life, most likely after she renounced her Anglican faith and became a Catholic in order to marry my grandfather in 1923.

Granddad Victor was born on nearby Darnley Island (Erub) in 1901, and was an experienced pearl diver and fisherman. He was the eldest of five children, including Silverio or 'Silver' (1903–1968), Maria Trinidad (1907–1930), Celestina (1909–unknown), and Philomena (1910–1911). His parents were Filipino migrant and pearl worker Juan Blanco and Annie Dupar (var. Dopar), a mainland Aboriginal woman. Juan Blanco was believed to have been born c.1864 in Pueblo de Calibo, Capiz (now Kalibo, Aklan]), in the Western Visayas region of the Philippines. Like the many hundreds of Asiatic and Filipino immigrants to Australia at that time, Juan was motivated by the financial rewards and opportunities provided by the burgeoning pearling industry; it was a chance for a fresh start and a new life. The Torres Strait also provided welcome refuge from the prevailing tensions and conflict associated with the Philippines Revolution (1896–1897), the Spanish–American War (1898) and the Philippines–American War (1899–1902). Little is known about Juan's earlier life in the Philippines, despite continuing efforts to trace his family history. Although there is no doubting his Filipino heritage, based on historical associations and other evidence, there is a suggestion that he changed his name either before or after arriving in Australia. It is believed he 'jumped ship' following his arrival in Sydney in the 1880s before making his way up to the Torres Strait.

Juan Blanco, Granddad Victor and Uncle Silver spent many years working the seabeds across the Torres Strait, off the coasts of Papua New Guinea and Irian Jaya, and up and down the east coast of Queensland. Pearl shells were once used to make buttons before the invention of the wood and plastic varieties in use today. The Torres Strait Islands, Broome in Western Australia, and Darwin were at the heart of the pearling boom that reached its peak in 1897 and began to wane in 1904.[6]

My great-grandmother, Annie Blanco, born c.1878, is believed to have been descended from the seafaring Yadhaigana (or Yaraikana, Yaraikanna) people on the eastern side of Cape York Peninsula. Like Grandmother Azey, Annie was also a widow when she met Juan Blanco. Annie had two children, Maidam Remo and Tako Gimai (Emily), from her first marriage to Murray Islander Ned Dupar, also known as Geas. It is unclear how Annie came to be a resident on Mer. She spent some of her earlier years living at Mount Adolphus Island (Muralag) on the tip of Cape York Peninsula, an area that served as a neutral trading ground between coastal Aboriginal groups and the Western, Eastern and Central Torres Strait Islanders and Papuans. It is possible that Annie journeyed from Mount Adolphus to Mer with visiting pearl luggers or island traders, or met her first husband, Geas, while he was working in that region.

Juan and Annie married in August 1900 amidst significant social change. The couple exchanged vows just five months before Australian Federation in January 1901. Fortunately, their union also occurred prior to the introduction of stricter State-sanctioned marriage controls. Under Section 9 of the *Aboriginal Protection and Restriction of Sale of Opium Act 1901* (2nd Ed. VII. No. 1.), Aboriginal people could not marry without written permission from the Chief Protector, acting on advice from the local Protector. The State legislated to intervene in marriages between Aboriginal women and non-Aboriginal men, and the restrictions were enforced after the Act was gazetted on 16 May 1902.

As a mainland-born Aboriginal, Annie Blanco was subject to the *Aboriginal Protection and Restriction of the Sale of Opium Act (1897)* and its various incarnations. Later in life, she was subject to the *Aboriginal Protection Act (1939)*. Even today, these pieces of legislation are often cited as 'the Act' or 'living under the Act' during public debate and discourse. The Act empowered Chief Protectors to regulate and control every aspect of Aboriginal people's lives, including their employment, savings and wages, welfare, education and freedom of movement.

Juan Blanco remained an unnaturalised alien until his death from tuberculosis in 1911. He was one of the many Asiatic migrants unfairly impacted by the introduction of the *Immigration Restriction Act (1901)*, commonly known as the White Australia Policy that was designed to limit non-European migration to Australia. The Commonwealth *Naturalisation Act (1903)* also excluded Chinese and other 'natives of the Pacific Islands, Asia, Africa and the Pacific' from becoming citizens.[7]

Annie Blanco re-married for a third time sixteen years after Juan's death. She and Robert (Bob) Quetta from Somerset, Cape York, married in August 1927 at Thursday Island, but she became a widow again when Bob died in 1941.

Granddad Victor identified as a 'half-caste Manilaman', a term used to describe early stage migrants from the Philippine Islands. Mum occasionally spoke of him, revering his contribution as a corporal with the 2/31st Battalion, Second Australian Imperial Force

(2nd AIF, 7th Division) in the Middle East and North Africa, and with the Royal Australian Army Engineers (1st Port Maintenance Company and 2/2nd Australian Docks Operations Company) in New Guinea during the Second World War. Granddad Victor sailed to Brisbane in December 1939 with the first batch of Indigenous and non-Indigenous volunteers from the Torres Strait, which included his mates Ted Loban, Charles Mene and Aboo 'Starchy' Ah-Wang. He became a significant figure in Torres Strait Islander history and a *cause celèbré* for Indigenous participation in the war effort. In January 1941, while stationed in England, Granddad Victor was interviewed for a segment on BBC Radio. He appeared twice on front page of the Brisbane *Courier Mail*, and was a regular face in the pictorial section of several Australian and British newspapers and magazines. I have only one memory of my grandfather. When I was six years old, he carried me high on his shoulders so I could glimpse Queen Elizabeth II during her visit to Cairns in March 1954. This was Granddad Victor's second brush with the British monarchy. He performed a traditional Torres Strait Islander dance before King George VI while stationed at Colchester, England, during the War.

While Granddad Victor was overseas fighting for Australia's freedom, his mother was still living as a second-class citizen under the Act. When Annie Blanco received an exemption from the *Aboriginals Preservation and Protection Act (1939*) on 30 September 1942 at the aged of 64, for the first time in her life she was officially free and 'at liberty to obtain employment without agreement' and 'generally manage her own affairs'. Sadly, Annie's independence was short-lived. She died three years later in 1945.

Mum had two siblings: a brother and sister. Uncle George Ganomi Blanco, born in 1923, was Mum's first cousin but reared as her brother in accordance with Torres Strait Islander customary adoption practices. Aunt Teama Celestina Blanco (or Aunt Tina) was born in 1924. She and Mum had a twin-like bond. Aunt Tina died seven months before I was born in 1948, and I was given the middle name Celestine in her honour. By the time I was born, both Grandmother Azey and Great-grandmother Annie Blanco had been dead for several years, so I never met them either.

And I never knew Uncle George Blanco. He remained on Mer for most of his life, where he worked as a Native Policeman. Uncle George was the second member of my family to support Australia's war effort when he enlisted in the Torres Strait Light Infantry Battalion (TSLIB) in 1941. He also continued the family legacy when he performed *kab kar*, a traditional style of Meriam dance before Queen Elizabeth II during her Australian tour in April 1970. Uncle George died from a heart attack in February 1972, aged 48.

My extended family were not part my life as I grew up, with the exception of Uncle Silver, cousin Aggie Dan and Mum's cousin, Auntie Theresa Zitha, who was the only child of Granddad Victor's sister, Maria Trinidad Zitha (née Blanco), and her husband, Horace Utan Zitha (var. Utan Walters). But Mum proudly identified as a Murray Islander on account of her own upbringing and socialisation. The notion of being a Torres Strait Islander did not exist in her time; the concept of a common, pan Torres Strait Islander consciousness did not evolve until well after the introduction of the *Torres Strait Islanders Act (1939)*, post the Second World War.[8]

Mum publicly acknowledged her Filipino heritage but rarely spoke about her Aboriginal ancestry. Perhaps she was fearful that, like Grandmother Annie Blanco, she too might be subject to the restrictive control of Queensland's Aboriginal Protection Acts. Mum's sense of identity may also have been influenced by the parochial views of mainland Aboriginal people held by some Torres Strait Islanders of her generation. The late Eddie Koiki Mabo candidly discussed this stigma in his biography.[9]

Mum's progressive migration from the Torres Strait to mainland Australia began at the early age of six, when she was sent to boarding school at Our Lady of the Sacred Heart (OLSH) School, New Guinea Diocese, on Thursday Island. The Sacred Heart Orphanage and Home for Coloured Girls offered boarding facilities to children, mostly of mixed race, from all the outer islands of the Torres Strait. Mum, Aunt Tina, Grandmother Azey and Granddad Victor all relocated to Thursday Island, and Mum started at the Sacred Heart convent school in January 1928. Aunt Tina was enrolled at the same school in the early 1930s. Uncle George remained on Murray Island to safeguard the family land inheritance.

3

TEMPTATION AND SATISFACTION

Although my great-grandfather, Juan Blanco, died a decade before Mum was born, his influence extended beyond the grave. Mum and Aunt Tina's early lives were pre-determined by their inherited Catholic affiliation. They became the second generation of the Blanco family to attend the Sacred Heart School and board at the Sacred Heart Orphanage and Home for Coloured Girls on Thursday Island.

At school, the sisters' island names, Temana and Teama, were axed in favour of more acceptable Catholic titles. Mum officially became Agnes Blanco, while Teama became Celestina; they preferred Aggie and Tina.

It is not that difficult for me to imagine the quality of life in a rigid, neo-colonial boarding school environment a few years either side of the Great Depression. The children endured a regimented, back-breaking cycle of boiling, soaking and stirring the Catholic sisters' habits and priests' vestments in a giant copper pot, along with all the linen and uniforms. The senior girls were tasked with ironing. Child boarders were also required to scrub and polish every floor and fixture, feed and milk the goats, collect eggs, and tend to the gardens in addition to regularly reciting the Angelus prayer and other incantations. Then there was school. It was a six day a week, six o'clock in the morning to six o'clock in the evening existence. Sunday was the only day the children were allowed outside the convent perimeter; the sisters corrected any wayward behaviour by withholding this privilege. Emptying the dormitory poo pans each morning was, understandably, every girl's worst nightmare.[10]

During these years, Mum had a tenuous relationship with her father, my Granddad Victor, which was compounded by his itinerant, pearl-diving lifestyle and his temporary exile from Torres Strait after the Thursday Island police branded him a troublemaker. In 1931, Granddad Victor also abandoned his family. He was ordered by a judge to pay four shillings and sixpence weekly for Mum and Aunt Tina's maintenance after Grandmother Azey took him to court.[11]

The following year, when Mum was twelve, the Chief Protector of Aborigines issued a Removal Order to transfer Granddad Victor to Mapoon, Cape York. The Chief Protector originally proposed that he be sent to Palm Island with his immediate family, then to Mabuiag Island. Some years later, in 1935, he was removed by the State to Lockhart River. Granddad Victor's continued absence left Mum without any strong male influence during her early years.

Mum's aunt, Sister Celestina Blanco (Granddad Victor's sister), filled a void. She served as a 'Handmaid of the Lord' at the Sacred Heart School and Convent from 1927 to 1933.[12] Sister Celestina was both a positive influence and a familiar face for Mum. Having a close relative on the school staff compensated Mum and Aunt Tina, in part, for their disconnection from family, and during the first six years of her education, Mum thrived under Sister Celestina's loving and watchful eye.

Mum also made a lifelong friend at the Sacred Heart. Marie Swindley (née Sim), whom we later came to know as Auntie Marie, entered the Orphanage in 1929. Auntie Marie's father was Filipino; her mother, Torres Strait Islander. Aunt Tina and Marie aside, Mum's other favoured companion was Connie the goat. The children fed and tended to their own goats, all the while knowing their 'pets' were destined for the dinner table. Connie became Mum's faithful friend and the object of her affection, and Mum was mortified upon learning she had devoured Connie for dinner one evening: Connie had been slaughtered and served up as stew without Mum's knowledge. The incident had a profound effect. Mum felt as if she had cannibalised a friend; a devout animal lover, she never forgot this incident and often credited Connie's slaughter with her gradual loss of faith in the Catholic Church.

Music and singing became a way for Mum to add joy to her world. She took music lessons at the convent, being tutored by nuns, and sang in the school choir. She learned to play the piano, although the ukulele was her favourite instrument. At the convent school, Mum also developed a beautiful style of handwriting. I have vivid memories of her licking the tip of her lead pencil before starting to write in order to darken the imprint on the page.

Fellow student, Monica Gould (née Walton), reflects on her time with Mum and Aunt Tina during those years in the convent:

Both Agnes and Tina were very attractive, being tall, slim, with long legs, and much admired by the younger girls on Thursday Island. They were both wonderful dancers as well as singers and would sing and dance to entertain the other kids in the convent. One song they used to sing was 'Keep Your Sunny Side Up!' and they would kick up their long legs.

> *Agnes was older but I used to admire her in Church. She could sing. Tina had thick wavy hair. I used to wish I had that wavy hair, because I had straight hair.*[13]

Mum left school in December 1937, one year before graduating. She often spoke of her bitter disappointment at not completing her education, but her rejection of rigid, convent school life was explained by her lifelong contempt for conformity. Mum stepped out from the convent and into the world with a suitcase full of self-confidence and youthful dreams. Her freedom, though, was limited.

Before the Second World War, Thursday Island, like most Queensland towns with large non-white populations, was racially segregated. The Catholic school and orphanage were not segregated but state schooling was, according to the racial classification of the period. Children of European, Japanese or Chinese descent attended the 'white' state school while the 'coloured' state school accepted children of other heritages.[14] The local schools, swimming baths, dance hall and open-air movie theatre (with its two entrances and types of seating, one for whites and one for blacks) were all segregated. Hotels were barred to anyone classed as 'Aboriginal'. Marriage, sexual relations and even friendships between blacks and whites were frowned upon. Vestiges of this pervasive segregation, and the culture and mentality it engendered, continued even into the early 1980s.[15]

Regardless of this, Mum and Aunt Tina ran amok during their years on Thursday Island. The misadventures of the two young women nicknamed Temptation and Satisfaction remain enmeshed in the minds and memories of many older generation Thursday Islanders. After Mum eventually found employment, she and Aunt Tina shed their Catholic names, along with the staid images that went with them.

Before long, the Temptation (Mum) and Satisfaction (Aunt Tina) duo was at the epicentre of the Second World War party scene on Thursday Island. Mum blossomed, attracting much male interest. She was on TI during the build-up of Australian and allied armed forces during the Second World War, with several thousand garrison members stationed on Horn and Thursday Islands. During her heyday, Thursday Island was to Australia what in the same era Honolulu and the Blue Hawaii represented to the United States.

Temptation and Satisfaction scandalised the conservative inhabitants of Thursday Island. Their sense of liberation was palpable as they discarded the drab white and blue tunic sack-like uniform and thick knickerbocker-style underwear for something much more provocative. Mum and Aunt Tina became the first girls on Thursday Island to wear tiny shorts, high heels and make-up. The tales of what they got up to set tongues wagging all over the island and provided regular fodder for some of the more gossip-prone residents.

Monica Gould remembers her mother and her Aunt Lena talking about how shameful it was that convent girls should conduct themselves in such a manner.

Agnes, after leaving the convent, wore short shorts, red lipstick and rouge and white powder. Mum and my Auntie Lena said to them: '*Wiswei* all that powder on your face, you're still black underneath.' But it was because they were suddenly free. (*Wiswei* derived from 'which way' is a Torres Strait Creole expression. In this example, it means 'why'.)[16]

Fellow convent pupil Rita Fell-Tyrell (1934–2004), better known as Rita Mills of the legendary Torres Strait Islander musical trio The Mills Sisters, recounted a similar story. Her face lit up when asked if she knew any stories about an unabashed woman named Temptation:

> *She used to babysit my sisters and I sometimes. She was real sexy. She would pluck her eyebrows so thin and she would do her hair up real sexy way.*[17]

When Rita said 'sexy', it sounded more like 'sexxxxxy' for added effect. She remembered Temptation as being the first woman on Thursday Island to walk the corrugated streets in high-heeled shoes. Rita cackled at the memory of seeing Mum hobbling shakily down the unpaved roads breaking in her new stilettos.

Rita's sister, Ina Titasey (1927–2014), remembered:

> *We had all the girls that lived in the convent and by that time Aggie had left the convent and worked in town. She was working in a shop. I can't recall what they were selling. But she was the most popular girl on TI when I was going to school then. She loved to sing. Everybody knew Aggie.*
>
> *If we went up town she would be sitting in the window of the shop where she worked. If there were no customers she used to sing when she had nothing to do. It was only a little shop. She would sing at the top of her lungs. She had a beautiful voice.*
>
> *When the sailors came into TI, the shop used to be full of sailors wanting to talk to her. She was a little temptation to everyone. They just went mad, all the men. She knew she was so beautiful too and she was a lovely girl. We all loved her.*[18]

Although we lived on the mainland, Mum raised us with some elements of island custom (*ailan kastom*). One time Mum and Uncle Silver took us all down to the Cairns wharf to welcome the fishing boats arriving from the Torres Strait. It was a jubilant occasion and a carnival atmosphere prevailed. Everyone donned their finest clothing.

Uncle Silver was immaculately dressed, wearing a perfectly ironed, crisp white shirt just like flamenco dancers wear. He always looked dapper. Then he changed into his *lap-lap,* a traditional male sarong made from cloth, also known as a *lava-lava,* and performed traditional island dances with the other men. There was endless singing and dancing while Mum kept pace singing along while playing her ukulele. I was wearing a pair of little red leather shoes and tapped around on the deck.

As part of the celebration, seafood was freely distributed. The coveted items were trochus and trepang (*bêche-de-mer*) meat that was exported to Chinese and other Asian markets as both a delicacy and aphrodisiac. Turtle eggs, turtle meat and dugong portions were also in great demand from the Islanders who came down to the wharf. It would have warmed the cockles of Mum's giant heart if I'd eaten the trochus shell meat she desperately tried to force-feed me.

'Come on, Patsy; you won't be a *prapa little ailan girl* until you eat trochus meat,' she laughed, dangling the reeking flesh in front of my face. Unaccustomed as I was to traditional island food, I had never smelt or tasted anything worse. I screwed my face up, tightened my mouth until it became impenetrable and that was it. Mum would have had more success breaking into a bank vault. In keeping with Islander custom, Mum often bathed us in dugong oil, which arrived on the boats from TI. Dugong oil was good for our skin, she said. She was right. Our skin always felt so smooth and velvety at the end of bath time. Like other Torres Strait Islander mothers, Mum also developed an obsession with talcum powder. We were doused in Johnson's Baby Powder after every bath; as an added measure of comfort, Mum sprinkled it generously between the bed sheets each night.

The turtle (*nam*), Mum carefully explained, was our family totem (*lubabat*), an animal with which we had a special connection and one that would offer spiritual protection. I was unaware this was a cultural practice at the time. Magaram and Teg Dauareb clan totems include the snake (*tabo*), whale (*galbol*), mackerel (*dabor*), dolphin (*bid*), dugong (*deger*) and the fruit dove (*dibadiba*).

Mum's Islander heritage explained her lifelong passion and knack for fishing. A skilled angler, she always seemed to know the best time to sit on the jetty, how to predict tides, and exactly where and at what time the fish would bite. She never came home empty-handed.

As children, we were also told about the Coming of the Light to the Torres Strait – or the 'Coming of the Whites', in Mum's parlance. This event commemorates the arrival of Christianity in the Torres Strait via the London Missionary Society (LMS) on 1 July 1871. Mum was forever expressing her disdain for the role that missionary societies played in eroding Indigenous practices and beliefs.

Mum spooked us with tales of our headhunter warrior ancestors who used the skulls of their victims to create magic and enhance their supernatural powers. Sorcery was central to Meriam life and customs in the old days and widely practised at the time. Mum spun exaggerated yarns of cannibalism to keep us all in check. She warned us to run for our lives if we happened upon any dark-skinned men with deep red mouths, inner lips and gums. These people, she said, were the last remaining cannibals on the prowl for new victims.

Mum's own form of spirituality reflected a fusion of her Catholic upbringing, superstition, and traditional and personal beliefs. I imagine she was raised hearing many tales of island magic. Her Grandfather, Misoa (or Waimer), was a *zogo le* (man with sacred or divine power) on Murray Island and reputed for his ability to 'make people of a village hungry and lean' through a process of flesh wasting (*gem kerar*) and through dysentery.[19]

We always covered household mirrors during electrical storms to ward off the bad luck caused by lightning. And Mum prohibited certain types of decorative feathers inside the house. The pretty spots on peacock feathers, she warned, would transform into our enemies' eyes and watch our every move. Shoes were never allowed inside the house, a common Torres Strait Islander practice. Photos of Mum are rare. She loathed being photographed, except on happy occasions or where she is proudly holding up her catch of the day.

We were raised non-denominational and rarely attended Church. However, because of her Catholic upbringing, Mum enlightened us about Mother Mary, Joseph, Baby Jesus and the Catholic saints. She taught us the Ten Hail Marys and Our Father. She was a firm believer in the power of prayer, particularly in times of crisis.

'Prayer is like an insurance policy,' she said.

I thought it odd when Mum stopped and blessed herself whenever she passed a church or cemetery. She always whispered a prayer when an ambulance sped past with its siren blaring and lights flashing. I once asked if she was talking to herself.

'Patsy!' she replied. 'Whenever we see people talking to themselves, we think that they are crazy. When I am talking to God, although he may be invisible, it's called prayer.' Once she had an unfriendly encounter with a local churchgoer, which resulted in her casting one of her more caustic comments: 'In view of your conduct, I understand why the Romans threw Christians to the lions.'

Mum was among the new generation of Torres Strait Islander migrants to the mainland during the Second World War. The dreaming had begun on TI with Mum yearning for a bigger and better slice of life beyond the limitations the tiny three-and-a-half square kilometre 'goldfish bowl'. Spurred on by endless tales of the carefree, glitzy lifestyle and the bright city lights to the south, Mum realised early that marrying a white man would increase her prospects of living the mainland life.

Presumably, Mum was not subject to Aboriginal Protection legislation because she, like other mixed-raced residents on Thursday Island, was considered a Thursday Island half-caste. In the 1930s, the Thursday Island-based local Protector had unsuccessfully attempted to bring Torres Strait Islander half-castes under the Act but he was thwarted by heavy opposition from local residents. The sheer numbers of mixed-race children born of relationships between Indigenous people and mainly Asian migrants made Protection laws difficult to enforce. Determining who was and who was not 'Aboriginal' or 'half-caste Aboriginal' became problematic.[20]

So, Mum considered marriage as her passport to opportunity – including the opportunity to not only experience a new way of living but also to participate in a new community beyond her island home. In her own words, it would have been ideal if love had figured in the plan. But the wanderlust coursing through her veins was impatient to be realised. Love would have to wait. Cupid struck his intended target and Mum's soon-to-be suitor and husband was John Francis Janke (1917–1961), also known as Jack. Jack Janke had worked as a tractor driver and earthmoving operator on Horn Island during the initial stages of the war effort. He was not a tall man, so they must have seemed an odd couple with Mum, at 177 centimetres, towering well above Jack's swarthy 162-centimetre frame.

The Jankes were among the initial flow of German migrants to Queensland in the 1880s. Patriarch Johann Ludwig Janke I (1842–1927) migrated to Australia with his family in 1879, becoming a naturalised British subject in 1887. The Janke family then moved to

German New Guinea in 1905, where Johann regained his German citizenship during the Protectorate era. Although he returned to Australia in 1910, the Home and Territories Minister refused him Australian citizenship when he reapplied in 1925.[21] Unimpressed with the Janke family changing citizenship to suit their personal circumstances, a Director of the Commonwealth Attorney General's Department described Johann as a 'hypocrite of the lowest sort', a man with 'low cunning' and 'no scruple'.[22] Jack's adoptive parents, Johann Ludwig Janke (1882–1970) and his wife, Julia, resided in the sugarcane community of Babinda, North Queensland.

After a brief period of courting, Mum became Agnes Janke when she married on Thursday Island on 28 December 1940; Mum was nineteen, Jack was 23. Mum's close friend, seventeen-year-old Flo Kennedy (née Savage), was Mum's bridesmaid. A simple reception was held at the Guivarra family house on Hastings Street.

The looming threat of Japanese air raids over the Thursday Island group probably influenced John's decision to return to the mainland. Emboldened by her vision of a new life and a renewed sense of emotional security with her then supportive husband, Mum left Thursday Island for Babinda in April 1941. She never returned to the Torres Strait.

4

THE LOVE TRIANGLE

Mum settled into domestic life with Jack in their modest first home at 10 Martin Street, Babinda. I imagine her thoughts frequently drifted the 850 kilometres north to Thursday Island, particularly during Babinda's heavy seasonal downpours; the town is known as Australia's wettest, receiving over 4,200 millimetres of rainfall annually. Mum quickly concluded that life among the sugarcane plantations fell disappointingly short of 'living the dream' on the mainland. She had gone from being the centre of attention on a small tropical island to being an unknown in a sleepy rural community seemingly in the middle of nowhere.

The arrival of unexpected visitors in January 1942 buoyed Mum's spirits. The Second World War was well underway in the Pacific by now, and Grandmother Azey, Aunt Tina, Uncle Silver's family and other Torres Strait Islanders were compulsorily evacuated to Babinda. All women and children from the Thursday Island group were resettled in the Cairns region as the threat of Japanese air raids intensified. The Queensland Government selected Babinda as a host destination, believing the Torres Strait Islander evacuees might 'all be of some assistance to the sugarcane industry'.[23] Other residents, including Great-grandmother Annie Blanco, were evacuated further afield throughout Queensland to the Sacred Heart Mission at Cooyar near Toowoomba.

The impromptu family reunion was complete when Granddad Victor returned from active duty in the Middle East with the 2nd AIF. He visited Babinda during his five weeks of home leave before being deployed to New Guinea in June 1942. Jack Janke also served with the 1st Australian Artillery Field Regiment from March 1943. He was stationed in New South Wales, although his service was frequently disrupted by bouts of painful arthritis. Mum remained in Babinda.

Within months of Jack's departure, Mum learned she was expecting the first and only child they had together. My eldest brother, John Francis Janke, was born in Cairns in December 1943. We were not raised with John. In fact, Mum never even told us that we had an older brother. News of his existence came as a major revelation much later in my life.

Mum's marriage to Jack Janke unravelled in the mid-1940s. Although they had separated by 1945, divorce proceedings were not finalised until July 1949. The divorce was bitter. Mum was named and shamed as the bad girl when their case was included in the 'Decree Nisi' column of the *Townsville Daily Bulletin*. Divorce proceedings were regarded as newsworthy events in those times. Jack told the court that Mum was more interested in partying and being a good-time girl than being a good wife. He claimed to have returned to Babinda on medical leave in mid-1944 to find her under the influence of liquor and in the company of two servicemen. Mum apologised and promised to 'go straight but did not altogether'. In June 1944, when seven-month-old John Francis was sick in hospital, Jack agreed to Mum's request to go to Cairns. A few days later, he read a report in the newspaper that she had been charged and convicted for public drunkenness. Jack claimed to have offered Mum a final opportunity to reform and save the marriage, but she seemed more interested in drinking and continuing her revelry. In December that year, Mum supposedly walked out on the marriage when she returned to the family home, packed her bags and moved to Cairns.[24]

Mum did not contest the divorce, forfeiting the right to tell her version of events. She lost custody of her first-born son. Jack, along with his parents, Julia and Johann Janke, raised John in Babinda. Years later, Mum told me there were several reasons for her unhappiness. She had a sour relationship with her mother-in-law. According to Mum, Julia Janke was unwelcoming and often lamented the fact that her son married a black woman. Conversely, Mum held a great deal of respect for her father-in-law, Johann. My sister, Johanne, appears to have been named after him.

Mum was also a victim of domestic violence during her marriage. Her abuse was common knowledge among close friends and family. An older cousin who socialised with Mum and Jack at the time told me that the beatings were so brutal that Jack's own father often intervened in the quarrels and took Mum's side during the bitter disputes. Ironically, it was a physical altercation between Mum and Jack that led to her walking out of her marriage and straight into my father's life.

Keron Patrick Glendon was already a married man with ten children when Mum arrived on the scene; he had six children of his own, three stepchildren through his wife Emma's first marriage to Basil Arthur 'Texas' Stewart and a child as a result of his involvement with another woman. Late one afternoon, Emma Glendon (1901–1984) was standing at her front door, looking out onto the street from their modest family home on Moorehead Street, Bungalow. At that very moment, Mum was walking by in a distressed state, crying and holding her swollen cheek. Jack Janke had savagely bitten her on the face. Emma took pity on Mum's circumstances, invited her in and offered her a cup of tea to calm her while she caringly tended to Mum's torn skin and broken spirit. In that moment, the two women struck up an instant but lifelong friendship.

Emma was fond of the occasional tipple. She was a generous, down-to-earth woman who possessed an endearing sense of humour which, at times, was irreverent and wicked. She had a raucous laugh to match. Fiercely independent, she put her children's welfare foremost. Emma and Mum spent hours yarning, at times bewailing their misfortunes at having met more than their fair share of unsatisfactory men – Dad included. Ultimately, Mum and Emma's shared circumstances would make them strange bedfellows.

Emma was empathetic to Mum's personal situation because it evoked painful reminders of her abandonment by her first husband, Texas Stewart. Emma offered Mum a helping hand, inviting her to stay with the Glendon family. Her board and keep would be paid in kind by assisting the household as a domestic worker. Working for the Glendons helped Mum to steady herself, financially and emotionally, following the unexpected deaths of her mother, Azey, at 45 and Grandmother Annie Blanco at 67 in 1945 and 1946, respectively.

The Glendons' 325-acre dairy farm at the Daintree near Mossman seemed the perfect environment in which to restore purpose and meaning to Mum's otherwise aimless existence following her separation. Employment with the Glendons marked a significant turning point and a fresh direction in her life. She flourished in the knowledge that her presence and work mattered to someone. Mum became a godsend as a companion and nurse to Emma through the pain she experienced after undergoing a life-threatening hysterectomy. Emma handed the reins to Mum to manage the daily operations of the dairy farm as well as the domestic chores, which included caring for the younger Glendon children. It was a busy existence tending to the 60 head of stock, including cows and heifer calves, sixteen pigs and 100 fowls. Aunt Tina also helped out on the farm from time to time, particularly with milking the cows. Granddad Victor also helped out on the farm from 1946 onward after he returned from active service in New Guinea.

Both Mum and Emma were probably at their most vulnerable when Dad's carnal desires began to stir. Still recuperating from the hysterectomy, Emma was incapable of having conjugal relations with him. It was only a matter of time before he turned to Mum, who to his mind was a nubile, exotic alternative to his wife rather than merely the hired domestic help.

Mum and Dad's developing liaison was no secret to Emma. The *ménage à trois* seemed convenient to all parties. As the 'man of the house' and breadwinner, Dad held the upper hand in the relationship. Mum and Emma depended on him for their livelihood and basic survival. Both women were fragile: Emma, physically; Mum, financially and emotionally. Neither offered any resistance to Dad's demands. Indeed, Emma's friendship with Mum continued unabated, irrespective of her knowing that Dad had transferred his sexual attentions to Mum. She remained indebted for the full-time care and support Mum provided to the family.

Dad was 20 years older than Mum and a year younger than Granddad Victor. He was a tall, sprightly and handsome man. His poster-boy looks and deep blue eyes complemented his charm. It was little wonder many women admired him. The demanding dairy farming work and his keen interest in boxing and, at times, pugilistic encounters meant he was no slouch when it came to defending his tough-guy reputation. Dad often bragged about the days when, as a nineteen-year-old, he had sparred with Jack Johnson's sparring partner. Johnson became the first African-American world heavyweight-boxing champion in Sydney in 1908.

Dad descended from Irish settlers. In a true immigrant love story, my paternal grandparents, Keron Glendon (1858–1927) and Emma Barry (1866–1929), met aboard a passenger ship, the *S.S. Zamora,* while en route from Liverpool, England, to Moreton Bay, Brisbane, in 1882. The Glendons originated from Callan, County Kilkenny, and the Barrys from Banteer, County Cork. The *S.S. Zamora* eventually reached Brisbane on 14 July 1882 after a protracted 102-day journey via the western and southern coasts of Africa and around the Cape of Good Hope. Keron and Ellen were just two of the 315 hopeful immigrants on board; 170 of these were unassisted Irish free settlers.[25] Within a year of arriving in Brisbane, the pair had saved enough money to be married, which they did in August 1883.

Keron and Ellen Glendon started a family, hitched their cattle and wagons, and arduously journeyed north to be among the early settlers in the Barron River, Biboohra and Deeral areas outside of Cairns. They established a farm, 'Glen Valley', which thrived as a result of their pure hard yakka. Dad was one of their nine children. He had several nick-names as a boy, including Paddy, KP (short for Keron Patrick), Kingy and Wonder Boy – the latter given to him by his mother because she often wondered where he disappeared to when chores needed to be done.

My children remember their paternal grandfather, affectionately called 'Pop', as an endearing old man whom they often visited at his little one-bedroom pensioner's cottage on Grove Street, Cairns. When the kids reminisce about those visits, they talk of how he spoilt them with a generous supply of multi-coloured, boiled humbug lollies and bottles of sarsaparilla. Dad's companion in those years was a viciously territorial Chihuahua named Paddy who thrived on a diet of milky tea mixed with cigarette ash; Dad believed this was a preventative measure for heartworms. Dad's grandfatherly demeanour was enhanced by his display of trophies and ribbons from the Cairns Agricultural Show. He regularly scooped the pool in the Best Garden and Prize Rose categories. His 'secret' formula was fertilising the rose bushes with leftover tea leaves straight from the pot.

The docile dad of his later years seemed at odds with the type of man he was in his heyday. If the expression 'where there is smoke, there is fire' is anything to go by, then Dad billowed from birth. As a youngster, he would often remove the catch pan from underneath the girls' thunderbox (outdoor toilet), pull out a big, soft feather and proceed to tickle his female classmates' 'fancies'. This behaviour continued until the day his teacher, Miss Kelly, used the toilet during recess. The rest, as they say, is history. Miss Kelly did not appreciate having her 'undercarriage' stimulated with Dad's feather. Dad was sent home with a note addressed to his mother with words to the effect:

Dear Mrs Glendon. Your son Keron's inappropriate conduct indicates he is too old to attend school. Would you kindly make alternative arrangements for his future? Signed Miss Kelly.

Dad left school at fourteen years of age and worked on the family farm. He landed his first job with the Biboohra Meat Exporting (BME)

Company when he was sixteen, and stayed in the meat business for several years before working in the timber and sugarcane industries. Mum often jibed Dad, mocking him for his philandering eye and his antipathy for hard, physical labour.

'The heaviest thing he ever lifted in his life was a woman's petticoat!' Mum once quipped.

Dad's wayward exploits increased in seriousness over the years and by the late 1930s, he and Emma were illegally selling alcohol to allied servicemen stationed in Cairns. Although Dad was the instigator of the sly grog scheme, he was rarely caught.[26] Emma and her son, Basil Robert Stewart, were charged and convicted for the illicit sale of alcohol following a string of undercover police raids in the 1940s.[27] Dad also supplemented his income by providing laundry services to American servicemen during the Second World War.

Income earned through his legitimate work in the meatworks and timber industries was supplemented by other activities. An astute investor and speculator, in time, Dad amassed an impressive property portfolio. He owned several houses, farms and commercial properties as well as a number of vintage vehicles, including a Goanna sports mobile, a Chevrolet utility, a 1940 Chevrolet Pullman sedan and a classic old Austin that he referred to as his 'antwique'. In later years, Dad claimed to support the Irish Republican Army (IRA) and said he remitted money for their cause. I do not know if this was true, but Dad had become a man of means and influence among his many connections, including publicans, bookmakers, sly-groggers, police and women.

'When money talks, angels sing!' Mum would say.

In her declining years, Mum often remarked that she knew a great deal about Dad's finances and activities.

'One day there will be a book about me, Patsy. I can't write it just now. I have to wait for a lot of people to die first,' she once said.

Family folklore also prevails about Dad's insurance fraud scams in the 1930s that allegedly involved setting fire to family property and assets and collecting on the policies.[28] Emma purportedly joined in on the act, earning herself the gangster-style nickname 'Firestick Emma'. Yet Dad had some noble qualities. He was 26 when he married Emma after Texas deserted, leaving her impoverished after he supposedly returned to his native South Africa, never to be seen or heard from again. Dad's marriage to Emma took place in spite of his mother's vehement opposition and family dissension. Emma was not Catholic and she already had three children – Bob, Jack and Mary. Dad was ultimately hunted out from his family properties and disinherited.

In 1946, the mutually beneficial 'arrangement' between Mum, Emma and Dad was shattered when Mum became pregnant with my brother, Terry. Dad maintained separate living arrangements from Mum after his marriage to Emma foundered, and Mum's devotion to Dad meant she mutely acquiesced to being hidden out of sight at the Daintree farm after she became pregnant.

My six siblings from Dad's marriage to Emma, all Glendons, include Keron Patrick (1926–2013), Kevon Barry (1928–2018), Margaret 'Megsy' Ellen (1932–2010), Keith 'Joe' Denton (1930–present), Glenda Patricia (1937–2010) and Kenneth Richard James (1941–present). Dad's other son, Edward 'Eddie' Clarke (1942–1984), was through his involvement with another woman of mixed Indigenous ancestry. I never met Eddie but Terry and Michael did. While some people in similar circumstances refer to such siblings as 'half-brothers' or 'half-sisters', I make no distinction and always refer to them as my 'brothers' and 'sisters'.

My brother Joe recalled his early memories of Mum:

We knew nothing much of the relationship Dad and Agnes had going because we were too young. By 1945 Dad had picked up with Aggie in a more or less compatible arrangement and then he moved out of home and went up to Hartley Street. I had lost touch with Agnes then. In 1946 I was supporting Mum and paying her my wages. Dad needed some extra help on one of the farms he owned over the river. He bought another farm and ran into trouble because he was working at the Meatworks and he was also with Agnes.

Mum asked me to go to the farm to help my father. At that stage I thought Mum and Dad were in the process of reconciling. When I got up there to Daintree Farm I did not know Agnes was there. That really threw me because I did not expect anyone to be there.

I remember it as though it was yesterday. I walked onto the property and the house was built on the sort of a hill and I must have arrived there between 4 pm and 5pm. Agnes the poor bugger, she was running that dairy farm, and she was pregnant too. I didn't know she was pregnant. I remember she was in a white dress when I walked up and she was chopping wood at the back of house for firewood and she was there by herself on the property with only the cows for company. I couldn't believe it.

She taught me the run of the farm. The farm had its own electricity and battery storage. She was cranking the diesel engines, making bales, milking the cows and separating the cream. Dad would have taught her that in a short space of time. Here she is, 7 months pregnant with Terry, running the farm alone.

Agnes blended in with the family because she was family. She treated us kids like a mother. She was a good guiding star. Because the love was there, the love she gave us kids. Honestly that woman in my opinion needs

> *a crown for what she put up with on that farm and for running it the way she did. I don't think Dad ever had any intention of marrying Agnes but she was the most loyal to him.*[29]

Although Mum was out on the farm, news of her and Dad's dalliance quickly spread within Cairns social circles. Some of the more narrow-minded labelled Dad a 'gin-jockey' (man who has sex with Aboriginal women) for openly flaunting his association with lower-class black people. Impervious to the gossip, Dad continued to live life on his terms. In these times, the weight of social judgment was a strong deterrent to mixed-race relationships and marriages. I listened with a retrospective sense of sadness as my sister Glenda told me of her ostracism; she was mercilessly teased at school and by some members of the close-knit Deeral community because our father had deserted Emma for a 'black gin'.

By the time I was born in August 1948, Mum's vulnerability had deepened following the death of her closest companion and only sister. Aunt Tina, then 24, passed suddenly from heart failure caused by the onset of tuberculosis in January while Mum was in the very early stages of pregnancy with me. She left behind a now-orphaned six-year-old girl, my elder cousin and Mum's namesake, Agnes Philomena Blanco. Fellow Torres Strait Islander Granny Jaira Dan (Catherine Jaira Dan, née Amboyn) took on the responsibility for raising little Aggie. Granny Jaira and her husband, Henry, had previously adopted a little boy, Henry Gibson Dan, back on Thursday Island. These days, Henry Dan is well-known in Indigenous and musical circles as the Australian Recording Industry Association (ARIA) award-winning musician 'Seaman Dan'.

Mum was inconsolable following Aunt Tina's passing. The deaths of her mother and grandmother were still fresh in her mind. Granddad

Victor continued to help Mum out on the farm until he moved to the Northern Territory in 1949. He came back to Cairns for a fleeting visit in 1954, but I believe Mum had no further contact with him after that.

When Mum's divorce from Jack Janke removed any legal impediment to her marrying again, she succumbed to the realisation that it was now up to Dad to divorce Emma or vice versa. Nevertheless, Dad continued to live like a single man, happy with his philandering lifestyle, bound to no one. He was free to come and go to the farm – or anywhere else – as it suited his needs, while Mum was left with the responsibility of raising the family. She continued to wait.

By April 1950, Mum was pregnant with Michael. It was around this time that Dad sold the Daintree farm and moved us to Hartley Street. I believe he'd had this property since the early 1940s and had plans to use it as a boarding house, catering for waterside workers. In the meantime, Dad never seemed to live in one place, flitting between Emma's place and Mum's. For a time, he preferred to stay in boarding houses in Cairns to maintain his 'single' lifestyle; he favoured the Heatherview Boarding House in particular.

Dad's *annus horribilis* was 1950, the year in which his character and activities would be vigorously scrutinised following his appearances as a witness at a murder trial and coronial inquest. One of these events would have disastrous impacts for our family and dash Mum's expectations of marrying Dad.

5

THE WITNESS

On 3 April 1950, Dad witnessed a fatal stabbing involving my godmother, Isabella Violet Nakamura. A genteel, thick-set, portly Caucasian woman, Mrs Nakamura was not the dainty Japanese woman her name evokes. Mum had entrusted her to be my godmother, and Mrs Nakamura (née Butler) played an active role in raising and nurturing me during my formative years. Her house offered sanctuary. She bathed me, fed me nutritious home-cooked meals during regular sleepovers and tucked me into bed. I loved snuggling between the sunshine-fresh linen.

Mrs Nakamura also sent Mum food parcels, usually brought over to Hartley Street by two teenage girls whom I presume were her daughters. One day the girls arrived when Mum was not home.

'When your mum comes home, please give her our regards,' they said as they handed over the food.

I passed on the message when Mum returned.

'Mum! Mrs Nakamura's girls were here today. They left a parcel but they also wanted me to give you their regards. I am sorry, Mum. I waited but they didn't give me anything.'

Mum laughed loudly.

'Oh, Patsy, don't you know what regards means?'

Mrs Nakamura's caregiving to us seems all the more remarkable in view of the tragic events in her own life. Hardship and heartbreak were her closest companions. She was a child bride, married when she was just fourteen years old. Her Japanese pearl-diver husband, Naka Nakamura, was well into his forties at the time of their wedding. Some years later, in January 1937, Mr Nakamura and their daughter Hazeline died in a drowning incident in the Mossman River. Hazeline was eight years old. Although Mrs Nakamura had separated from her husband four years before this terrible event, such a traumatic loss would have been difficult to bear.[30]

In April 1950, Mrs Nakamura was charged with the murder of her second partner, café owner Mick Poulos (Mikhail Dimitropoulos), after she stabbed him to death with a kitchen knife in self-defence. She went to trial in July 1950. Mick, 47, had received seven stab wounds to his upper body, including two inflicted to the heart. Family legend tells that Mick was disembowelled but the coroner's report states otherwise.[31]

Mick was a formidable opponent, even while heavily intoxicated. A 167-centimetre, 115-kilogram Greek-Albanian ex-professional wrestler and all-round standover man, Mick also had a penchant for biting off and chewing chunks of glass from tumblers. He could also bend the silver and copper threepence coins with his fingers. At the murder trial, Mrs Nakamura told the jury that Mick subjected her and her daughter Nellie (Mick's stepdaughter) to unspeakable acts and years of brutal abuse. He had forced her into prostitution and slashed her with a razor to keep her in line, she said. She further claimed Mick was a violent drunk who sexually abused Nellie over many years.[32]

By this time, Dad was a fellow tenant at the Heatherview Boarding House with Mrs Nakamura and Mick. He was present at the time of the stabbing and testified in Mrs Nakamura's favour. During the trial, Dad recounted the events of that day and the lead-up to the violent event. He spoke of Mr Poulos's aggressive character and his previous pattern of alcohol-related rage. Mick had once tried to slash Dad with a jungle knife. The defence team established a compelling case with Dad's help. Mrs Nakamura was found not guilty after a jury acquitted her of murder on Friday, 28 July 1950.[33]

Dad became embroiled in more scandal two days later. Another unfortunate incident had culminated in Dad courting and eventually marrying a younger woman, Eileen Cynthia Tooth (née Ludwig). Eileen was a pretty woman of mixed Aboriginal and German descent who hailed from Yarrabah Mission outside of Cairns. Eileen was also married at the time but that would all change following an ill-fated Sunday social outing at which Dad was present. On Sunday, 30 July 1950, Eileen's first husband of three years, Gordon Keith Tooth, plunged 210 metres to his death over the Tully Falls in North Queensland. Eileen, her sister Florence Leitch, her brother-in-law Alexander 'Dusty' Leitch, their infant daughter and Dad were all there when the accident occurred. The group were all known to each other. Eileen claimed she and Dad first met at Northern Plywoods when she worked as his offsider on the benches two and a half years before. And Dad was already well acquainted with the Leitch family on account of him and Dusty being colleagues at the Queerah Meatworks.[34]

A coronial inquest into the accident was held in December 1950 and continued in July 1951. Dad, Eileen and several other witnesses were called to give evidence. The coroner heard Gordon Tooth, a cattle station worker of mixed Aboriginal and Malay ancestry, had allegedly been throwing sticks over the falls, lost his footing and fell. His body re-floated nine days later when it was caught temporarily in a water pool but disappeared again with the strong currents. His remains were never recovered.[35]

Gordon Tooth's mother, Lizzie Boyd, informed the coroner that she resided at the Heatherview Boarding House, the same place where Mick Poulos was killed and where Dad was still living. I do not know if Dad and Lizzie Boyd were acquainted, but can only assume that their paths would have crossed at the boarding house at some point.[36] The inquest reviewed the extent to which, if any, Gordon's life insurance policies may have been a factor in his death. Gordon and Eileen had jointly taken out a £500 accidental death insurance policy and a separate £500 endowment policy in October 1949, six months before the accident. Eileen was the sole beneficiary for both policies.[37]

The coroner subsequently determined that Gordon's death was accidental, attributing no blame to any person. But this incident was not an isolated one. At least two other visitors died in similar circumstances at the Tully Falls. A tourist, George Walters, had fallen to his death in November 1939, and in July 1954, a picnicker, Hugh Mullins, had met his death the same way.[38]

Presumably, Eileen and Dad sought solace in each other's company, the traumatic experience bringing them closer. Dad did not take long to declare his romantic interest in Eileen. He remained unperturbed by talk of his appearances in Mrs Nakamura's court case and at Gordon Tooth's inquest. If anything, the public spotlight only served to inflate his ego and glamorise his 'bad boy' reputation. A string of casual liaisons with other women ensued. Mum began to notice the by-now familiar, telltale signs of infidelity, including lipstick smears and perfume scent, as she laundered his shirts. Family rumour has it that Dad fathered several children to women other than Mum and Emma as a result of his frequent womanising, which reminds me of another of Mum's favourite phrases: 'A standing prick has no conscience!'

Dad's indiscretions with other women were no surprise to Mum; she was always looking for evidence of his affairs. She once recounted an incident in which she succeeded. I believe this encounter occurred before I was born, at a time when Mum, Dad and Terry had left the Daintree farm and were living together in Cairns. Mum had left the house on the pretext of visiting a friend, but she made a surprise return to find a lady, a family friend, massaging Dad's foot that was resting on her lap. Dad and his love interest sat smug and cosy, unaware that Mum was outside, watching and listening. The woman giggled, occasionally throwing her head back in laughter. The lovers continued canoodling, pausing only to take a sip of tea from the china cups.

Mum restrained her anger as she walked in unannounced. Dad and his date were startled. Mum said nothing, just calmly went about clearing the china teapot and matching cups and saucers from the table. Uncertain as to Mum's next move, Dad and his playmate simmered in awkward silence, waiting for the expected emotional outburst. Mum whisked the tablecloth off the table, flicking it swiftly aside, matador style. She paused, glared at the woman and issued her cold retort.

'I don't care what you do with my man, but you are certainly not welcome to drink tea out of my good tea set.'

According to Mum, Dad's ego wasn't the only thing that deflated that evening.

Mum became disheartened, exhausted by her continual attempts to dissuade Dad from womanising. She suspected the blossoming romance between Dad and Eileen. She didn't know why but their obvious attraction made her wary of their intentions. She wrestled with a new kind of jealousy and decided to take action. Mum hatched a plan to challenge the status of Dad and Eileen's relationship. They had maintained for several years that they were just good friends, but Mum invited them to our Hartley Street home in an attempt to force the issue of them being an item. When Eileen went to the toilet, Mum told Dad Eileen wanted to see him. Once Dad was at the toilet door, Mum pushed him inside, promptly locking the door behind him.

'Don't play me for a fool,' she shouted. 'If you want to be together, get it over and done with. Just spare me the lies.'

She then left, leaving them captive in the toilet until Dad kicked the door open. In some respects, Mum's action that day freed her from the anguish created by uncertainty and self-doubt. But it also finally ignited the flame that had flickered between Dad and Eileen. Mum was crestfallen.

'Hunger makes coarse meat sweet!' was Mum's usual retort when alluding to Dad's infidelities. She had fallen victim to her own hunger and neediness when she put all her eggs in one basket with Dad. Perhaps humourist Dorothy Parker's wit best captures Mum's situation: 'She put all of her eggs in one bastard!'

—

Michael was born in 1951. Mum, bound by her misguided loyalty, continued dressing Dad in the garments of her dreams, investing him with qualities he simply did not possess. She naively continued to believe Dad would marry her. Johanne's arrival in May 1952 brought Dad's tally of children with Mum to four, but there was still no wedding on the horizon. To maintain consistency, Mum decided to give all of us the Janke surname even though Jack Janke was not our father.

In October that year, at Dad's request, Emma filed for divorce, on the grounds of desertion.[39] She agreed to the divorce with a curious caveat – that he marry Mum. Although Dad agreed in principle, it never happened. In 1954, Dad, now 52, married Eileen, aged 27. No doubt distracted by his efforts to support and please his new wife, Dad's contact with our family was reduced. Mum reckoned that Eileen might not have been keen about Dad spending too much time with us during their honeymoon period, let alone happy about their money being spent on our upkeep.

To say that Mum, like Dad's first wife Emma, was left holding the babies is something of an understatement. At the time, while we knew her as Auntie Eileen or Aunt Eil, Eileen seemed like an older sister figure to me; this was reinforced by her constantly referring to Dad as 'Daddy'. Mum did not handle the break-up with Dad very well and increasingly sought to soothe her sorrows in the bottle. She embarked on prolonged drinking sessions, often referring to alcohol as the poor person's psychiatrist. But if Mum was struggling coming to terms with the dramatic shift that Dad's marriage to Eileen had created within her life, then outwardly she never showed it. Her life continued to be one big party and she was intent on keeping up appearances.

Dad and Eileen gradually became regular drinking associates within Mum's social circles. Over time, there were occasional gatherings, with adults and children mingling on the banks of the Mulgrave River, picnicking and swimming with the music from the phonograph wafting in the background. In a curious echo of Emma and Mum's inexplicable bond, Mum and Eileen managed to remain on relatively good terms. But there was clearly no love lost between Emma and Eileen, evidenced by a civil action in which Eileen recovered £150 pounds plus costs owed to her in 1954.[40]

Eileen was duplicitous and dismissive of me as a young girl. I was involuntarily bonded to her and found it irksome when I learned we shared the same birthday. I believe she resented my having any contact with Dad. Maybe it was because I was a reminder of his relationship with Mum. Whatever her reasons, Eileen assumed a 'street angel, house devil' persona with me. She was sweet and charming toward me in public or at social functions, but whenever I tried to visit Dad at their Scott Street residence, she would chide me and stridently shoo me away. I never let her 'wicked stepmother' behaviour deter my visits to Dad though.

Even as a child, I struggled to understand how Mum could stay friendly with Dad and Eileen after the heartache their marriage had caused her. It still saddens me to think of Mum's nightly sobbing and my own helplessness to make things better for her. I did my best to comfort her, innocently believing her sobbing would stop with my beseeching. 'It'll be all right, Mum,' I'd whisper. 'Terry, Jumbo, Johanne and me are still here.'

I was too young to know that however heartfelt my words were, they were not enough to divert Mum from her grief-stricken turmoil. I was also too young to appreciate the significant impact Dad's marriage to Eileen had upon Mum. Years later, Mum told me that her acceptance of Dad's betrayal and ultimate rejection of her and us, his children, in favour of a much younger woman, was worse than coming to terms with the death of a loved one: the loved one is dead and buried, yet Dad was alive and kicking and gadding about in the same social circles, heartlessly flaunting Eileen's presence in his life. Irrespective of how she tried to mask her heartache, the pain of Dad's rejection left Mum with a gaping wound within that marred her attempts to pick up and move on. Mum's downward spiral had commenced.

6

LITTLE BIG GIRL

I was Mum's 'Little Big Girl'. It was her special name for me. I was her apprentice. We shared household chores and I took care of my younger siblings. In reality, she was grooming me for a shared burden of the responsibility of maintaining and supporting our family, a role I now appreciate the value of, during the period when Mum's relationship with Dad disintegrated.

My bond with Mum developed as I monopolised much of her time and craved her attention and presence. Mum relied on me as much as I leaned on her, and the enduring influence she had in my life was formed while I was her Little Big Girl. My siblings did not share this same kind of bond or close relationship with Mum. I was always being teased for being 'Mummy's little pet' as I began to boss my brothers and sister around, assuming the role of the mini-matriarch of the family. Mum showed me how to clean the house, to make the beds, and to sweep and mop. Sometimes her lessons were unconventional. One time Michael was stung by a jellyfish while on a visit to Yorkeys Knob beach. Mum's attempt to have Terry pee on

Michael's leg to alleviate the sting still makes me laugh whenever I think of jellyfish.

As Mum's confidante, I listened intently as she spent countless hours sharing stories with me and pouring her heart out on the back steps of the house. I snuggled beside her, sucking my thumb while she articulated her problems. Our bond was so close that she breastfed me until I was almost six years old. This was my idea, not hers, and the breastfeeding only stopped after Mum threatened to come down to school and pull out her *susus* (breasts) in front of all the other children and feed me.

Because of Dad's rejection and infrequent child support, Mum remained the centre of our universe, always working hard to stave off poverty and provide for our needs. She worked as a laundress at the Central Hotel in Cairns, a typical two-storey pub with a big veranda on the second level that was always full of beer-thirsty patrons. With child minders in short supply, whenever possible we accompanied Mum to work. We darted back and forth and slid about on the wide wooden floorboards while Mum buried herself in mountains of linen and garments. She was an immensely proud woman and it showed in the detail and quality she applied to her work. Occasionally, I would pause and admire the way Mum energetically washed, starched and ironed all day long while cheerfully humming tunes. The heat from the heavy wrought iron magnified the intensity of the humid tropical weather. It was hot, hard work, but nobody could press a crisp business shirt like Mum or produce linen that was so white. Her toil was done when she neatly folded all the pressed linen and put a dry towel over the top of the basket.

Mum took on extra loads of ironing for private customers to increase her hard-earned but paltry income. There was very little in the way of social and financial support from the government, other than small child endowment payments, which were received monthly. So often Mum worked several jobs, which usually came piecemeal, to generate additional income. On occasion, she worked at Glasgow House as a kitchen assistant and part-time cook for Mrs Hickey, a rather matronly woman with a glass eye. Glasgow House on Spence Street catered for single male wharf employees, seasonal labourers and immigrants. One evening, Mrs Hickey gave true meaning to the idiom 'keep your eye out' when hers plopped out and became lost somewhere inside the house. Mum was horrified as she ladled Mrs Hickey's glass eye from a pot of hot chowder, serving it into a soup bowl before a startled boarder before she fully realised what was happening.

Mum was eye-catching in the physical sense too (pun intended). It is said that 'there is only one beautiful baby in the world and every mother has it'. But Mum was truly beautiful – and she belonged to us. She had a sassy, haughty presence and retained a sense of pride, which was fastidiously focussed on her appearance. Tall and shapely, Mum was always very aware of her presence, confident of her ability to attract attention, male and female alike. Her lovely long legs were her best physical attribute. I used to lie on top of the bed and watch her dressing, enthralled by the manner in which she applied improvised cosmetics to her face. With some gentle twisting, plaiting and tucking, her soft frizzy hair would be transformed into an elegant style in moments. Mum never wore jewellery or accessories, not even a watch or necklace. She dressed simply, being one of those exceptional women who could buy a ten-dollar dress and look a million dollars in it.

Mum's preoccupation with her appearance was motivated by part-vanity and part-pageantry. A regular in-house busker, Mum supplemented our meagre family income by hustling for tips as a seasoned cabaret performer, singing at local pubs. Mum was good for business. She was often invited by publicans to entertain in their establishments. Flanked by her loyal entourage and admirers, Mum always managed to pull a crowd. Her performances enlivened a number of Cairns venues during the quieter periods of trade. Mum thrived on the charity of pub patrons and the sentimentality of drunken sailors. Patrons rewarded her musical renditions with spare notes, loose coins and in kind – with Mum's favourite being bottomless, free beers. Alluring and beguiling, a sultry songstress, in next to no time she had hotel drinkers and her regular partying companions eating out of her hands and competing for her rendition of their favourite songs. That suited Mum. She was always styling up big time and revelled in being the centre of attention.

A born entertainer and a true one-woman variety artiste, Mum sang a cappella and played the piano. She introduced the ukulele to her routine and amused the crowd with a hula, her voice sounding a little like Sarah Vaughan's or Billie Holiday's. We grew up listening to the repetitive strains of her favourite numbers – 'Harbor Lights' by the Platters, 'Mona Lisa' by Nat King Cole, 'Pearly Shells' by Hank Snow and 'The Philadelphia Lawyer' by Woodie Guthrie. To please Dad and the overtly Irish pub patrons, she also had a repertoire of Irish songs: 'Galway Bay', 'Forty Shades of Green', 'When Irish Eyes Are Smiling', 'Danny Boy' and the humorous 'Paddy McGinty's Goat'. She often performed Torres Strait Islander classics including 'Old T.I.' and 'What's A Matter You Last Night?'

Mum's talent and confident demeanour became her licence to infiltrate the exclusive, segregated whites-only areas of many a drinking establishment. Buchanan's Hotel in Townsville was one such.

It imposed a colour ban during Mum's heyday. A 'coloured' patron needed to be a sponsored guest of a white Australian or European in order to drink there. Mum was a sponsored guest of a member from Dad's side, the white side, of the family on one particular occasion. A younger lady of mixed English and Aboriginal descent walked into the lounge, demanding service. She had previously been involved in an altercation and entered the lounge looking shabby, sporting a black eye – a disincentive for the publican to respond to her drink order. He refused to serve her. The lady became abusive, outraged not to be served on the basis of her colour. The publican's stubbornness only inflamed the situation. When the lady caught a glimpse of Mum, a fellow black woman, enjoying a beer in a corner of the lounge, she ventured towards Mum, her chest pumped and lips pouted, hell-bent on engaging Mum in the dispute.

'Well, what have you got to say about my not being able to get a drink? Look at my colour compared to yours! You're blacker than me!' she ranted.

Mum maintained her composure.

'Leave me out of it,' she calmly retorted. 'I don't know what your problem is but the publican's clearly colour blind! Please go away!'

The woman went off in a huff. Other patrons marvelled at Mum's wit in handling the matter. Over the years it took the sting out of some deeply hurtful and humiliating situations. Once a patron abused Mum in a crowded bar by calling her a *gin* (pejorative term for an Aboriginal woman).

'If you don't mind, I prefer to be called Gilbey's!' she retorted, citing the popular English brand.

Mum often told us this story, and plenty of others like it.

'It takes a special person with an equally special attitude to bounce back from life's setbacks,' she'd say. 'Remember, a thick skin is a gift from God.'

—

Mum's drinking increased with shrinking regard for our basic care and welfare. She claimed to be a social drinker before meeting Dad, but her alcohol consumption since Dad's marriage to Eileen had become habitual. While Mum went about her business and socialising, we amused ourselves in a small park near the pubs and played on the swings, slippery slide and a carousel. She was always close by and we were never troubled by strangers or scared of playing by ourselves. We spent as much time in that park as we did at home. George Manning's pie van was nearby and we were among his most regular customers. I had the task of running across to get some money from Mum whenever we became hungry or thirsty. Mum's drinking companions and other pub patrons often reacted with shock when they heard me call her 'Mum'.

'How can it be?' one of them once asked. 'You are black-skinned but your child is white?'

'Hey, buster,' Mum quipped. 'Haven't you heard of the black hen that laid the white egg?'

It was like winning a mini-casket prize whenever Mum's drinking buddies reached into their pockets and pulled out loose coins. We'd spend them on food and drinks, or pool them to save up to spend at the school tuckshop. If they were really generous with their tips – or as Mum called it, our lucky dips – we would feel pretty spoilt at being able to buy milkshakes and Paddle Pop ice-creams rather than the usual spread of potato chips, hot chips, pies and sausage rolls. This kind of largesse could be expected on the wharfies' weekly payday. Although some were married with their own families to feed, they liked Mum and felt good about lending her a helping hand.

Sometimes Mum left us at home alone before returning much later in the evening. I recall one visit by Child Protective Services (CPS) when we lived at Hartley Street. Terry and his friends were running through a large vacant allotment adjoining the street. The lot had just been back-burned, leaving patches of ground carpeted with smouldering embers. While trying to keep pace with his friends, Terry tripped and fell into a ditch that was lined with hot ashes. He required a skin graft after receiving second-degree burns to his feet and lower limbs. The local Health Department staff made several house calls to obtain Mum's formal consent for the procedure but she was not at home. We were reported to the CPS for being left unsupervised, but I'm unaware what action, if any, was taken against Mum at the time.

—

Hartley Street was next to the entertainment area and within short walking distance of the lively pub hub of Cairns, known locally as the Barbary Coast. The Barbary Coast was dotted with popular pubs, which included the Pacific Hotel, the Great Barrier Reef Hotel and the Oceanic Hotel. All contained a lounge section, which was separate from the public bar. Mum provided cabaret entertainment in the lounges. She and her drinking companions were such a regular part of the scene that they considered they virtually owned the strip. After closing time, the party would move to our house. Mum and her disparate companions, whom she had us call Aunties and Uncles, entertained themselves by partying frivolously, drinking, dancing and singing into the early hours of the morning. Aunties Nancy, Phyllis and Del were regular female revellers. Mum's friend from the Sacred

Heart School, Auntie Marie Swindley, was not interested in drinking but came for a good time and Mum's company. Her husband, 'Uncle' Clarrie (Clarence) Swindley, was also on the scene from time to time. Auntie Marie went mad for Mum's *ailan* singing. Some nights I would stay with Mrs Nakamura; her house was quiet compared to the cacophony at Hartley Street when Mum's parties were in full swing.

Mum also developed some celebrity status among the Scandinavian labourers and wharfies, who were among the new generation of immigrants to Australia. Hartley Street soon became an informal Scandinavian embassy in Cairns; it was a place where men from various parts of Europe – Denmark, Sweden and Norway in particular – intermingled. The second incarnation of the Assisted Passage Scheme had opened to Scandinavian migrants in 1952. Since then, Australia had received a significant increase in the number of skilled labourers, tradesmen and other workers, including carpenters, plumbers and cheese-makers who found ready employment with local businesses in Queensland's metropolitan and rural areas, Cairns included.[41]

During impromptu home visits and social outings, Dad would stir Mum, arguing with her, accusing her of fraternising with Nordic men because of their fabled larger endowment. She scoffed at his crude remarks. Mum really enjoyed winding up the Welshmen. She referred to them as 'blow away Danes', recounting the early history of raids by the Vikings, and stirred the pot a little more by reciting tales of Norse mythology and Erik the Viking.

Our favourite visitor was 'Uncle' Hans Hvid, a gentle, caring man from Denmark. Short and bow-legged, his darting cross-eyes made him an odd-looking fellow. He used to regale us with tales from the high seas, stories of pirate adventures and, of course, Hans Christian Andersen fairy tales. I loved 'The Ugly Duckling', 'The Little Mermaid' and 'The Little Match Girl'. Because of his interest in making us laugh and befriending us, Uncle Hans stood out among Mum's companions and friends.

Mum and Uncle Hans had a close, platonic bond throughout this time. Uncle Hans was placid, steady-natured, and from the outset, always tried to influence Mum's life for the better – quite different from the rowdy revellers who were just about always on the scene. He was a good boxer too and could defend himself when needed. He never backed down. One time he broke a truck driver's arm during an altercation. An experienced carpenter-cum-boat builder and seafarer, Uncle Hans rejected the landlubber life. He preferred to live on a boat moored near Cairns inlet at Portsmith or in one of the nearby estuaries.

Auntie Marie, like Uncle Hans, was a staunch supporter of Mum. Both she and Uncle Hans were very protective of my mother. They badgered her constantly in the hope that she'd give up the self-destructive party lifestyle in favour of giving herself and us children a better, happier life.

Mum's enduring, 'starstruck' love for Dad was another story. Because of the unconventional nature of their relationship, her capacity to fully enjoy herself without his presence was diminished. Although Mum had no shortage of male companions, nothing compensated for Dad's absence. Mum craved the stability and certainty of a loving relationship. As her love for Dad went unrequited, she became ever-receptive to the attention of other men.

For a short time, Mum took in Scandinavian boarders for extra income. Kris Bergman was a lanky, two-metre tall Swede who was Mum's temporary live-in companion until he assaulted her. One evening, upon hearing Mum's agonised screaming, Terry and I raced into her bedroom. She and Kris were arguing. He tried to bar her from reaching for the door to escape his rage. In his fury, Kris had grabbed hold of her hand and was trying to pull her away from the door; in the process, he twisted and broke Mum's hand. Her little finger protruded, bent back and broke out of shape.

I leapt to Mum's defence, my foot charging directly into Kris's balls. Terry intervened with a shoulder charge. Kris surrendered by rushing through the house and outside onto his clapped-out pushbike. He never set foot in the house nor bothered Mum again. We kept a watchful eye on Mum as yet another relationship 'bit the dust'.

—

On 8 June 1954, my future stepfather, Kaj Aron Svend Eggertsen, stepped off the Norwegian merchant ship the *Kvernaas* carrying little more than a giant suitcase full of demons all the way from Copenhagen, Denmark. Kaj Eggertsen, whom we called Uncle Kaj, was already a chronic alcoholic when he arrived in Australia. He also suffered from depression and was prone to dark moods. His brother, Ejnar, who suffered from similar afflictions, had suicided by gassing himself back in Denmark some time before Uncle Kaj's arrival in Australia. Uncle Kaj was contracted to work with Cairns Ship Building on Lake Street but then drifted as a seasonal labourer.[42] His and Mum's worlds intersected during a drinking session at one of her usual pub haunts.

At the time of their meeting, both Mum and Uncle Kaj's lives were fraught with self-destructive behaviour. They were both struggling to cope with the breakdown of their last relationships. Both were looking for a new beginning. Kindred souls, inextricably drawn together by unhappiness and common adversity, they found comfort in being together. It was as though they were on a quest to restore some measure of happiness to their own and each other's lives. They abandoned their personal strife, though, by resorting to their mutual love of alcohol. And Kaj had a case of 'uncork the bottle, uncork the demons'.

Mum, now 34, and Uncle Kaj, 32 years old, became inseparable. They married on 30 May 1955 at the Central Methodist Church in Aplin Street, Cairns. I was almost seven years old at the time. Their marriage represented yet another metamorphosis for Mum; she became known as Mrs Agnes Eggertsen. Despite his own addictions, Uncle Kaj's attempts to stabilise Mum's unsettled domestic life made him seem a far better influence than Dad. In marrying Mum, Uncle Kaj inherited a ready-made family of four children who were not his, but we never called him Dad, just Uncle Kaj. 'When you take the cow, you have to take the calves too,' was a saying Mum inherited from Emma. Uncle Kaj's outwardly sentimental displays of affection for Mum were clear indicators of not only how besotted he was with Mum but also how he was putting his love to the ultimate test by marrying her. The initial honeymoon period, with Mum and Kaj both bathing in matrimonial delight, was a time we all enjoyed.

I recall Uncle Kaj being a kind, hard-working stepfather when the bottle did not get the better of him. I used to think how lucky Mum was to have such a handsome husband whose blue eyes and blond Nordic features set him apart from other fathers in our neighborhood. He was also tall, standing at 175 centimetres, and had a small rose tattooed on his left arm.

Uncle Kaj tended to flit between jobs. Although his work was seasonal, he was sometimes dismissed for turning up drunk or not turning up at all. We would crowd around the radio each morning waiting to hear if his name would be called live on air to go to sign on at the Cairns wharf. If we heard his stevedoring number on the radio, we would run down the corridor and into the bedroom, pushing and shoving each other aside.

'Uncle Kaj, Uncle Kaj, you have to go to work. Your number was on the radio.'

On paydays he would become scarce, preferring to spend more time drinking than being at home. This wasn't a bad thing. Uncle Kaj could become quite sentimental and argumentative when he was drinking. But he also could be very generous, showering us with treats when he came home from the pub. And he must have been observant as he quickly adopted the standard Aussie practice of Fridays being fish and chips night.

Although we never understood a word of it, we enjoyed his nostalgic singing and toasting – '*skol*!' – in Danish. Uncle Kaj said he did not miss Denmark. Australia was home now and it was warmer. He would often speak amid tears and fond remembrances about a little girl named Judy who was back in Denmark, telling me she and I were the same age and how much we would like each other. He promised that if he ever won the lottery, he would take me to Denmark to meet her. Sadly, Uncle Kaj's lottery dream failed to materialise. The furthest we ventured together was to a new house on Progress Road in an outer suburb of Cairns.

7

PROGRESS ROAD

Life became harder around November 1955 when Dad moved us all from Hartley Street to a new house on Progress Road. An emerging suburb of Cairns, in that era White Rock was quite some distance out of town. The houses were situated on large plots of land. We lived on a corner block, and I recall no more than six houses within our immediate vicinity, although our neighbours' houses were not tightly clustered together. Families in the area included the Felminghams, the Khalus, the Cowards and some local Aboriginal families who lived closer to Skeleton Creek. Mr Colin Swann lived further out near Cannon Park and allowed us to ride horses on his acreage.

Although Mum was now married to Uncle Kaj, Dad still provided the roof over our heads. I'm not sure why he chose to move us so far out of town. Progress Road was closer to the Queerah Meatworks where he was Manager. Perhaps he sold the Hartley Street property. Or our move to White Rock could have been a ploy to put some distance between Mum and her regular drinking companions, whose ongoing presence disrupted Dad's domineering influence over Mum. Whatever the reason, the move destroyed all our lives in the most catastrophic manner possible. Such was the irony of 'Progress' Road.

White Rock itself was picturesque and set among the canefields but living there imposed a particular hardship on Mum. Instead of being able to walk the short distances to and from Cairns central business precinct, it was now necessary for her to catch the rail motor, approximately a 40-minute one-way trip. She would leave White Rock early in the morning and often return late in the evenings, by taxi, usually in company of several friends. Uncle Kaj was also at work, and subject to his staggered stevedoring roster, he usually joined Mum when he knocked off and usually accompanied her home at night. There would be happy times. There would be argumentative times.

Like other children of our generation, we became latchkey kids, left to manage ourselves during Mum's working hours. As months passed, her excursions to town became more frequent and her absences longer; she was now, more than ever before, in full pursuit of the alcohol-fuelled 'good life'. So much so, she gradually relinquished her parental and maternal responsibilities.

The move to White Rock also meant we could no longer walk to the Tropical Picture Theatre as we did in Hartley Street. Most weekends we either hitchhiked or rode into town on stolen pushbikes Terry gathered from neighbourhood yards, local shops, or nearby playgrounds and parks. At the end of the movies, we'd all ride back to White Rock and Terry would return the bikes or rearrange them so the owners never knew they were missing. We were real little urchins, just like those rascal kids in *Oliver Twist*.

Mum taught us about stranger danger and warned us against hitching rides.

'Don't be hopping in cars with strange men or people you don't know. Even if they tell you Mum sent them,' she said.

But if no pushbikes could be found, Terry would decide on hitch-hiking. I was the front person in these escapades because Terry believed that a girl would have more success at being picked up by a passing motorist than a boy. This proved to be a foolproof method. We always managed to score a free ride into town.

Despite Mum struggling to provide for the four of us, soon there was another mouth to feed after Mum became pregnant with Elin, her only child with Uncle Kaj. We tried to take advantage of Mum's incapacity during her pregnancy with Elin, always running wild, generally ignoring her orders, cheekily poking fun at her and taunting her, secure in the knowledge that she was unable to discipline us because her big, fat belly impeded her chances of getting hold of us. But regardless of her condition, Mum tolerated no nonsense.

It was game over one particular day when Mum casually picked up the nearest stone, took aim at me, then fired her missile. Direct hit. It was target down as the rock struck me in the back of the head. I still have the four-stitch scar. I fainted more at the sight of the blood than I did from the pain. But I never messed with Mum again.

One would think Mum's style of retribution would have resulted in my putting such childish capers aside forever. Not long after being downed by the rock she hurled at me, and overjoyed at the pending arrival of Elin, one afternoon I took three neighbourhood children into Mum's bedroom, where she was sleeping. Slinking onto the bed, we took up vantage points. Our eyes focussed on Mum's swollen belly. I was willing for a sign – any movement from baby Elin would do. We waited. The only movement on the bed was Mum's and ours. Suddenly she woke, flustered, and hunted us out of the bedroom.

Baby Elin's arrival temporarily bonded our close-knit family even more tightly. By coincidence, Elin was born on 8 June 1958, exactly four years to the day that Uncle Kaj arrived from Denmark. We fussed over our baby sister, encircling her at bath and feeding times, and secretly disturbing her by gently pulling her fingers and hands while she was asleep. Sometimes, I would deliberately wake her so I could pick her up, nurse her, cuddle her and get a whiff of her Johnson's Baby Powder smell. Elin was much more fun and interesting than my doll, Penny.

Mum gave me a crash course in nappy changing, just as she had when Johanne was born, emphasising the importance of holding my fingers in a particular way when pinning the nappy so as not to pierce her delicate skin. Baby Elin slept in a makeshift crib in the bottom of our pull-out chest of drawers. Johanne liked singing lullabies to her and Elin, like others over several generations of our family, was hummed to sleep by the melodic tune of Hank Snow's classic song 'Pearly Shells'.

After Elin's birth, Mum continued to commute to Cairns to find casual laundry work, socialise and drink. Uncle Kaj also began to disappear, sometimes for days on end. Mum expected Terry to stay home and babysit Elin and Johanne while she was gone. Michael and I were supposed to attend school. This did not happen.

While Terry initially took charge of the household, he soon became unreliable, preferring to roam the neighbourhood and create mischief. As Little Big Girl, I had no choice but to step in and take charge. I was nine years old at the time. Elin was three weeks, Johanne five years, Michael six and Terry eleven. I meticulously measured and prepared the Lactogen infant formula. I changed Elin's nappies and spot-bathed her with a face cloth. She was tiny, the same size as my doll.

Our school attendance became more infrequent. Although I enjoyed school, I preferred the outdoors, self-paced, disorderly lifestyle

Our only family photo taken at Hartley Street, Cairns. Mum centre, Terry, me, Michael with Uncle Hans Hvid partly obscured, Johanne and Aunty Marie Swindley.

Mum on a flattie.

Mum's only sister, my Aunt Tina, (Teama) Celestina Blanco.

Great Grandmother Annie Blanco and her third husband, Bob Quetta, in their canoe off Hammond Island. *Pic courtesy Blanco family collection*

Mum's brother Uncle George Ganomi Blanco performs a traditional Meriam 'kab kar' warrior dance before Queen Elizabeth during her royal tour in 1971. *Pic courtesy Getty Images, Hulton Royal Collection*

Photo of Meriam dancers, 1921, the year Mum was born.
Pic courtesy National Library of Australia, Frank Hurley Collection

My Grandmother, Azey Leyah Sari (alias Mary Blanco) pictured standing rear with family members.

ASKING A POLICEMAN. **Victor Blanco, the only Australian aboriginal soldier at present in London, asking a policeman for information. In civil life Victor was a pearl diver at Thursday Island.**

Granddad Victor in London with the Australian Imperial Forces during WWII.

My grandfather, Victor Blanco performing a traditional dance, circa 1940, for fellow Australian Imperial Forces (AIF) troops at Colchester, England during WWII. *Pic courtesy State Library of Victoria*

Mum's first husband, John 'Jack' Janke, working on the Horn Island Airport Construction, circa 1943. *Pic courtesy of the Loban family*

Dad, Keron Patrick Glendon.

Dad's first wife, Emma Isobel Glendon (née Simpson). *Pic courtesy of the Glendon family*

A photo of my Irish-Australian family taken in April 1912 at the wedding of Mary Ellen 'Nellie' Vallely and John Glendon in Mareeba, North Queensland. The elderly couple on the far left are my grandparents Keron Glendon (1858-1927) and Ellen Glendon (née Barry, 1866-1929). *Pic courtesy of my cousin Ellen*

Mum's party pal and close companion,
Danish migrant 'Uncle' Hans Hvid.
Pic courtesy National Archives of Australia.

My stepfather and Mum's second husband,
'Uncle' Kaj Eggertsen. *Pic courtesy National Archives of Australia*

where I was not confined to a classroom with the irritatingly repetitious spelling and arithmetic. Instead, we attended the 'University of Life'; our campus was out and about, playing in the sunshine and wide-open spaces. Desk-bound biology and earth science lessons were replaced by frequent excursions to Skeleton Creek. We dashed about the embankment searching for tadpoles, chased and caught butterflies, trapped red and black ladybirds and put them into bottles with punctured lids so they could have oxygen. We swam when the creek was flowing with full force after the seasonal downpours. We played with clay on the banks, making mud cakes, often taking Elin with us, carting her around in a wheelbarrow with the dogs, Bjørn and Tige, running closely behind.

Floating down Blackfellow Creek on sheets of galvanised iron was fun. If we were not swimming, we engineered hand-made mini-steamrollers from empty Sunshine powdered milk tins filled with sand and hauled them along using cotton reels for wheels and coathanger wire for handles. Other days, we cruised around the neighbourhood on billycarts. Our imagination and creativity were limitless. I became the local marbles champion for two successive years, defeating all the boys. Our activities became cheekier, more daring and dangerous, including playing chicken with trains on the track or dodging the rail motors as they traversed the overhead bridge at Skeleton Creek. We placed pennies and coins on the railway tracks and waited for the trains to run over them.

'Stay away from those train tracks or you will end up like Auntie Topsy!' Mum cautioned. Mum's drinking buddy was said to have died after being run over by a train as she slept on a railway track while under the influence of alcohol.

Dad did not value education as much as Mum because of his abrupt departure from Miss Kelly's class in his earlier years. If anything, he aided and abetted our exploits by dumping huge blocks of dry ice and cow bladders from the Queerah Meatworks into Skeleton Creek. The mist and vapour would rise from the water with eerie effect. We learned to blow up the cow bladders and bull testicles and use them as water polo balls or footballs. Mum was never aware of the extent of our truancy. Fearful of retribution, I forged her signature on our school report cards, carefully writing her initials A.P.E. before returning them to school, where they were blindly accepted without any comments.

Terry, Michael and I were obliged to go to school when Mum stayed home, of course, and it was not unusual for us to go without lunch on those days we attended Hambledon State Primary School. Although there was no shortage of mischief in Progress Road, there was a food shortage. Stuck out at White Rock, we could no longer rely on the charity of strangers, nor could we steal Mrs Harding's pies from the fence. Starving, I scavenged through the school rubbish bins looking for half-eaten apples, fruit, sandwiches, any leftover lunchbox food. I often wished my schoolmates would waste some of their packed lunches. I surveyed the common areas, sat back and quietly waited for students to toss their leftovers. I went to the rubbish bin and salvaged what I could. Michael was always hungry. His nickname wasn't Jumbo because he was skinny. He wouldn't eat the food if he knew I had retrieved it from the bin so I pretended to eat the food scraps, nibbling at the edges and then offering them to him to eat.

Our mixed racial heritage was never an issue until we moved to White Rock. Somehow or other, it filtered around the neighbourhood that the Janke children were the coloured family on the block. I never really understood what colour they were referring to. Yellow? Pink? Red? Blue? At Hambledon State Primary School, Hilary Barnard was my friend. In fact, she was my only friend apart from my siblings.

We hung around together, and one day, after school, she invited me to her home to play. She ran ahead to ask her mother for permission. Waiting on the back steps of Hilary's house, my excitement was shattered when I overhead Hilary's mother's response.

'Tell her to go home. I am not having any coloured kid in my house. I don't want you being friends with her either!' Mrs Barnard declared.

Hilary looked awkward and embarrassed as she approached me. She said her mother did not want me in the house and she was no longer allowed to play with me. I felt hurt at being rejected but also sad for Hilary. I knew she liked being my friend and having fun with me. As I walked home, I kept touching and looking at my skin. I could not understand what Mrs Barnard's fuss was about, as my skin didn't seem to be that much darker than Hilary's. After her mother's outburst, Hilary avoided me when we played near each other in the schoolyard. I had gone from being her best friend to a *persona non grata.* I don't know what her true feelings were about this. We never spoke again.

It was a miserable time for me. The loss of Hilary's friendship profoundly blighted my capacity at that early age to ever want another friend. Mrs Barnard's words really gnawed at me. I knew from her tone and inflection that the word 'coloured' meant 'dirty'. I was not good enough to be Hilary's friend. I wanted Mum's comfort and reassurance so badly. I needed to place the gut-wrenching hurt somewhere.

But having contemplated Mum's impulsive nature and fearing the consequences, I never told her what Mrs Barnard had said. Throughout the almost 65 years since, as I have gone about my professional and personal life, whenever I have watched, heard, encountered or engaged in debates on racism and how it feels to be discriminated against on the basis of race, Mrs Barnard always comes to mind.

8

TROUBLED TIMES

Mum and Uncle Kaj had had arguments about the household budget from the outset and they continued to disagree over money, mainly the lack of it. Although Uncle Kaj became the family breadwinner, we survived on his crumbs. Our wellbeing, including food and clothing, was secondary to feeding his and Mum's addictions. What little income was earned was quickly spent on beer and the Temple Bar and Camel-brand cigarettes that he smoked. Once, in a moment of curiosity, I decided to sample Uncle Kaj's cigarettes. I took his Temple Bars from the table and went down to the backyard. Shielded by a lemon tree, I was hoping to be magically transformed from a nine-year-old into an adult just by lighting up. The only transformation was my face as it contorted with the choking fit that followed. Mum would have been bitterly disappointed in me had she ever known of this, but luckily she didn't have a clue what I'd been up to.

After a while, Mum, Dad, Uncle Kaj and Eileen resumed a cordial relationship, often socialising at the pub and going on outings, including picnics. Dad's visits were more regular at Progress Road than they'd been at Hartley Street. Emma, meanwhile, moved in her own social circles, being now in an established de facto relationship. My much older siblings, Keron (Kingy), Kevon, Keith (Joe), Kenneth (Scotty), Margaret (Megsy) and Glenda were all busy maintaining separate lives too; I didn't have any association with Emma or that branch of the family at this time, and only developed a closer connection with the Glendons through Dad, Megsy and Glenda from 1967 onwards.

As much as Mum cared about Kaj, her heart still belonged to Dad. Often, upon her return home after a night out, she became emotional. Her moods swung like a pendulum between optimism and pessimism. Many a time during those episodes, Mum pulled me aside for a mother–daughter session.

'Promise me you will never marry or have children, Patsy,' she said. 'Women start off with bright hopes and dreams like shiny new pennies only to end up as loose change in some man's pocket or discarded on his dresser.'

Mum would flick her hands as if tossing a coin on the ground. Then she'd sob as I tucked her into bed. Sometimes, I snuggled in beside her until she fell asleep. Her heartbreak and despair were tangible. I know she also felt the pressures of providing for her children. Dislocation and distance had made things much more difficult for her at White Rock, economically and socially.

Mum still felt obligated to Dad as he continued to exert his Svengali-type influence over her. Theirs was an unusual dynamic. Although Dad had rejected Mum and married Eileen, he remained possessive about Mum's personal interests and activities. He did not like the thought of her being with anyone else – Uncle Kaj included – in spite of all the picnics and parties. Dad thrived on power and control and used his financial support as leverage. He often reminded

Mum that we were living in his house at his discretion. We could be made homeless at his whim.

Effectively, Mum was relegated to being a single mother doing her best to raise five children with dwindling financial and practical support. Uncle Kaj, grappling with his own demons, tried his best but his reduced income from blowing shifts at work compounded his – and our – problems. To the best of my knowledge, Dad didn't provide Mum with much cash but what little support he offered was gratefully received. Mum persevered as best she could, trying to make up any shortfalls by doing piecemeal work. But her income could not offset the expenses of her drinking habits and our upkeep. Drinking remained Mum's chosen method for numbing out the harshest aspects of her life, which included looking after us.

Nonetheless, Mum usually had a plan. She improvised whenever there was a shortage of food or money. On several occasions she took us down to the waterfront along the Cairns Esplanade. She huddled us under an upturned dinghy beached on the shore, then disappeared. I had the responsibility of looking after Michael, Joanne and Elin. Terry was there but, being his usual disobedient self, as soon as Mum was out of sight, he would skedaddle off to do his own thing.

Mum would return several hours later laden with groceries, ice-cream and lollies. Impatient to eat the treats, we did not need to be hurried up to head home. Sometimes, Mum would chat briefly with male strangers as we headed back to White Rock. They would give her cash before parting ways. As a child, this all seemed a part of Mum's outgoing nature; she'd always enjoyed male company so such meetings seemed just a normal extension of her cabaret engagements at the local pubs.

In time, I came to accept that Mum had resorted to sex work. And that Dad knew about this. It caused tremendous friction between them. I remember one of their confrontations clearly.

'I suppose you've been lying on your back again, haven't you?' Dad asserted.

'What do you expect? We can't live off what little money you give us,' Mum replied.

That evening, Dad came back to the White Rock house and went into Mum's bedroom while she readied herself to go into town for another cabaret session. Dad intervened. He became angry at her insistence on going out. Desperate, he accosted her, pushing her onto her bed. All the while, Mum was trying to repel his attack so she could continue dressing. Family folklore has it that Dad pulled a razor out, but it turned out to be a shaver. It was on top of the bedside dresser. Agitated, he restrained Mum and proceeded to shave both her eyebrows off. Then he left the house.

Mum did not react. She regained her composure and, straightening her dress, sat down at the dresser, drew the mirror closer and began to apply her make-up. She lit two matches and watched them burn for a split second before snuffing them out. Then, placing the charred matchstick between her fingertips she neatly pencilled on two new eyebrows. Down to the Esplanade we went.

Being only ten years old when this happened, I didn't understand what Dad meant when he accused Mum of 'lying on her back'. Mother's Day was coming up when Miss Lynne Mills, my teacher at the Hambledon State School, asked the class to write an essay. The topic was 'Why I love my mother'. The best essay would receive a prize. I scribbled frantically, hoping to win. My turn came to stand before Miss Mills and the class and read my composition aloud. I walked to the front, stood firm and proud as I waited for Miss Mills to prompt me. She nodded when it was my turn.

'I love my Mum because she lies on her back to give me, my brothers and my sisters clothes, story books and lollies.'

Before I could finish the rest of my composition, Miss Mills stood, walked toward me and gave me an almighty slap across the cheek. I was ordered to leave the classroom. Miss Mills was a big woman, so it hurt when she struck me. I flinched but I did not cry. I waited outside the classroom, hoping Miss Mills would explain what I had done wrong. That did not happen. My composition was not returned. Distressed, I wandered out of the schoolyard and onto the road for the four-kilometre walk home to Progress Road.

This was another school matter that I did not want Mum to know about. After that incident, I don't recall ever returning to Hambledon State Primary School. Nor do I remember ever seeing Miss Mills again. My education in Cairns ended months short of my tenth birthday. It was not until I was eighteen that I learnt the vulgar inference in Dad's remark to Mum. This revelation enabled me to release the longstanding resentment I'd harboured towards Miss Mills but it did not allow me to forgive her mistreatment.

—

Since our move to White Rock, Mum also became increasingly frustrated by Terry's troublesome antics. He continued stealing, shoplifting, fighting and bullying kids in the parks, disappearing from the house all day and wandering at will. Mum expected that Terry, being the eldest, would behave himself and lead his younger siblings by good example. Instead, he not only continued to misbehave, but he would also take advantage of Michael's innocence by coaxing him into engaging in acts of petty theft together.

At some stage, Mum's tolerance ran out. She took to beating Terry regularly, at times severely. Michael, Johanne and Elin were too young to understand that Mum's mistreatment of Terry shouldn't be allowed to happen. One time, after watching Mum hit Terry and then lock him out of the house, forcing him to sleep downstairs with the dogs, I pleaded with Mum not to treat him so cruelly. I implored her not to lock him outside; she had already punished him enough.

'Please let him sleep inside with us,' I begged.

My plea fell upon deaf ears. Mum tried to excuse the severity of Terry's punishment, stating that something serious needed to be done to get his misbehaviour under control. Mum was concerned that his misbehaviour, particularly stealing, would attract yet more unwanted attention from the police and welfare authorities. She also became annoyed when Terry's pranks could have had serious repercussions for Michael's health. Once he'd dropped a bug into Michael's ear canal while he was sleeping. Michael woke up alarmed while Terry thought it was a great joke. Uncle Hans came to the rescue with a spoonful of heated castor oil, a cotton tip and a torch. On another occasion, Terry pushed my head into a plough, resulting in a sizeable gash to my head. He also copped a hiding after he stole Mum's money from underneath her pillow while she was sleeping. He went to the store and bought lollies for the neighbourhood children. Mum was livid because he had stolen her drinking money. She really got stuck into Terry that day.

Mrs Coward, a neighbour, intervened after another incident in which Mum was heavy-handed with Terry. Mrs Coward took Terry to her house for the night. She rubbed his welts with a mixture of cold butter and flour to reduce the swelling and ease the stinging. Not long after this, two welfare workers, presumably from Child Protective Services, visited us at Progress Road to investigate reports of maltreatment. They were critical of the perceived deficiencies in

Mum's child-rearing capabilities, citing our truancy and unfettered roaming around the neighbourhood, and her absences from home. Dysfunctional misfits, we clearly did not conform to society's standards for a nuclear family. Mum was indignant about the welfare workers' officious stance and lack of recognition for the hardships she endured and cursed them.

'Yes! I may have fallen short in difficult times but I don't see the government handing out any spare tits to help me feed the children. Come back and see me when you've got something other than lip service!'

Terry's troublesome antics intensified at Progress Road. Recognising that Terry was the cause of Mum's growing frustration, Dad took more of an interest in him. He decided to have Terry accompany him to local building and construction sites at the weekend. He also gave Terry driving lessons in his Chevrolet, and organised sparring sessions in a makeshift boxing ring. The bouts would exhaust Terry, deterring him from engaging in more troublesome antics.

Occasionally Dad kept Terry overnight at his Scott Street residence but Mum became suspicious of Dad's motives for doing so. Dad continued to ingratiate himself with Terry in order to gain information about Mum's general activities and whereabouts. Terry, in his innocence and wanting to please Dad, unwittingly told him snippets of Mum's comings and goings. If Dad was not pleased with anything Terry had let loose, he would confront Mum about it, demanding an explanation from her.

Mum resented Dad's sly intrusion into her life again. Even after all this time, she still had not come to terms with his rejection of her in favour of Eileen. With Dad now living in Cairns and some distance between them, Mum vented her rage on Terry, punishing him by locking him outside with the dogs again. This time, behaving more cruelly, she restricted Terry's movement by attaching a dog chain. It was a rainy night. I could see his cowering silhouette, huddled against the dogs as the lightning flashed across the sky. Again, I pleaded with Mum, again unsuccessfully. The rain became heavier. I tried to ignore the fact that Terry was out in the middle of it. In the end, I caved. Shuddering, but unafraid of the consequences, I raced downstairs and unchained him. There was a change of dry clothes hanging on the undercover clothesline downstairs. We grabbed them, crept upstairs and snuggled into the double bed beside Michael and Johanne.

Listening to the raindrops on the tin roof and with Terry tucked in bed beside me, I worried about our safety. Mum could appear at the bedroom door at any tick of the clock. I prayed, asking God to watch over and protect us, especially Terry. I expected a backlash from Mum the next morning but she didn't say a word about anything out of the ordinary. It was as if she had simply expected that someone would look after Terry's welfare that stormy night.

As Mum's second-in-charge, it was difficult for me to ignore her forceful behaviour. We were all affected by her escalating loss of control. She had never used that level of violence on any of us until our move to White Rock. Michael and Johanne never got a smack, ever. Mum kept them in check by chiding them or depriving them of treats, playing outside or other recreational outings. She left it to me to mete out their discipline, but I never smacked them either, following Mum's example.

When it came my turn to be disciplined, it was the usual whack about the legs with the circular leather strap from an old Singer sewing machine. It sure packed a sting. From memory, I never copped it more than three or four times. Terry still drove Mum to her wits' end though. He was whacked in similar fashion to me until Mum could no longer control him. His juvenile misdemeanours piled up: his bad influence on Michael, ceaseless mischievous escapades and, of course, 'pimping' to Dad about Mum's private life. Still worried about Mum's mistreatment of Terry, I somehow plucked up the courage to be angry with her. Having to ignore her in such a sulky way hurt me deeply though.

'What's the matter, Patsy? Come, don't be cranky. Give Mum a cuddle,' she beckoned.

Finally, I responded.

'Mum, I am the child. You are supposed to be the grown-up, our mother. At the moment, it is the other way around.'

The maturity in my words stung her. Stepping backwards, away from me, she looked me over.

'My Patsy, such horrible words from sweet lips,' she said disdainfully. 'Who taught you all you know? Come, give Mum a cuddle.'

There she stood, looking vulnerable and innocent, yet claiming full credit for my mini-matriarch deeds. She seemed oblivious to my criticism, and it was difficult to maintain my anger; she always used her persuasive sweet-talk to break down any emotional defence mechanisms. Not only did she have a mighty way with words, but she was also equipped with a seductive manner. She sure knew how to charm the anger – and sometimes the hurt – out of me.

—

Mum and Uncle Kaj experienced their ups and downs like any married couple, but at White Rock, their domestic disputes intensified over time. Uncle Kaj's absences from home became more extended. Sometimes he was gone for days. The Edmonton police were called to the house on one occasion after Kaj received a laceration on his arm during a dispute with Mum. She'd cut him with a broken bottle. It was the only time I recall any physical altercation between them. When the police arrived, Kaj claimed the injury was accidental. The sergeant, Stan Whyte, pulled me aside.

'Nothing will happen to you if you tell the truth,' he said.

I was the only witness to the fight, but my first loyalty was to Mum regardless of her addictions and changing behaviour. I remained silent, refusing to betray her.

Terry recalls the occasions when Mum and Uncle Kaj left us at home unsupervised for lengthy periods without any food. He claims they were sometimes absent for almost a week but I believe it was never for more than two days at a time. We both remember Elin crying from hunger after the Lactogen formula had run out. I improvised and fed her a bottle full of black tea and sugar instead.

On 16 July 1957, Mum and Uncle Kaj appeared before the Cairns Children's Court charged with neglect following an intervention by the Edmonton police. They were admonished and cautioned by Magistrate Hickey to behave more responsibly. Unfortunately, paying scant regard to the court edict, their lives continued on a downward spiral. In 1958, the police intervened again.

9

WARDS OF THE STATE

I was ten years old when I was locked up with Terry, Michael and Johanne at Cairns Police Station. The cells were gloomy and colourless, a far cry from the daily freedoms and fresh air and sunlight we were used to. They were located in a slightly raised wooden structure at the back of the police station that was visible from the street. The veranda was encased by thick diamond mesh that extended from the ceiling to the floor. The sleeping areas and toilets were in the same section. Although my recollections are fuzzy, our cell seemed to have been hurriedly prepared, with bedding placed on the floor in a haphazard manner. We were detained in these cells because child welfare centres and family refuges did not exist at the time. At the time of writing, the practice of detaining children in police cells still continues in some remote locations throughout Western Australia. Our anxiety at being in this caged environment intensified as we became increasingly fretful over Mum's absence.

Neither Mum nor I were at home when the police initially took Terry, then eleven years old; Michael, aged seven; my sister Johanne, who was six; and four-month-old baby Elin into custody. My siblings were transported by paddy wagon from Progress Road to the police station on the Esplanade. Elin was admitted to hospital. Under Part IV, Section 20 of the *Queensland Children Act (1911–1966)*, the police were empowered to take neglected children into protective custody without a warrant, pending a court hearing.

On 9 October 1958, Mum appeared alone, unsupported by any family or friends and without any legal representation, before Stipendiary Magistrate Mr Thomas Hickey in the Cairns Children's Court. The hearing relied exclusively on hearsay evidence contained in the deposition of Constable Stan Whyte, who was stationed at the nearby Edmonton Police Station. Misspelling and typographical errors are consistent with the original Court deposition.

Childrens Court,
Cairns
9 October 1958

SUB INSPECTOR M. McDONALD APPEARS TO PROSECUTE.
NO APPEARANCE OF KAI ARON SVEND EGGERTSEN
AGNES PHILOMENA EGGERTSON APPEARS.
STANLEY WHYTE sworn states:

I am a Police Constable attached to Edmonton Police Station. I know the Defendant and children now before the Court. I also know the mother Agnes Philomena Eggertsen now before the Court. I also know the father Kai Aron Svend Eggertsen. At about 1pm on the 8th October, 1958, a complaint was received at the Edmonton Police Station by a Mrs Felmingham of White Rock stating that her house had been broken into by Terrence Eggertsen and One Pounds worth of crackers were stolen.

I immediately proceeded to White Rock … I asked Terrence when he had last fed the baby and he said 'About 10 o'clock this morning'.

I said 'Where is your mother'?

He said 'She hasn't been home for a couple of days'.

I said 'Have you had anything to eat?' He said 'No'. I said 'Has your father been home'?

He said 'Yes, he came home, had his tea, got dressed and went out again'. I noticed on the table there were two bottles of wrapped beer that had been drank.

Further enquiries were made and it was ascertained that Agnes Philomena Eggertsen was arrested on 2nd October, and on the 7th October for drunkenness. I later located Agnes Philomena Eggertsen at White Rock where I questioned her concerning this matter and she stated that she 'had a row with her husband and she had a cancer on the lip and she hasn't got much to live for so I might as well get on the grog and have a good time'.

I said to her 'I have just put Elain Eggertsen in the Cairns Base Hospital and Terence Michael and Joanne are being looked after at the Cairns Police Station'.

I said to her 'Where is Patricia'? She said 'At some friends place in Cairns'.

Today I went down to a Mr Danns place of Morehead Street, Cairns where I located Patricia. Mrs Dann stated that a Mrs Canendo found Patricia wandering around the streets of Cairns on 2nd October and taken her to Mrs Danns place to be looked after.

I later informed Mrs Eggertsen that I would be charging the children as being neglected children, and that she was an unfit person to be in control of them …

I do not think that the mother and father of the children are fit and proper persons to have control of the children, as they have been warned on numerous occasions by the Police stationed at Edmonton. I endeavoured to serve notice to Kai Aron Svend Eggertsen who is employed as a Waterside worker at Cairns. He was paid this morning and absented himself from work. I have made diligent enquiries to his whereabouts and I have been unable to locate him. He is well known to me and other members of the Police Force. To my knowledge he has been before this Court on charges of drunkenness. He is addicted to liquor. On numerous occasions he absents himself from his family home. He absents himself overnight and sometimes he is gone for a couple of days.

Mrs Eggertsen is addicted to liquor and seems to associate with lower class coloured people on the waterfronts and there is nothing much I can say in her favour. She has been before the courts on previous occasions for drunkenness. Quite frequently she leaves the kiddies at home and catches the early bus into town and never comes home until the late bus at night.

I have visited the family home on a number of occasions in recent times. The appearance of Terence, Michael, and Johanne this morning is much better than they generally are. The same can be said of Patricia. One previous occasion the mother approached me and asked me if I could get them into a home as the husband was drinking all the time and would not give her any money. I instructed her to go to the C.P.S (Child Protection Service) Office at Cairns, and obtain the forms.

I would say that in all my visits the children were in unkempt condition. I informed the mother last night that the baby had been taken to the Cairns Base Hospital and admitted to Ward 5, as I could not find her. I informed the mother this morning that the hospital authorities told me the baby when admitted was in a starved condition and suffering from a cold that would have to be given attention to.

XXD MOTHER
No questions

S Whyte
CASE FOR THE PROSECUTION.

I was not at home when the police took my siblings into custody. Constable Whyte said I was found wandering the streets in Cairns but I have a quite different memory of walking to Mrs Nakamura's house. According to Terry, Dad dropped by the police station on 8 October with new clothes for us to wear at the hearing, but I missed his visit.

Representing herself, Mum offered little defence. The result was a foregone conclusion. Magistrate Hickey issued Committal Orders and Warrants of Detention in accordance with Section 27 (1) and Section 27 (b) of the Queensland *State Children Act (1911).* We were immediately removed from Mum and Uncle Kaj's care. The magistrate declared each of us Wards of the State until we attained the age of eighteen years.

—

Being declared Wards of the State came with a legal duty of care and an implied guarantee: as neglected children, we would ultimately receive a higher standard of care and protection from the State Children's Department compared with the home environment from which we were removed. Nonetheless, our confinement at Cairns Police Station painted a grim picture of the life that lay ahead for us. We were placed in custody in the same section as adult offenders. Several men were detained in the adjoining cells. Most were drunk. Some were raucous while others remained quiet as they contemplated their own misfortunes. Some inmates swore and pulled at the mesh, behaving worse than monkeys in a zoo. It was the staring, somewhat leering nature of their actions that scared me the most. The drunken detainees frightened us when they called out and tried to engage us in conversation.

'What trouble did you kids make to find yourselves in here?' one asked.

I remember Terry toughing it out about the place and showing little outward concern or emotion about our detention. He was allowed to join us through the day but at night had to return to a special padded cell with a small viewing window. Michael and Johanne were too young to understand what was happening. They just wanted Mum, both of them crying out for her and defiantly pushing my hands aside as I reached out to comfort them. They wanted nothing to do with me.

Mum visited us during her authorised access visits. Her presence brought immediate calm and soothing reassurance to our troubled minds. Thank God! No more worrying. She had come to take us home. Terry aside, we could not contain our jubilation, delightedly skipping about, climbing all over her, overwhelming her with hugs, pushing and shoving each other as we vied for her exclusive attention.

Mum also solved the problem with the noisy cellmates. She disappeared for a moment. The noise and their antics ceased abruptly. It was as if she knew them personally or held sway over them. I liked to believe that Mum had magical powers to warn off scary events and shoo bad people away. She was my talisman, protecting me from the clutches of the bogeyman lurking under my bed and shielding me from the strange, menacing creatures I had concocted in my mind that were hiding out in the bedroom. They disappeared upon Mum's caress or being moved to the security and safety of her bed.

Terry was a non-believer when it came to Mum's mystical abilities. He reckoned the cellmates' silence came after Mum threatened to have them beaten up by Dad, who still had a notorious reputation about Cairns because of his involvement in pub and street brawls. Nevertheless, I still chose to idolise Mum and her protective powers.

I cannot recall Dad visiting us in the cells. Regardless, his appearance would not have made an iota of difference to our predicament. But Mum came back and forth at regular intervals during our confinement. She helped us shower and dress, then supervised us at meal times. She distracted us from being afraid by plying us with a generous selection of lollies, soft drinks, comics and Disney storybooks. She also used these treats as a form of blackmail to exercise some control over our growing restlessness. If we did not cooperate, stop crying or sulking, she would threaten to leave us and take the treats with her.

For the most part though, whenever she visited, Mum sat by our side, almost stoically, speaking softly. She continued to reassure us, saying that everything would be okay, encouraging us not to be scared of anything, no matter how bad it was being cooped up in a metal cage like little birds. Her 'little chickadees', she affectionately called us. The most important thing, she said, was that we stayed together as children and as a family. I believe it was Mum's special way of preparing us for the separation.

When I became a mother myself, I realised what an agonising moment that must have been for Mum: attempting to maintain her composure and keeping up an appearance to protect her children from the grief and trauma of indefinite separation. I cannot imagine how she felt knowing we were about to be removed and her feeling powerless to prevent it.

Mustering all of her strength, and suppressing her regret and sorrow, Mum savoured every remaining moment of contact with us. She showered us with endless warm embraces, kisses and cuddles. There were some unguarded, solemn moments when she must have imagined what her life would be like without us. Despite Mum's efforts in putting on a brave face and reassuring us that everything was going to be okay, I just knew in my heart that our family togetherness, as it had been, was now shattered.

Mum never mentioned Elin. She ignored my questions about her whereabouts and welfare. Although I knew Elin was too young to be confined with us in the police cells, she was still our four-month-old baby sister and I was concerned about her.

—

Just when I started to succumb to the belief that I may never see Elin again, she appeared on the platform of Cairns Central Station on 10 October 1958. She was wearing a white bonnet, and Mum was nursing and caressing her.

I remember a lot of brightness on the day of our separation, maybe because we had been confined and had walked out of the darkness of the cells and into the sunshine. Our beautiful mum was wearing a white nylon dress; her hair had been styled into a French roll and, although her face was etched with sadness, she looked exquisite.

Mum had brought us new clothes to travel in. Sadly, our best-dressed day, the day Mum dressed us up so resplendently, was the day we were going away. The excitement of going on a train journey was somehow intermingled with trepidation and sorrow. Our joyful greetings to baby sister Elin were replaced with tearful goodbyes to Mum.

Some of Mum's friends showed up to farewell us, but Dad and Eileen were no-shows. Michael has a memory of Uncle Kaj being at the railway station. I do not. I have often wondered what part, if any, Dad may have played in our removal. He was notable by his absence during the court hearing and in the days after. Our removal would have suited his and Eileen's domestic situation. Unknown to me at the time, I would have no communication whatsoever with Dad for the next eight years.

Cousin Aggie Dan rode down to the train station on her bike that had a woven plastic basket strapped to the frame below the handlebars. Fearing she had missed us, she came rushing over. She reached into her pocket and firmly pressed a white handkerchief into the palm of my right hand and pulled my fingers closed.

Mum reassured us that she would see us very soon. She promised we would be reunited. She showered us with endearments, hugged and kissed us. Then a nanny escort took Elin from Mum and onto the train. The conductor blew his whistle. Mum started to withdraw. She backed away, still holding my outstretched hands as it was now our turn to get on the train. I caught a final glimpse of Mum and everyone waving on the platform through the thick, wooden-framed windowpane as the train began its slow chug on the journey southward.

We clutched each other, crying, scared and uncertain about what lay ahead. Amid the emotional turmoil, I hadn't noticed that Terry was not in the same compartment as Michael, Johanne, Elin, the nanny and myself. Then I saw him in the compartment next to us. He was handcuffed, apparently separated from us because of concerns that he might attempt to jump from the train as it approached White Rock. A police escort accompanied him.

I struggled to understand why all five of us, in the company of strangers rather than with Mum, were leaving our home in Cairns on a train bound for Townsville. The whole episode had been deeply traumatic: our confinement in the cells at Cairns Police Station; the initial separation from Mum when we were taken into custody; our final separation from her at Cairns Central Station; and the sight of her standing heartbroken on the platform as the train left the station.

The train travelled out of Cairns Central Station, tracking right past our home on Progress Road, White Rock. I still regret that somehow I missed the chance to see our house that final time or catch a glimpse of the dogs prancing around the yard. Perhaps I did and I've forgotten. The trauma of our separation from Mum obliterated many memories. If only I'd known that would be the last time we would be together as a family, I would have paid more attention and treasured every moment of that day.

10

THE LETTERS

13 October 1958

The Inspector of Police
CAIRNS

Dear Sir,

On the 9th instant, five children named JANKE & EGGERTSEN appeared before the Children's Court and were committed to the care of this Department.

To enable us to determine the best way in which to provide for these children, it would be appreciated if you could supply as much information as available, regarding the circumstances leading up to their committal, as well as the nationality and parentage of each children.

With the exception of the infant, of four months, who is rather dark, the remaining children are fairly light skinned and probably would not be accepted at Palm Island.

It would be an advantage if this woman could be questioned regarding her own nationality as well as the nationality of each of the children. And also obtain from her the particulars of immunization, if any, received by each of the children in respect to diphtheria, whooping cough, tetanus and poliomyelitis. If this information is not complete, we can check with the various Health Authorities if it can be ascertained what localities the children have resided in.

Have either of the boys come under the notice of Police in respect of stealing?

For your general information, we have a record under the Infant Life Protection Act, of a woman named Agnes Philomena Janke, who originally resided at 31 Hartley Street, Cairns. This woman is apparently identical with the mother of these children.

In 1951 at the time of the birth of the child, Patrick, whose correct name is Kieran Patrick; she was described as a divorcee aged 29 years, residing with a man named Glendon. Reference was then made of two other children, Terence Patrick Janke and of Joanne, whose surname is now shown as Eggertsen.

At the time of the birth, the mother's name was shown as Jarne, apparently meant for Janke.

Is she married to Eggertsen, and when did this take place?

Yours faithfully
District Officer

—

14th October 58.

The Director,
State Children's Department
BRISBANE

Dear Sir,

Enclosed are copies of the Orders of Committal in connection with five children named Janke and Eggertsen admitted to the Townsville Receiving Depot on the 10th instant. We are awaiting full particulars regarding the circumstances from the Police.

These children have different fathers and various degrees of colour. Some are comparatively light-skinned and I do not think it would be fair to send them to Palm Island. Never-the-less they will present a difficulty here in respect of boarding out.

Yours faithfully
District Officer.

—

14th October 58

The District Officer
State Children Department
ROCKHAMPTON

Dear Sir,

Some time ago, when in this locality, the Superintendent of St. George's Home called at this office and in general conversation stated he would not be adverse to taking children from this locality.

At the present time we have nineteen children in the Receiving Depot here, most if not all unsuitable for Boarding out. As a result we have no reserve accommodation for any further new additions.

Included in the children are a family of five, boys aged eleven and seven years, and girls aged ten and six years and four months. These children all have coloured blood but the white predominates and we could not send them to Palm Island. On the other hand, there is no likelihood whatever of finding a foster-home for them. We were wondering whether, if there are some vacancies, the older members of the family could be transferred to St. Georges Home.

I would mention that the children have only just been received through the Children's Court as neglected. With the exception of the baby, they are good physical types and so far have conducted themselves quite well.

Yours faithfully,
District Officer.

Handwritten note on file: NB Question of maintenance to be kept in mind if Eggertsen is the father of any of the children.

—

17 October 1958

State Children's Department Rockhampton

Dear Sir,

With reference to your letter of the 14th instant, concerning vacancies at St. George, Parkhurst, I regret to advise that the conditions obtaining at the time of the Superintendent's visit to Townsville and at the present time have altered considerably.

At the time, the three Homes, namely Boys', Girls' and Infants' were operating, and accordingly, there were some vacancies for additional children. Approximately two months ago, because of financial embarrassment, the Committee were compelled to close the Infants' Home and amalgamated children into the Boys' and Girls' Home, with the result that these are both full.

At the present time, despite repeated efforts to obtain Foster Mothers, there are sixteen children at the Rockhampton Receiving Depot, many of whom as in your case, are unsuitable for board. I have had to refuse a considerable number of applications for admission over a long period, owing to the shortage of accommodation, which is almost always acute, except in the case of Roman Catholic children.

If the position improves at some future date, I will be pleased to assist you.

Yours faithfully
District Officer.

—

17th November, .58

The Director
State Children Department,
BRISBANE

Dear Sir,

In reply to Mr Harris' letter of the 13th instant, without reference, regarding an approach by the Native Affairs Department in Brisbane concerning the Janke or Eggertsen children, we did make some approach to Mr Bartlam at Palm Island but more in the sense of a general inquiry as to whether he had any previous knowledge of these children.

On many occasions, Mr Bartlam has a remarkable memory and was able to give the family history on referring the name. We had touched on this matter in our letter of 14 October when forwarding copies of the Orders of Committal. All caste children are a problem as they belong to neither race. We have no hope of a Foster Home and they will be permanent inmates of the Receiving Depot.

These children were committed on the eve of my departure on the Northern tour and enclosed is a copy of the written instruction I left for Mr. Jessop. The children range from eleven years to four months and it would have been of great assistance if a Foster Mother could be found at Palm Island for the young baby who is very dark skinned. Enclosed also is a spare copy of the Police Report since received. It will be seen that the mother is a caste of Filipino-Murray Island descent and would be very dark skinned. She married a man named Janke an Australian born German obviously white. Four of the children were registered in his name but at the time of the birth of Kieran Michael in 1951 she was living with a man named Glendon who was apparently also a white man. This man could also be the father of Johanne, born in 1952.

In 1955 she married Eggertsen who is a native of Denmark and extremely fair. I have seen this man. This man admits paternity of the baby who is, however, extremely dark skinned, and in view of this woman's standard of living it does not necessarily follow that any of these three white men are the fathers of the children. At the most, the children are half white, one quarter Murray Islander and one quarter Filipino. Of course they could be more coloured depending as to who are the correct fathers of the children.

Terrence is very dark, tight curly hair. Patricia is fairly dark, as is the infant. Kieran and Johanne are much whiter, but of course, not white.

Yours faithfully,
District Officer

—

STATE CHILDREN'S DEPARTMENT, TOWNSVILLE

23rd October 58

Mr. Bartlam
Superintendent,
Aboriginal Settlement
PALM ISLAND

Dear Sir,

We have in our care at the present time, five coloured children aged 11 yrs., 10 yrs,. 7 yrs., 6 yrs., and 4 ½ months. These children were committed by the Children's Court in Cairns as neglected and as yet we have inaccurate information about the circumstances leading up to their committal.

Three of the children, named Terrence 11 yrs., Patricia 10 yrs., and Elaine 4 ½ months are quite dark skinned, whilst Michael 7yrs., and Johanne 6 yrs., are of much lighter colouring, although their coloured blood is quite obvious. We have no definite information as regards to their racial ancestry although we do know that the three youngest children have white fathers.

We understand that their mother, Agnes Philomena Eggertsen, formerly Janke, nee Blanco is almost 100% coloured and there is a suggestion she is of Kanaka descent.

As you will realize, it is almost impossible to find suitable Foster Homes for such children and they do not fit in very well with white children in institutions such are conducted by this Department.

It would be greatly appreciated if you could advise whether it would be possible to admit all, or some of these children to Palm Island. It has occurred to us that you may be able to locate a suitable Foster Home for the baby.

Any assistance or advice that you can give would be greatly appreciated. At the moment we have over twenty children in the Receiving Depot here and our Resources are severely strained.

Yours faithfully
D. Jessey for
District Officer.

NB: Discuss ancestry of children and mother with Eggertsen when he calls.

—

Cairns District
Edmonton Police Station
3rd November, 1958.

Dear Sir,

I have to report with reference to the above and attached that I have interviewed Agnes Philomena EGGERSTEN whose five children were admitted to the care of the State Children's Department, Townsville, and the following information I have obtained from her.

Court Depositions were handed to me by Mr H SPICER, of the C.P.S Office, Cairns relating to this case and are attached here-to:

Agnes Philomena EGGERTSEN when interviewed regarding her nationality she stated that her mother was a Murray Islander and her father a Filipino.

Terence and Patricia, Michael JANKE have all been immunised against Diphtheria, Whooping cough, Tetanus and Poliomyelitis, Johanne and Elaine have not received any injections whatsoever.

John Francis JANKE is an Australian Born German and Kai Aron Svend EGGERTSEN is a native of Denmark coming to Australia in 1953.

In relation to Terence and Michael they have often come under the notice of the Police at Edmonton for stealing pedal cycles, food but they have not been punished. Terence, Patricia, Michael JANKE and Joanne EGGERTSEN appeared at the Children Court, Cairns before Mr T. Hickey on 16-7-57 as neglected children and were admonished and discharged to the care of their parents.

Agnes Philomena EGGERTSEN formerly resided at 31 Hartley Street, Cairns and is the same person mentioned in the attached report.

The Inspector of Police.
CAIRNS

—

INTERNAL DEPARTMENTAL FILE NOTES

Re children in Depot.

No prospect of sending Janke children to R'ton. You might explore the possibility of Palm Is. As I understand it – Palm Island is for aboriginals but where coloured children are <u>convicted or uncontrollable</u> we send them if any islanders.

We do not know what these children are but we now know the names of the parents. I suggest that you phone Mr Bartlam who could generally know something of coloured people.

Terence in particular is dark with tight curly hair – probably kanaka. Patricia is also fairly dark. Kieran and Johanne are the fairest. The infant is very dark – apparently Eggertsen is her father.

Even if a foster mother was found there for the infant it would help but we would have to move wisely, as children are neglect cases and as yet we have no information re the cause.

Handwritten note in file:

Eggertsen called earlier this week. He has not yet started work on the wharf here, but expects to do so this week. Staying temporarily at the Empire Hotel, South Townsville. His wife will come down when he can obtain accommodation.

This man is a very fair Scandinavian type. It was quite early in the day when he called, but he smelt strongly of drink, although he was quite sensible to talk to and is not difficult to handle. He says he is the father of Johanne and Elin. Claims to have married this woman at the Cairns Methodist Church in 1955.

Admits his wife is a heavy drinker and that he does most of the cooking and caring for the children. Claims his wife has given up the drink since the children removed and that he will see that she reforms. They propose to set up a home here with a view to getting the children back. Told they will have to prove themselves first.

Permit to visit 22/10/1958

—

INTERNAL DEPARTMENTAL FILE NOTES

22/10/58

Case discussed with Mrs. Reid. She will look into the matter of the baby present in the Hospital and advise.

She believes many Torres Strait Islanders etc. at Palm and that anyone of coloured extraction would be accepted there.

I have written to Mrs. Parker Nursing Home Keefer re the baby. She has received a child of Chinese extraction. However I doubt whether she would accept this child.

—

PALM ISLAND ABORIGINAL SETTLEMENT

27th October 1958

District Officer
State Children's Department
TOWNSVILLE

Re: Coloured Children
Your Ref: T5277

As these children appear to have little or no aboriginal blood further enquiries are being made. You will be advised as soon as possible.

Enquiries are also being made regarding a possibility of having the baby cared for here.

Signed
Roy Bartlam

—

INTERNAL DEPARTMENTAL FILE NOTES

3 November 1958

Kindly allow Mr & Mrs Eggertsen to see the children on Saturday morning, 8th November.

Handwritten note:

Eggertsen is not sure whether wife will come down by next Saturday. He will visit, in any case.

He now denies paternity of Johanne and says he does not know who is her father. Admits only paternity of Elin.

Says Glendon is the father of Terrence, Patricia and Michael. Says Glendon is Irish.

Says wife is half-caste Torres Strait Islander – her mother now deceased was an Islander, and her father is now living in Darwin, a Filipino.

Still at Empire Hotel endeavouring to obtain accommodation. 3/11/58

Additional Handwritten Notes:

Maintenance and Immunisation

Police say children not bad but mother away all day drinking. (11/11/58)

—

13 November, 1958.

Dear Sir,

The Department of Native Affairs has just telephoned me concerning five children named EGGERTSON who were recently committed to the care of the Department.

I understand that you have requested their transfer to Palm Island.

I should be pleased if you would furnish a full report on the facts of the case, intimating the degree of colour of each child.

Thanking you in anticipation,

Yours faithfully,
Director.

—

1.12.58

Mrs Eggertsen called on 27.11.58. She was clean, well dressed and suitably conducted during the interview. She came to Townsville and is staying temporarily at the Empire Hotel where Eggertsen boards. They have been trying to find accommodation but she will probably return back to Cairns at the end of the week.

She states her husband is Janke who is of German descent is the father of only an 18-year-old boy in his custody. This man divorced her.

She thus worked for some years on a farm belonging to a man named Glendon who is of Irish-Australian extraction. He is the father of Terrence, Patricia and Michael.

She commenced drinking only about five years ago when Glendon took up with another woman whom he has since married.

Johanne's father is a man named Andersen of Scandinavian nationality, who is a member of crew of a visiting ship.

She has since married Eggertsen who is a white man of northern European extraction who is the father of the baby.

Before coming to Townsville she was staying at White Rock with the man Glendon and his wife and she will probably return there. She admits Terrence was beyond her control. She also admits evidence given in the Children's Court.

Actually she is rather a superior type for a coloured woman. Her mother was Philippino and her father a Murray Islander.

None of the children have been immunised in respect of whooping cough, diphtheria or tetanus and Johanne and Elin have not received poliomyelitis vaccinations.

Signed,
District Officer.

11

THE RECEIVING DEPOT

The Sunlander train pulled into Townsville station around 8pm. A man from the State Children's Department met us. Terry, Johanne, Michael and I were driven in a black Ford Customline motorcar to the State Children's Receiving Depot. The Depot, which looked more like an industrial warehouse than a children's home, had operated as an orphanage from 1878 to 1934. As a State-run facility, its role was to temporarily care for and eventually foster children to new homes and families. At some stage, I noticed Elin was not with us. When I asked where she was, Mr Jessop said she was with the nanny in another car.

Upon arrival at the Depot, the duty night nurse helped us settle in. The scent of hospital disinfectant permeated the building. Johanne and I were in separate sleeping quarters to Terry and Michael, who were taken to another part of the building.

The Depot was home to approximately nineteen children and a full-time staff of eight, who worked on rostered shifts. It was a large property fronting 42 Warburton Street, North Ward. The building was divided into several wings comprising the administration section, the living quarters and the dormitories, including showers. The dining room, library, laundry, kitchen and inventory were all in the living quarter section. When the physical condition of the Depot was discussed in the Queensland Parliament in 1962, the Member for Townsville North, Perc Tucker, noted:

> *The depot itself is old and dilapidated. Its appearance is made to look worse in contrast to the Cootharinga home for crippled children, which we point out to visitors to Townsville as one of the highlights of the area. Again the home for sub-normal children is a very attractive building. In comparison with those two buildings the receiving depot is a sorry sight. Although it is situated on a splendid site, it looks like the poor relation. The present buildings have a depressing air about them, which must have an effect on the children, especially when they see the children next door in better surroundings.*[43]

At the time, the Queensland Minister for Health and Home Affairs, Dr D.W. Noble, said he felt 'completely disappointed' following a visit to the Depot. He observed it was riddled with termites and supported calls for its demolition.[44]

It was difficult to relax in the girls-only ward. The feel of the starched white sheets against my skin made me feel unclean, as if I'd not had a proper shower. Everything seemed to be white, from the towels to the crockery. The stern-faced night nurse wore a starched white uniform, which gave the impression that the Depot was a children's hospital. I began to look about for Johanne but couldn't see her. I panicked when I realised this was the first time we had not shared the same bedroom. The ward was the complete opposite of our warm but basic room at home. Cold. Sterile. The combination of the starched sheets, the smell of disinfectant, and my feelings of loss, isolation and uncertainty overwhelmed me. I vomited. The night nurse was dispassionate about my distress, quite cranky about the added work of having to bathe me and change the soiled bed linen.

Physically and emotionally exhausted, I finally surrendered to fatigue. When I awoke the next morning, I anxiously searched about the Depot hoping to find my sister and brothers. But I didn't see one familiar face among all adults, teenagers and children. Foremost, I wanted to find Elin. I'd assumed we'd see her again once we got to the Receiving Depot, thinking there may have been a babies' nursery attached to the building. At breakfast time, I was at last reunited with Terry, Michael and Johanne. Still confused about our predicament, I drew Johanne and Michael to me. We huddled together.

Later that morning, I happened upon a lady, also dressed in a white uniform. She was the lady in charge, Matron Ross. I asked if she knew where my baby sister was, but she fobbed me off, casually telling me that I would have to await the arrival of Mr Vic Linthwaite or Mr Jessop. While both these men maintained an active administrative involvement with the Depot, they worked from the State Children's Department office in Townsville's CBD. Occasionally, they would be called upon to discipline boys who had engaged in unruly conduct.

Like many State children's institutions during that time, the Depot in Townsville operated within very rigid, regimental disciplinary boundaries. Children would be seen but rarely heard. These institutions ensured that children received the basic necessities – safety, health care, shelter, food, the opportunity to be educated academically as well as religiously and ethically. But our emotional wellbeing, mental health, any feelings emanating from being separated from our parents were never taken into consideration.

Mr Linthwaite was senior to Mr Jessop, but both men went about their business in a dour, dictatorial manner. I do not remember what both men looked like but I certainly remember their gruff attitude and demeanour. Somehow I was able to find Mr Linthwaite and ask what had happened to Elin. He carefully explained to me that she was very sick, suffering from meningitis, and had been admitted to hospital the evening we'd arrived.

'There's no need for worry. Elin is not with us anymore. She has gone to a better place,' he said.

His words were crushing. I was left to interpret what he meant. He counselled me in a reserved manner, directing me to settle into my new home while assisting Johanne and Michael to do the same. No further explanation was given, other than to be firm and accept Elin's circumstances. There was no mention of Terry. Mr Linthwaite thought he, being the eldest, had the capacity to look after himself. But what did all this mean? My sister had died overnight! I would never see her again. There was no mention of a funeral. Bewildered by Mr Linthwaite's insensitivity, I retreated, recalling Mum's strict words.

'Patsy, you should stay quiet! It is rude to interrupt when grown-ups are talking,' she'd often counselled.

I did not want to be perceived as a nuisance. That had already happened when I vomited in bed. I needed to wrap my grief in an all-embracing hug and find a shoulder to cry on. Mum was good for that but it was clear there would be no love or sympathy in the Depot, where I'd already figured several unwritten rules were enforced: know your place; never ask questions or challenge authority; settle in the best you can; if in doubt, do not ask. There would be dire consequences if children were disobedient or considered to be a disruptive influence.

Corporal punishment seemed to be the standard practice, based on what Terry told me of his experiences. His propensity to engage in mischief included fighting, petty theft and being stubborn. Mr Linthwaite and Mr Jessop would strip him of his shorts, have him bend over a bench and then lash his bare buttocks with a thick leather belt. Children's rights were non-existent at this time: the *United Nations Convention on the Rights of the Child* was only effected in 1990. Additional punishments included deprivation of recreational activities, visits and treats, and isolation by solitary confinement in the library. In the event of severe breaches and rebellions against authority, staff threatened children with removal to harsher institutions, such as Neerkol, near Rockhampton, or Westbrook in Brisbane. Like a prison environment, all correspondence, both incoming and outgoing, was vetted. In places like these, mail was censored or completely withheld if any information in the correspondence was deemed to be distressing for the recipient.

The Receiving Depot was often referred to as an orphanage or 'The Home' but I did not meet one orphan during my two-year stay. Most of the other inmates were children who were deemed 'neglected' or 'uncontrollable'. 'Uncontrollable' was a way of branding a complex set of behavioural disorders, which, in the 1950s and 1960s, mostly went undiagnosed and medically untreated.

Initially, I was reluctant to befriend anyone. Aggrieved, I wanted only to be with Terry, Michael and Johanne. The unencumbered life we'd enjoyed had been replaced by stifling restraint and repression. I yearned for the return of our freedom, our family togetherness. But in their stead were discipline, supervision, restrictions and regimentation.

In short, it was a cheerless existence. I became a daydreamer, manufacturing a multitude of thoughts to cloud the harsh reality of life in the Receiving Depot.

—

Within the first few weeks of our placement in Townsville, Mum and Uncle Kaj came to the Receiving Depot for their first authorised visit. A State Children's Department duty nurse supervised. Mum's arrival was a surprise. I couldn't believe she was there. Just her physical presence swept aside the anguish I'd been feeling since being separated from her. As we shared this precious time together, Mum reassured us that she was doing her best to have us returned to her care. Excited at the news of a family reunion, we hopped and skipped about energetically, our sagging spirits revived. Moving to Townsville to be closer to us was the first part of her plan.

Uncle Kaj relocated to Townsville ahead of Mum to commence work on the wharf. I had a list of questions in my mind. How did Mum feel about baby Elin's death? Did Mum miss us as much as we missed her? Why couldn't she be quicker in getting us out of the Receiving Depot? What were we waiting for?

We could never predict when Mum would visit us next. She appeared sporadically. In many ways, her visits were bittersweet affairs; joyful hellos were replaced by tearful goodbyes. In between her visits, time moved on agonisingly slowly. When Mum was not with us, my mind always reverted to her and our home in Cairns. Mum had suffered a devastating loss when Terry, Michael, Johanne, Elin and I were removed from her care. By comparison, mine was an easy road to hoe. Not wanting to be perpetually immersed in sadness, I realised that I had to compose myself. I was determined not to 'drop my bundle', irrespective of any hardships in the Depot. In Mum's absence, I had to step up and be the second-in-charge that she had trained me to be. She still expected me to be her Little Big Girl, continuing to provide Michael and Johanne with motherly care.

—

Matron Ross was supported by a team of carers, including Nurses Hall, Hansen, Crowther and Piccio. Matron Bruce was the alternate head carer, who later took charge of the Receiving Depot. She was transferred from a nursing position she had held previously at a hospital. It soon became apparent that we could make our lives heaven or hell according to the way in which we interacted with staff and, indeed, with fellow inmates. We were encouraged to be useful and helpful. I was always putting my hand up for various chores in my attempts to engender goodwill and respect from the staff.

Nurse Hall was very strict and aloof. She did not seem to like children very much and injected little compassion into her care of us. We certainly avoided her as much as possible. Other staff simply performed their duties and went home. On the other hand, Matron Bruce, Nurse Ivy Hansen and Mrs Anderson, the laundress, exuded great warmth towards the children in their care. All three were grandmotherly types who took a genuine interest in our welfare.

Mrs Anderson was a jolly woman who always had some words of encouragement and good humour; she often placated my despair by reassuring me that, no matter the problem, I would be okay. She was a lovely lady. Her kindness mattered to me. She was surprised by my inquisitiveness and genuine enthusiasm to learn the different facets of her trade. I never told her that my interest stemmed from Mum's working at the pubs and doing the laundry. She always praised me for my interest and the occasional advice I gave: I showed Mrs Anderson different ways to mix the knobs of Bluo-brand bleach with starch, and demonstrated ways to press and fold clothing and linen just like Mum did at the Central Hotel in Cairns.

Mrs Anderson did not seem to mind me hanging about as she worked. If she did, she never said so. She indulged me, giving me the gift of her attention. I became her offsider; she said she appreciated my company, expressing concern if I did not turn up to help her each day.

'Patricia, you must have been a regular little sunbeam to your mum with your helpful ways. I bet she misses you. If I had a busy little girl like you, I'd miss her,' she told me.

I gravitated towards Mrs Anderson. Her affirming words fed my self-esteem and sustained that part of me that wanted to be needed and loved.

—

We all gradually adapted to the new regime at the place we now begrudgingly called 'home'. We were enrolled at Central State School, and soon I began to make friends in the Depot and at school. We were constantly reminded that 'life is great in the Sunshine State' and endured the compulsory singing of the Queensland State Anthem during the daily parade. Being in the Depot instantly regulated our attendance at school. There was no tolerance of truancy.

The immaculately groomed Miss Castellanos, my English teacher, took a dislike to me from the outset, treating me differently from the other students in her class. The tone and the manner with which she addressed me were particularly gruff and condescending. I was perplexed by her behaviour because she was of Greek heritage and significantly darker than me in complexion. In view of her own ethnic background,

I thought she might have been more empathetic towards children of colour. I was wrong. She often detained me after class under the guise of completing additional revision work. I was also targeted for frequent rounds of corporal punishment and rapped across the knuckles with a thick wooden ruler for seemingly no good reason. As hard as I tried to please Miss Castellanos, it became clear that my apple, even if it were the pick of the crop, would never find a prominent place on her desk.

I had the good fortune to be taught by one dedicated teacher who actually loved teaching. Her passion for her profession offset Miss Castellanos' behaviour. Miss McKeon was my favourite because she took an active interest in not only my education but also my personal development and the circumstances that had brought me to the Receiving Depot. Miss McKeon encouraged me to share my feelings with her. But I did not divulge much, and she believed I was an orphan. She never fully understood just how much succour I derived from her genuine concern for me, an impressionable, waif-like eleven-year-old girl, with a store of pent-up emotions.

Mrs Bligh, another senior teacher with a warm personality, encouraged me to work harder. I got to know her daughter, Deidre, who also attended Central State School. Even at that age, I could tell the difference between teachers who regarded their occupation as an eight to three job and those who invested their time and effort in their students and encouraged them to shine. Eventually I came top of my form, while also excelling in swimming. I participated in the school carnivals, winning certificates and ribbons for my placings. It took me some time to master all the strokes but swimming was a welcome way to vent some of my frustrations.

—

Word of my swimming must have drifted back to the Depot. On occasion, Matron Bruce arranged for me and several other inmates to visit the Cootharinga Crippled Children's Home next door to participate in the recreational activities with the residents who were partially incapacitated. Matron Howlett, who was in charge of the complex, organised swimming in the heated indoor pool. We would also have wheelchair races where our hands and legs were mildly restrained to enable us to compete on 'equal' terms. I preferred the swimming activities, being too clumsy and uncoordinated for the wheelchair events. Matron Bruce and Matron Howlett clearly wanted to educate us about the limitations of being disabled. Nonetheless, it was always enjoyable to escape the Receiving Depot and have some fun in the pool.

At the invitation of Laurie Lawrence, Nurse Crowther regularly took a group of us to the Tobruk Memorial Swimming Pool for swimming lessons. The Australian Olympic swimming team were using the pool at this time during a training camp. Swimming sensations the Konrads twins, Ilsa and John, were present, as were Dawn Fraser, Murray Rose, John Devitt, and Lorraine Crapp. I was fascinated to see all the different swimming styles and took note of their techniques and strokes. It was wonderful to be in the presence of Australia's swimming elite. Although I was not a fan of any of them prior to this, I began to take an interest in their careers and achievements. I was dismayed some years later when Dawn Fraser's career ended following her suspension by the Australian Swimming Union after the 1964 Summer Olympics in Tokyo.

Still, some days, swimming and the Olympics were the last things on my mind. Terry was still getting into mischief, and Mr Linthwaite and Mr Jessop were still being called upon to discipline him. In the hope of correcting his bad conduct, they decided to flog him. When this failed to control him, an alternative option was identified.

12

AND THEN THERE WERE TWO

Despite Mum's visits, we were still paraded before groups of adults each month. The staff at the Receiving Depot never explained the reason for these parades nor that we could be placed with other families. Most of the information came from the older girls. It did not take long to conclude that these were potential foster family visits. I feared the Department's 'split the litter' mentality would impact on our family. For each parade, Matron Bruce and the nurses dressed us in our best clothes, paying extra attention to our appearance and generally making sure we all looked adorable and behaved respectfully for the visitors.

For a still young girl, I was already learning one too many lessons. I became acutely aware that life does not come with any guarantees. Our fates were reduced to a game of chance – including to whom we could be fostered and where we might end up.

As Wards of the State, we could not be legally adopted, but we could be fostered out through short- or long-term care arrangements. Legal adoption removes the rights and responsibilities of a child's birth parents and transfers this to the adoptive parents. In our situation, the State remained our legal guardians and fully accountable for our welfare; at the time, we didn't know the difference between adoption and fostering. All I saw were children, including Johanne, going to new families.

I remember the confusion and anguish when Johanne was fostered to Oswald and Annie Stephenson, who were of British heritage. Mrs Stephenson was the cleaner at the school, and even though she was familiar to us, it was quite surreal seeing my little sister taken out of my life by strangers who could then claim her as their own as if no former family life or ties existed. The Stephensons lived locally in Townsville. As much as I continued to see Johanne at school each day, I knew all too well our fates could change in an instant, and all four could be scattered to the winds.

Initially, I delighted in hearing reports from Johanne about her new home. I was intrigued by her updates and excited descriptions about the strange world in which she now lived; I was incredulous on hearing that she received money after losing a tooth one evening, and had been visited by a weird little mythical being called the 'Tooth Fairy'. Mrs Stephenson had also started sending Johanne to school with a little handkerchief with tuckshop money wrapped in it, pinned neatly inside her top pocket.

I yearned for Johanne's company more than ever, especially being one of only about eight girls at the Depot. My curiosity about her new life was overwhelming. I hatched a plan to visit Johanne at Mrs Stephenson's. My new friends from the orphanage, who were several years older than me, sisters Margie and Kathy Gilboy, became my co-conspirators. Together, we arranged for the younger orphans to catch the school bus to Central State Primary School, which was several street blocks away, but within safe and comfortable walking distance of the Depot. The rest of us went by foot.

I was still only very young but Matron Bruce had entrusted me with the responsibility of handling the bus fare money. Unbeknownst to her, I saved the change and unused bus fares to buy Johanne a small, inexpensive doll for her seventh birthday. In exchange for the older inmates' help, I was asked to smuggle letters to a lady friend and an older man, who was the boyfriend of one of the girls. At the time, both the lady and the man were hospitalised in Townsville General Hospital, which was adjacent to Central State Primary School. On the day I visited the hospital with the letters, I changed out of my uniform and hid it beneath a bush at the Presbyterian Church on Warburton Street; I attended this church on occasion to participate in the Path Finder Youth Group. I had to skip school for two afternoon lessons but I accomplished my mission.

Mrs Anderson, the laundress, knowing how much Johanne meant to me, helped me to buy a doll that would keep Johanne company during our separation. She was swept up in the excitement of Johanne's surprise and wanted to be a part of it. I don't know if she breached Depot policy by purchasing Johanne's present on my behalf, but it was evidence of her compassion and empathy for my situation that she helped me so much.

I eventually found my way to Mrs Stephenson's house on Eyre Street and could barely contain the joy of being able to give Johanne her gift. I knocked on the door, excitedly clutching the doll in one hand. I was excited at the thought that I had never bought a gift for anyone before. But when Mrs Stephenson opened the front door, the scowl on her face was as repellent as her words.

'What do you want?' she shrieked. 'Stay away from my house. Don't ever come here again, or I will report you to the authorities!'

The shrill tone of her voice startled the joy from me. Not expecting her response, I was speechless, which was unusual for me, having gained enough self-confidence to express an opinion. Given the circumstances, however, Mrs Stephenson's rage gave her the edge over me. She ripped the doll from my hand, ferociously dismembering it. She tore its head off first, followed by its arms. Gathering the body parts together, she then hurled the pieces back at me while pushing and poking me in the chest. I was more bewildered than terrified. I did not see Johanne amid the ruckus but later told her about my encounter with her foster mother. She was too young to understand the extent of the awfulness of what Mrs Stephenson had done.

I resolved never to surrender my sisterly love, and remained persistent in my attempts to see Johanne. I refused to give up and kept going back to the Stephensons' house. Johanne was my family, not theirs. Mr and Mrs Stephenson sensed my determination. After a while, as a compromise, they allowed me to sit outside on the kerb with Johanne when I visited her.

I felt really hurt when, in her innocence, Johanne proudly began to show me photos of her with her new family. It seemed intolerably cruel that the rest of us, her 'real' family, were being slowly cast adrift. There were no photos of us in her album. I taunted her, reminding her that we were her true family and she should never forget it. It would be many years before I learnt that Johanne's life with her foster family was anything but idyllic.

Johanne still remembers her days with the Stephensons:

My foster parents, Oswald and Annie Stephenson, had four biological children – two boys and two girls. Three of them were mainly out of the picture by the time I arrived. The eldest daughter had moved to Brisbane. The eldest son worked for Queensland Rail at the time. He was always very good to me, a kind person who spent time with me when he came home from jobs in west Queensland. He was a fettler. He made good friends with an Aboriginal fellow at work and brought him home one day. Mum and Dad Stephenson were just horrified. Mum Stephenson was like that. The other daughter married and moved out earlier on. Allan, the youngest, was the only child who was raised with me the whole time.

The only vivid memory I have is of my Mum coming to the shop next door to where we lived. She came in to say hello to me. That would have been 1958 or 1959. I have flashbacks and remember running out of the shop and going home. Mum Stephenson must have demonised Mum in some way. There must have been something she instilled in me to make me run away from my own mother. My running must have had a devastating impact on Mum. Mum Stephenson would also have put a stop to Mum's informal visits at the shop by saying she was a bad influence. The initial visits with Mum were held at the State Children Department head office in town.[45]

I can only imagine that Mum really struggled with the indignity of seeing her child placed in long-term care with an unknown family. To add to her injury, Mrs Stephenson supervised the scheduled visits at the Department. No wonder Mum stopped visiting Johanne. She would have been powerless to withstand the bureaucratic scrutiny and expectations of her maternal behaviour. Unsurprisingly perhaps, she continued drinking to ease her ache. A Departmental file note from 1959 stated:

Mrs Eggertsen was seen about 3.20pm in the street. The appointment was between three and four. I have seen Eggertsen in the street 'Rolling Drunk' on two or three occasions. Both Mr & Mrs Eggertsen work and they are only liable for £1/5 weekly. Mrs Eggertsen failed to keep a 3pm appointment with the District Officer last Friday 31st July.[46]

Meanwhile, Terry was proving to be an ongoing handful for the Depot staff, particularly Mr Jessop. I begged him to behave, fearing he would draw unnecessary attention to himself. But Terry, being the thick-headed and stubborn child he was, continued to generate strife. He was a big, solid kid with a naturally strong Islander build. If anything, he became even more pig-headed. The more they tried to break him, the further he dug his heels in, as this file note attests:

Already Terrence has given Matron considerable trouble and had to be punished more than once. He has engaged in several occasions of stealing, one instance being from his teacher's desk, and is the leader of much unruly conduct in the Home. One of the younger boys aged nine was admitted to the Hospital last Thursday with concussion. He had a number of slight facial abrasions and two severe bruises on his forehead. The boy himself cannot give any coherent of how he received these injuries and we cannot altogether discard the theory that Janke who is a very sturdy lad, may have had a hand in the trouble.[47]

—

The Receiving Depot frequently organised weekend outings and we were sometimes taken on excursions with local families. Michael was rebellious, resistant to leaving the Depot for a short day out, fearing he would miss Mum if she happened to call by. Besides, the day outings were generally non-eventful. On one occasion, Michael was left to play with an old lady's border collie dogs for the entire day.

There were also occasional excursions and entertainments sponsored by local wharfies, butchers and service clubs, including Lions and Rotary. Michael and I, along with other inmates, were eager participants, jumping at every opportunity to have some fun and gobble rarely available treats such as ice-cream, fairy floss, hamburgers, Cheerios and fizzy soft drinks. Terry never got to enjoy any of these outings. He was deprived of privileges as a form of punishment. Instead, he spent time in the sandpit playing with toy soldiers and animal figurines. Two other boys with behavioural problems became his companions, which did little to curtail either Terry's recalcitrance or his rebellious attitude.

We all loved the recreational activities and celebrations associated with Labour Day at the Black River. We went as invited guests, with Trade Union members and their families. There were competitive races galore, including the three-legged foot race, potato sack and barrel races, apple bobbing, egg-on-the-spoon race, and sprint races and relays on the dry, sandy riverbed. These occasions provided us with an opportunity to interact with good people who were genuinely interested in our lives. I remain grateful that these families cared enough to give up their time for those in less fortunate positions and make us feel special.

In January 1959, Matron Ross casually informed us that Terry was going on a picnic. I was envious that he was going to have fun while Michael and I had to stay behind. Terry was strutting about, being boastful and looking really pleased that he was going on a special adventure. He was kitted out in picnic attire with a small pannikin tin cup attached to his knapsack. He looked like a Boy Scout as he walked down the path fully decked out for his big adventure.

Later that day, I had an awful feeling in the pit of my stomach when Terry did not return to the Depot. And there was no information to be had from Matron or any other of the staff as to his whereabouts. He had just disappeared. I pestered Matron Bruce, but despite her usual warm disposition, Matron Bruce seemed unconcerned about Terry's absence and was dismissive of my anxieties. Perhaps she believed that what I did not know could not hurt me.

A day turned into a week, that week into a month and then into a year. Our family had been whittled down, just like the five little Indian boys depicted in Agatha Christie's novel *And Then There Were None.* We had commenced our fateful journey as a family. One by one, my siblings had gone. And then there were two.

I settled back into the routine of the Depot, partly because I feared for Michael and myself. The callous way we'd been split up played heavily on my mind, as I reflected sadly upon what our family used to be and what it was now was. Even then I felt that an unfair process of separation had been inflicted upon our family. Michael, being only eight years old, mutely accepted the situation and never asked after Terry. But even if he had, I would not have been able to give him any answers.

Around this time, Mum stopped making random visits to the Receiving Depot and instead began to show up outside the back gate at school several times per week. She made us promise not to tell anyone she was there. We always looked forward to seeing her, if only for a brief while, to hear her tell us that she loved us and entice us with the promise of us all being together again. Sometimes she would slip us pocket money or sweets. There was never any mention of Terry, Johanne or Elin.

Then everything began to change. Mum became more distant. She stopped coming to the school grounds. I would occasionally catch sight of her waving at us from afar. Uncle Kaj had already stopped visiting with Mum so he too disappeared from our lives. Mum had explained that he had become depressed about his inability to find permanent work and descended further into an alcoholic abyss. Mum and Uncle Kaj were experiencing marital difficulties as well, and their relationship was fragile. And, of course, I was unaware, at the time, that the State Children's Department was hounding Uncle Kaj for child maintenance payments.

The State was mandated by *Queensland Children Act 1911–1966* (Part IV, Section 50) to compel the parents of Wards of the State to make maintenance payments to offset the costs of clothing, medical support, nursing, training and education; the payments were paid directly to the State Children's Department, by cash, cheque or money order. The demands for payment and notices of arrears may have acted as a deterrent to Kaj's visits to the Receiving Depot. Besides, with Elin gone from our lives, perhaps his interest in us, his stepchildren, had waned.

Mum slowly began to retreat from every aspect of our lives. After a while, I would only receive messages and some pocket money through another child. I felt hurt that she refused to come and give me pocket money herself anymore. Then there was silence. No visits, no letters, no messages and no pocket money. Had she abandoned us too? I wondered if her love for us had diminished. I felt so alone. Needless to say, her visits – and her absences – had not gone unnoticed by the authorities.

INTERNAL DEPARTMENTAL FILE NOTE

13/3/59

Mrs Eggertsen is visiting the children several times a week outside the school grounds and tells them she is taking them home soon.

Write her.

—

OFFICIAL LETTER

17/3/59

Mrs K.A.S. Eggertsen
c/- Wyben
Housing Commission Estate,
Lonerganne Street,
Garbutt,
TOWNSVILLE

Dear Mrs Eggertsen,

Kindly call at this office first available opportunity as there is a matter concerning your children, which I desire to discuss with you.

Yours faithfully
District Officer.

Handwritten comment on document: Mother has been seeing children 2–3 times a week outside school holidays.

—

INTERNAL DEPARTMENTAL FILE NOTES

20/3/1959

Mother was called and she was severely warned she must not have contact with the children, other than on authorised occasions. Eggertsen has had little work (I do know the wharf has been slack). A warning re maintenance was also issued. Mrs E. proposes visit to Palm Island to see Terry. She is to write to Supt. and will advise us his reply. She has friends on the island.

Undated

Kindly allow Mr & Mrs Eggertsen to see their children on Saturday morning 27th instant. Handwritten note: These people failed to turn up on two successive Saturdays. Matron saw them both drunk in the street both Saturdays. Only one maintenance payment made.

29/5/1959

Mrs Eggertsen has again been visiting the children at the school, in spite of a strong warning issued by me some little time ago. Final warning to be issued at first opportunity. Maintenance discussed with her early this week by Mr Linthwaite. There has not been much work on the wharf. Nevertheless she works also and they have no other responsibilities. Further 14 days.

3/9/1959

I saw both Mr & Mrs Eggertsen come out from a nearby hotel yesterday and enter a taxi. We understand they are both working. Apparently they can afford to drink and ride in taxis but cannot find £1/5/ per week towards the baby's support. Only £22/5/ paid since 1st payment on 17/12/58 av. about 12/- per week. Present arrears over £36. Final Warning

20/10/59

Matron advises that Mrs Eggertsen is giving one boy who lives at the same residence money to hand Patsey at school.

—

20 November 1959

Mrs AP Eggertsen
32 Hale Street
City
<u>TOWNSVILLE</u>

Dear Mrs Eggertsen

It is understood you have made a practice recently of sending sums of money to school with a boy who resides at the same address as yourself, for Patsy.

I am strongly opposed to this and must insist that this practice cease immediately, failing which I shall be forced to take some action against you.

Yours Faithfully
District Officer

Handwritten comment written on file: Matron says she had heard Mrs Eggertsen gave birth to <u>twins</u> (Authors comment: Not true.)

13

A NOT SO MERRY CHRISTMAS

As Mum's visits became irregular and finally ceased, Michael and I learnt very quickly to fend for ourselves. At times, those in authority perceived this as stubbornness. I also became involved in amateur fisticuffs with some of the bigger boys at the Depot, who took cowardly delight in bullying Michael, who was no match for them. They were five to eight years older than him – in fact, the same age as Terry and of a similar sturdy build. Although only seven years old, Michael stood up to them, refusing to take a backward step, but thereby putting himself in harm's way. Hence the need for big sister to roll up her sleeves and rush to his defence.

Michael seemed to have inherited his pugnacious attitude from Dad, who always fancied himself as a tough street brawler.

'I am not worried about him,' Dad had said once in reference to one of Michael's larger competitors. 'He couldn't knock the skin off a custard.'

As a five-year-old, Michael shadowboxed on the edge of the makeshift ring in Cairns where Dad trained Terry in the art of self-defence. Because of his size, Dad would encourage Michael.

'Remember, Jumbo, it's not the size of the dog in the fight, but the size of fight in the dog!' he'd say. Or, 'Little axes can bring big trees down!' he'd remind him. 'It's not about the strength in your fists. Put the force of your shoulder into the punch. Maintain focus, follow their fists and not their face.'

Mum would put her two bob's worth in by telling Michael the story of David and Goliath. 'Don't be a powder puff. If you are knocked down six times, make sure you get up seven,' Mum said. I never agreed with Mum and Dad's philosophy. Sometimes when you know you are licked, it is better to stay down. Better still, don't pick fights you know you can't win.

Around this time, I had a crush on one of the older boys I pushed and poked in Michael's defence, but puppy love was sadly sacrificed on the altar of brotherly love. Still, this boxing experience gave me a salutary lesson: boys do not like aggressive, domineering girls who can protect themselves. Instead, they become smitten by timid, defenceless, damsel-in-distress types, a girl who they think needs a strong, capable male by her side.

—

I had my first Christmas celebration while at the Depot in Townsville. Mr Bainbridge and his wife, Sylvia, took a fellow inmate, my friend Monica Tolbert, and me for a tour of a milk and soft drink factory. I had never seen so many lollies in my life. It was a cornucopia of confectionery, with every sweet treat imaginable. The Christmas feast was made complete with gifts, balloons and decorations. I can't recall ever feeling so special – or, along with Monica, being the centre of attention. The Bainbridges were in their late thirties, possibly early forties, a reputable family. They owned a well-established local business, and Mr Bainbridge had some association with the Department of Defence.

After lunch, Mr Bainbridge took us for a swim in their home swimming pool while Mrs Bainbridge busied herself clearing away the table and tidying up. There were about eight other children in the pool including Monica, me, three of the Bainbridge children and others I assumed were extended family members. I was still high from the excitement of Christmas.

Mr Bainbridge was in the middle of the pool and he playfully engaged us in a game of catch and throw. He beckoned, coaxing us children to swim into his outstretched arms. He would then twirl us around a few times in the water, lift us up and propel us halfway across the pool. Then we would line up again. It was all great fun until Mr Bainbridge pulled the crotch of my bathers to one side and inserted his fingers in my vagina. I broke free, as he tried to hoist me across the pool, and swam as fast as I could away from him to the other side of the pool.

Mr Bainbridge then turned his attention to Monica. I knew from the startled look on her face and the way she also swam away that he tried the same thing with her. I knew too that his actions were disgusting and wrong, but I did not know what to do about it or how to approach Monica to gain her opinion. And, admittedly, I was reluctant to spoil the family's Christmas festivities by telling anyone what Mr Bainbridge had done.

Now being older, wiser and educated, it is clear that Mr Bainbridge had perfected his technique so that his actions went undetected. And he selected vulnerable children from the Receiving Depot like Monica and me to prey on. I didn't inform Matron Bruce about the incident, believing we might be punished and not allowed to go on other outings. Instead, I brooded. But 35 years later, I came across an article about the Bainbridges in a regional newspaper; Mr and Mrs Bainbridge had received a Community Service Award in recognition of their contribution towards bettering the lives of children and youth in care.

One day, while we were playing together in the sandpit at the Depot, fellow inmate Tony Rich put his hand up my dress and began to 'finger me', as he put it. I was about eleven years old at the time. I was upset and ran away from him. As was the case with Mr Bainbridge, I was fearful of what might happen to me if I spoke up.

Not long after, Tony sexually assaulted Rachel Forbes, a defenceless special-needs child, in a shed that was used to store chopped firewood. Rachel would have been about fourteen at the time. The wood shed, as it was called, was at the back of the Boys' Dormitory; the chopped logs were stacked in there. It was chilling to think I could have suffered the same fate as Rachel.

Tony Rich was an older boy, wiry and muscular, with fine hair across his top lip, the makings of a moustache. In hindsight, he must have been struggling with puberty. But his deviant behaviour did not go unnoticed. Nurse Hansen in particular took to segregating him indoors and restricting his recreational activities to board games in the library.

The Depot became a frenzy of activity when it was discovered that Rachel Forbes had been abused. Mr Linthwaite and Dr Leslie (Les) Halberstater, the Government Medical Officer, scrambled about, doing their best to contain and downplay the situation. But their sullen faces told the true story: something very serious had happened. The whispers of concern exchanged between care staff and the older inmates soon trickled down to younger inmates like me.

Throughout the years, whenever the inescapable sway of memory takes me back to those times, I am overcome when I recall Rachel

Forbes' brother John and the confused look upon his face. John was a forlorn sight, his stooped figure shuffling aimlessly about the Depot. He and Rachel were inseparable, not only bonded because they were siblings but also because they'd both been born with Down Syndrome.

As the investigation continued, I realised that it was best for me to remain silent. My mind went into overdrive. I was terrified of what would happen if I said anything about Tony Rich, fearful that I would be sent away. News of the assault had been conveyed to me via Marjorie (Margie) Gilboy, who was eighteen, and her sister Kathy, sixteen. Mrs Anderson and some of the nurses mentioned it too. It was impossible to contain reports of such a significant event.

'Mr Linthwaite and the Matron won't be happy. They will be in trouble for not looking after the place properly,' someone said. So that was what Margie meant when she'd said, 'Holy Shit! This is big trouble. Heads are going to roll!'

I was beset by dilemma once again. Do I speak? Do I stay silent? Who would look after Michael if I was sent to another home? Gradually, torn between decision and indecision, I began to trivialise what had happened to me. It could have been worse, I told myself, comparing my situation to Rachel's.

I learned of Tony Rich's immediate transfer to Westbrook Boys Home in Toowoomba from Margie Gilboy. Tony's younger sister, who was also resident in the home, confirmed that Matron Bruce also told her of his transfer to Westbrook. I was astounded at the double standard; Tony's fate was readily known whereas there was only a wall of silence about the disappearance of Elin, Johanne and Terry from Michael's and my lives.

—

Even with such events occurring, the Receiving Depot management maintained its usual façade. Children were still regularly paraded for placement with foster parents. Many of the prospective carers were drawn to Michael, making an immediate beeline to him. He was a handsome little tyke with his big green eyes and sandy hair.

'Would you like your own bedroom?' the visitors might ask, attempting to coax him. 'Would you like to have your own new little toys?'

Enticed by the dream, Michael would emphatically answer, 'Yes! Yes! Yes!'

Then I would butt in and remind him we needed to stick together.

I found ways of disrupting the line-up. Sometimes I kicked the visitors in the back of their ankles. On one occasion, I 'accidentally' pushed one bloke aside by planting my foot on his backside. However awful and selfish my conduct was, I justified it as necessary to keeping the last vestige of my family intact. With our three siblings gone in less than two years, there was no option other than to resist, in whatever manner, any attempt to separate Michael and me.

Whether it was the power of prayer, my steadfast spirit or the staff at the Depot taking pity on our plight, after a while Michael and I were no longer placed on the foster parent parade. Instead, we were confined to the library, watching as the other inmates hurried by, no doubt eager at the prospect of being among the chosen ones.

—

In June 1960, Margie Gilboy, who by then had the job of cleaning the administration office, inadvertently discovered that Michael and I were being sent to Palm Island Aboriginal Settlement. It sounded so idyllic! I had not long before read *Treasure Island* by Robert Louis

Stevenson. And while mature enough to know that there would be no pirates or buried treasure, I did think it would be exciting for Michael and me to play on the windswept sandy beaches, fish and perhaps climb coconut trees.

When I looked up, Margie was crying. With all my daydreaming, I'd not taken too much notice of Margie's tears when relaying the news. In hindsight, would it have mattered if we'd known the reality of our ill-fated journey? Regret, in that regard, is useless, as the records and our experiences attest; bureaucratic expediency triumphed any genuine consideration of our plight.

August 2, 1960 has never left my memory. I was nineteen days shy of my twelfth birthday. Matron Bruce, the other staff and the inmates bade us farewell. Perhaps to soften the blow of leaving and any of the uncertainty about our future, Matron confided that we could expect to see Terry upon our arrival on Palm Island. This was good news, but all I wanted to know just then was if Mum would be waiting at Townsville wharf to see us off.

Michael and I didn't get a chance to say goodbye to Johanne. She continued to attend Central State School and no doubt would have realised after a few days that we had gone – as if we had just disappeared overnight. Nobody told her where we were going and, more significantly, there was no consideration of our family's further separation and loss. As a result, any contact with Johanne was lost for the next six years.

Carrying nothing other than two small bags containing our personal belongings, we were bundled into a car. Mr Jessop was the chauffeur. Among my possessions was a new book, *The Snow Goose* by author Paul Gallico; my school friend, Robyn Cunningham, had given it to me as an early birthday present.

After a short ride from the Receiving Depot, the car pulled up near the Hales Wharf on Sturt Street, Townsville. Mr Jessop told us to hop out. We waited near the car as he walked back and forth, impatiently looking at his wristwatch. He then came closer, pointing in the direction of a boat docked at the wharf. He told us someone would meet us on arrival at Palm Island. He then hopped back into the car and drove off.

I looked about for Mum, recalling our farewell in Cairns. I was afraid and confused. I had no other instructions other than Mr Jessop pointing towards the wharf. There was nobody around at the time but we could see a boat. It turned out to be the Palm Island passenger-cum-cargo vessel, the *Kiru*.

Not long afterwards, some very peculiar looking people started walking in our direction. They were laden up with suitcases and bags full of shopping, and looked just like the people I had read about in my social studies book in the section about the Dark Continent. I assumed they were from the Congo or some other African nation. They were real black, pitch black, not a shade inbetween. The colour of their skin made their teeth look so white and I could barely see their eyes, although I had no interest in eyeballing them for fear of being abused. Most children are taught that it is rude to stare, us included. I recalled Mum's reprimands whenever she saw us inquisitively gawking at people who were either disabled or just looked odd. Until that point, these individuals were probably the darkest people I had ever seen.

I never had a sense of colour or race until that moment. Even though Mum was a Murray Islander and she had other friends who were Aboriginal or were of mixed heritage, we had never really witnessed a congregation of Aboriginal people. In those days, Aboriginal people could not roam around freely in public unless they had a government exemption – even then, Aboriginal people were seldom seen in large groups, at least in metropolitan areas. There was no police presence or any form of supervision; it was a first-come, first-served situation. The ferry was a free service provided by the Palm Island Aboriginal Settlement.

More people arrived. We were too terrified to speak when they said hello. Then they began whispering and chattering, occasionally speaking English with a strange accent. The same wharf that was quiet just one hour before, suddenly transformed into a flurry of activity. The prevailing silence gave way to the noisy hustle and bustle as the boat prepared for departure.

Panic set in. I knew boats were associated with long trips or big occasions like the arrival of the pearling luggers in Cairns. This was our first time on a big boat. Only there was nothing happy about this occasion. The mood was more solemn than celebratory. Then we were ushered by a white man, later known to be Mr Fred Whiting, Captain of the *Kiru*. He told us to get on board. For two unaccompanied minors, the scene was frightening. We comforted each other as I tried to hide from the gaze of curious onlookers.

Michael was confronted and distressed by the scenario. Anxious, I began to cling to him for support, clutching hands, taking slow steps toward the boat.

'Where are we going?' he asked, visibly upset.

The shock hit me as a thought entered my mind. Perhaps Palm Island was not part of Australia.

'Shhh, Michael! I think we are going to Africa!'

Telephone 2922
P.O. Box 213

Please quote Ref. No. T 5277

State Children Department

VL:MW Townsville 21st June, 1960

The Superintendent,
Aboriginal Settlement,
PALM ISLAND.

Dear Mr. Bartlam,

Reference is made to the boy Terence Patrick Janke, now aged 13 years, who was transferred to your control some time ago.

We would appreciate some information from you regarding this lad's progress, and in particular how he has fitted into the community at Palm Island. Would you also give your views as to whether his brother and sister are suitable subjects for your settlement?

The two children in question are Patricia, born 21.8.48, and Keiran, born 19.1.51. These two children have been in our Home in Townsville for more than two years, and in view of their very dark colouring, have not been assimilated into the white race. Every effort has been made to place them in a foster home without success because of their colour.

We believe that all three children have the same parentage. Certainly the same mother. The mother is of mixed Murray Island and Filipino descent, and has no white blood at all. We believe that the father of all three children is of white European descent. However, the dark colouring predominates in all the children.

We realise that any transfer, if acceptable to you, would have to be approved by the Department of Native Affairs.

Yours faithfully,

District Officer

14

YOU DON'T BELONG HERE

After a four-hour journey across the choppy waters of the Coral Sea, Michael and I arrived at Palm Island Aboriginal Settlement. Palm Island is a paradox. Its idyllic, tropical surrounds belie the island's dark and confronting history. Almost every book or article written about Palm Island highlights its breathtaking panoramic, picturesque beauty and natural wonders. Predictably, the descriptions become less flattering as the island's chequered history is explored. Palm Island has been described by a plethora of names, including an 'Aboriginal Alcatraz', the 'Black Hole of Calcutta', 'a hellhole', 'the Devil's Island', 'a concentration camp' and 'a Gulag'. In 1929, the *Sydney Morning Herald* described it as an 'Abo's Paradise', where natives could once again 'enjoy a freedom reminiscent of the dim, distant days before Captain Cook'.[48] Eighty-three years later, the same newspaper described it as 'Paradise Lost'.[49]

Named by Captain Cook when he passed by in 1770, the Palm Island group consists of thirteen islands, each with its own eclectic history. Palm Island Aboriginal Settlement was officially declared an

Aboriginal Reserve by the State of Queensland in 1914. The island received a new influx of residents when it became home to displaced Aboriginal people from Hull River whose settlement had been destroyed by a cyclone and tidal wave in March 1918. The island later morphed into a penal colony, becoming a dumping ground for the state's worst Aboriginal and Torres Strait Islander criminal offenders, who were perceived as social outcasts and misfits.

Palm Island was one of several designated Aboriginal Settlements and Reserves throughout Queensland, including Yarrabah, Cherbourg and Woorabinda, where undesirable 'natives' were routinely shuffled out of public view. Aboriginal Settlements and Reserves were established by the State but missions were established and operated by religious and church groups. A leprosarium was established separately on nearby Fantome Island to ensure that lepers and other disease-ridden people remained quarantined from the rest of the mainland population. Prisoners condemned to a life of hard labour served penance in the hills. The more serious and serial offenders were contained within their own isolated compounds, complete with high iron and barbed wire fences. Recalcitrant residents were exiled by the superintendent and sent to Eclipse Island, known among locals as 'Punishment Island'; here they were forced to eke out a subsistence lifestyle, living off the land and surviving on basic, minimal rations, supplied weekly. Nearby Esk, Falcon, Havana and Curacoa islands were also gazetted as for the 'benefit' of the Aboriginal people of Queensland.[50] In contrast, neighbouring Orpheus Island was an opulent, privately owned holiday resort for the rich and famous, whose guests boasted *Gone With The Wind* star Vivien Leigh, Sir Laurence Olivier and Mickey Rooney.

Originally home to the Manbarra (also called Manburra) traditional owners, Great Palm Island, also known as 'Palms' or

'Palm', subsequently became host to a hotchpotch of more than 40 Aboriginal language groups from across Queensland, who were forced to live together haphazardly within an oppressive, segregated environment. The later arrivals became known by the traditional name of Bwgcolman. Torres Strait Islanders had also been exiled to Palm Island from the 1920s onwards but were always outnumbered by the dominant Aboriginal groups.

—

The arrival of the *Kiru* from Townsville was a major social occasion, especially for residents who waited expectantly for visitors, families returning with newborn babies, parcels of shopping, gifts or to receive news from family resident on the mainland. There were sightseers and, in general, stickybeakers. The boat anchored amid a sea of black and curious faces, not one of them familiar to me.

Unlike the other passengers who were on familiar ground and in a hurry to get to shore, Michael and I were among the last passengers to disembark. A smaller boat, the *Doodlebug*, ferried us halfway ashore. We had not befriended any fellow passengers on the journey so were left to second guess where we were going. Coconut trees lined the beachfront. I could see several small dinghies pulled up onto the sand as we drew closer to the large gathering of adults, children and dogs on the shore.

The tide was out and the *Doodlebug* became stuck in the soft sand not far from the shoreline. We all alighted into ankle-deep water and waded ashore. Michael and I were left to find our own way. The scene that greeted us was confronting, and we felt overwhelmed and isolated at being surrounded by predominantly dark strangers. In this unfamiliar place, our fair skin was a point of distinction. As the large gathering of onlookers and arrivals dwindled, with talkative people departing in different directions, it quickly became clear that Mr Jessop's parting words to us – 'somebody will be there to meet you when you arrive at Palm Island' – did not ring true.

I approached a bystander and asked directions to the police station. It was a relief to learn it was located on Main Street, less than a ten-minute walk from the jetty. Michael and I picked up what little personal belongings we had, hoping for assistance or for the person who was meeting us to materialise. I was conscious of people staring at us; the awkward shuffling of our feet could be clearly heard amid the discomforting silence as the eyes of strangers appraised us from head to toe.

It was early afternoon when Michael and I entered the Palm Island Police Station. Two Native Police Sergeants, Esrom Geia and Jim Stanley, were manning the office. Sergeant Stanley, surprised by our arrival, immediately thought we were white children who had caught the wrong ferry and inadvertently ended up on Palm Island.

'I think you kids got off at the wrong place. You should have hopped off at Magnetic Island,' he said.

I told the sergeants that we'd been sent by the Receiving Depot in Townsville and that our brother Terry was already on the island. Sergeant Geia went across to the Main Office to see Palm Island Aboriginal Settlement Superintendent, Mr Bartlam, while Sergeant Stanley went to the Palm Island State School to collect Terry. We stayed behind at the police station.

A short time later, I caught sight of Terry crossing the road. It had been eighteen months since I'd last seen him, when he'd skipped cheerily down the footpath at the Depot in anticipation of his picnic. Neither of us were aware then that this supposed outing was in fact a callous guise, concocted by the State Children's Department to hide his transfer to Palm Island. Despite the feelings of estrangement, our reunion was emotionally charged as we hugged and cried. But I was pulled up short by Terry's first words.

'Have you got any comic books or money?' he asked. Then as though our arrival on Palm Island was by our own choice, Terry began to berate us. 'You should not have come here; it's a bad place,' he said.

Although he was pleased to see us, he also knew the horrible treatment awaiting us.

'It's a bad place!' he said again. 'You're a lot whiter. You shouldn't be here!'

Terry had grown since we had last seen him. Now thirteen years old, he had become more masculine in his behaviour and appearance, and seemed very different to the mischievous larrikin I remembered. His muscular build was similar to that of a big Islander man. As I still worried about Michael's welfare, it was comforting to know that he would have the protection of his big, solid elder brother.

The decision to send Terry ahead of us to Palm Island was made on the basis of him being 'very dark'. Correspondence from the State Children's Department at the time indicated the authorities believed he was 'thriving among people of his own colour and race'. The moment Michael and I arrived on Palm Island, we became entrenched in a caste system based on antiquated classifications and notions of racial superiority. Percentiles and fractions of black and white 'blood' defined our existence. A 'full-blood' was the term used to describe an Aboriginal whose genetic purity remained undiluted and unmixed with any other race. 'Half-caste' was the name used to describe bi-racial individuals, usually children of one Aboriginal and one Caucasian parent. A 'quarter-caste' or 'quadroon' was the label awarded to an individual with one 'full-blood' grandparent. In some instances, race labels extended to the labelling of 'octoroons', who are one-eighth Aboriginal by virtue of having one great-grandparent who was an Indigenous Australian. British colonial ethnographers applied this same system of race classification in other countries throughout the Americas, Asia and Africa.

—

Terry, Michael and I were summoned to Mr Bartlam's Office. Mr Roy Henry Bartlam (1906–1982) was a tall man, a towering giant compared with us. At first sight, he reminded me a little of Santa Claus minus the beard, with his snowy white hair and lily-white skin. I tried not to stare at the red blotches on his face, possibly the result of a skin condition or photosensitivity, or at his portly midriff.

It was immediately apparent, from the interaction between him and Sergeants Stanley and Geia, that Mr Bartlam was the person with authority. From the outset of our meeting with him, he had a commanding presence and the demeanour of a school headmaster. For a brief while, he stood silent, gazing at us from beneath his furrowed brow. It felt as though he was comparing each of us and sizing us up; we were not who or what he had expected. Fortunately, his mood softened as he became aware of our predicament, and I was struck by his immediate compassion and concern for our welfare.

'How was your trip over from Townsville? Have you been on a boat before?' he asked.

When we told him we'd been scared and did not know anyone, Mr Bartlam struggled to hide his bewilderment. It was very clear, in his view, that our transfer to Palm Island was the result of an administrative bungle. He'd been expecting darker children. We would most likely be sent back to Townsville, he told us, because we did not belong on the island among the Aboriginal and Torres Strait Islander population. Mr Bartlam contacted Mr Pat Killoran, Head of the Native Affairs Department in Brisbane, to plead our case, but the State Children's Department did not quite know what do to with us. No guidelines existed regarding the care and placement of 'coloured children' in those times. The decision was upheld. Palm Island would become our new home, albeit on and off, for the next seven years.

Sergeant Geia, a Torres Strait Islander, escorted us from Mr Bartlam's office to the Palm Island Girls' Dormitory (or Small Girls' Dormitory) Administration Office, where we met Matron Noela Bartlam, the superintendent's wife, and Matron Kath Barnett. Michael clung to me as both women rummaged through our bags and exchanged some of the clothing we had brought with us for dormitory clothes. We were issued with a regular set of clothes made by the senior women at the local home training centre. This clothing, known as 'free issue' was replaced every three months or upon necessity. My birthday gift, *The Snow Goose*, was confiscated. Matron Bartlam expressed surprise that I would own a book of this type. I never saw it again. I was quite upset, not only because it was my favourite story at the time but because it was a gift and had sentimental value.

The matrons told me that Michael would have to leave soon and be admitted to the Boys' Dormitory. As I held his hand, he clutched mine ever more tightly, as though in fearful anticipation of our being separated again. This would be the first time in our lives that we would not be living under the same roof, playing with each other, sharing meals and being accessible to each other, not confined by any restrictions. Michael's distress was evident. He was only nine years old and about to be separated from not just his big sister but, in many respects, his surrogate mother. Heartbroken, I watched from the porch of the Girls' Dormitory Administration Office as my little brother was escorted away.

And then there was one.

—

Over the following week, I learned that other women witnessed Michael's distraught state and felt sorry for him. However, given circumstances were beyond their control, they were powerless to attempt to comfort him. Mary Gallagher, a resident in the Women's Dormitory (or Big Girls' Dormitory) and a cook at the Boys' Home, was among the women who passed Michael on his way to the Boys' Home that day. In 1994 when I was travelling to Mornington Island, I renewed my acquaintance with Mary and she still recalled this incident.

I consoled myself with the knowledge that Michael wouldn't be alone, that he would have Terry's companionship and protection. As for me? Soon to turn twelve, I was so distracted by concerns for Michael's welfare that I barely focussed on my own situation. Surveying my immediate surrounds, I did not have to be Albert Einstein to know that it was going to be an uphill battle for me to overcome the odds. I consoled myself that I had done all I could to uphold the responsibility Mum had given me. That realisation was enough to lift my otherwise sagging spirits. I was determined to surmount any strife that lay ahead.

I developed my own self-styled faith based on my observations of Mum's Catholic idiosyncrasies, my earlier participation in religious instruction at the various schools I attended and my involvement with the Presbyterian Pathfinders Group in Townsville while resident at the Receiving Depot. I prayed to God for guidance and for the protection of my family and myself. I also invoked Mum's presence, drawing upon the strength of her love for us and her belief in me. I recalled her words and would hold conversations with her in my mind, willing my thoughts to be telepathically transferred to her wherever she was. I wondered if she knew where we were.

After Michael had left, I was sent to the kitchen to have something to eat while our paperwork was processed. In the kitchen, I noticed some dormitory residents gawking at me as if I was a zoo exhibit. Then Matron Bartlam accompanied me through the building, introducing me to several inmates along the way. I met Moira Benn, an Aboriginal residential dormitory supervisor, who took me on a housekeeping tour. I later found out that Mrs Benn, accompanied by her two young children, had been seconded from the Women's Dormitory.

My lifelong friend and fellow Girls' Dormitory resident, Irene Doyle (née Simpson), still remembers my arrival:

> *I remember the day Patsy first arrived on Palm Island. She wore a pale green and white chequered dress with a sash attached that tied into a bow behind her back. The dress had puffy sleeves and a white collar rounded at the ends. She wore black patent shiny shoes, her hair was short black and curly and her skin was white as could be except for her sunburnt chubby cheeks. Patsy was in the kitchen of the Small Girls' Dormitory eating cold meat and salad with a knife and fork while trying to avoid our staring eyes.*
>
> *It intrigued me how slowly and daintily this girl ate. We just gulped our food down with our hands or a spoon. To see someone young, handle a knife and fork well, I was personally impressed as were the others who whispered agreement with me. The only thing we couldn't work out or handle was, why is this white girl here? She should be living with the* 'migloos'. *(*Migloo *or* migaloo*, a common Queensland Aboriginal term*

> *to describe a 'white' person.) We resented the fact that she was going to be living with us. None of us ever lived with a white person before.*
>
> *Later that day I found out Patsy had a brother Terrence Janke already living here for two years and another younger brother Michael who arrived on the same day as Patsy. I discovered Michael crying by himself under a battered-up banana sapling. He had blue eyes and white skin but I felt sorry for him because he was sobbing. He was going to live at the Boys' Home with his older brother Terry. My mother was in charge of the Boys' Home at the time and I informed her how upset this boy was, that she should do something about it to comfort him. She just said 'Don't worry, he'll get over it.' Terry, his brother, had island hair and darker skin and was accepted by others straight away!*[51]

I had no concept of racial segregation, racism or bigotry until I was sent to Palm Island, where Michael, Terry and I were plunged head first into a 'reverse-assimilation' scenario. On the mainland, we all attended non-segregated schools, and lived a life of relative freedom, which included sneaking into a non-segregated picture theatre in Cairns. We had a Danish stepfather and an Australian-Irish father; we fitted into free society. Yet, we were removed to Palm Island because the State Children's Department maintained we had not been assimilated into the white race. Deracinated from our former life in Cairns, Michael, Terry and I – well, on paper at least – were now deemed by the State to be 'Aboriginal' children. Any rights and freedoms we'd enjoyed up until now disappeared with the requirement to live under The Act. Moreover, although we were raised non-denominational, the State Children's Department had classified us as Methodist during our separation in 1958, presumably because Mum and Uncle Kaj married in a Methodist Church. Nonetheless, in other correspondence, we were classified as Church of England, whereas in view of Mum's upbringing, we probably should have been classified as non-practising Catholics. In 1960, on Palm, we got another religion; the Department of Native Affairs designated us as Aboriginal Inland Ministry (AIM).

15

PALM ISLAND ABORIGINAL SETTLEMENT

In the 1950s 'assimilation', social and cultural integration became a widely-accepted goal for all Aboriginal people. All State and Territory Governments adopted it as policy. Although assimilation was first proposed in Queensland in 1951, the Director of Native Affairs, Cornelius O'Leary, formally announced its adoption in 1956; Queensland's policy initially focussed on the provision of education and housing for Indigenous people. Other State and Territory Governments pursued separate assimilation policy agendas until April 1961. The definition and aims of assimilation were brought together during the Native Welfare Conference in Canberra in April that year.[52] Championed by the Commonwealth Minister for Territories, the Hon. Paul Hasluck, the accepted goal of the policy was the way in which:

> *All Aborigines and part-Aborigines will attain the same manner of living as other Australians and live as members of a single Australian community enjoying the same rights and privileges, accepting the same*

> *responsibilities, observing the same customs and influenced by the same beliefs, hopes and loyalties as other Australians.*[53]

Journalist KG Kennedy, a public affairs specialist, on behalf of the Northern Territory Department of Interior, wrote:

> *Paradoxical though it seems, the very basis of Australia's new approach to the salvation of this once dying race is the very factor that once caused its decline – close contact with white people … both the Australian Federal and State Governments now agree that the general problem of the future of the aborigine reduces itself to one of assimilation which means in simpler terms that to survive and prosper the numerically small aboriginal group, within a vastly larger white Australian group, must learn to live and work as the majority do.*[54]

Aboriginal settlements and missions throughout Australia gradually morphed into 'centres of assimilation' during this policy era. Their function was to spearhead the wholesale re-socialisation and integration of Australia's largely 'unskilled', 'unsophisticated' and 'uncivilised' black population into mainstream white society. Settlement and mission dwellers would receive social skills, education and training with a view to becoming fully contributing, upstanding citizens. Internationally acclaimed artist, Albert Namatjira, and opera singer, Harold Blair, were hailed as exemplars for what every assimilated Aboriginal could potentially achieve.[55]

—

In 1960, Palm Island Settlement was home to almost 1400 residents, approximately 1300 of whom were Aboriginal; a few were Torres

Strait Islanders. The Settlement was managed and supported by 70 to 100 non-Indigenous support staff. The Palm Island community was a relatively young one, with roughly 40 per cent of residents under the age of 21.[56]

Not all Indigenous residents were legally compelled to live on Palm Island under the Act during the time I was there. State Care and Protection Orders applied to less than half the population. The remaining inhabitants were supposedly free to live and work on the mainland at their leisure[57] but the majority had little incentive to leave Palm and opted for the security of a sheltered life. Food, health care, education and training opportunities were provided in exchange for two-thirds of residents' social services benefit.

The older Aboriginal residents seemed hardened by their experiences on Palm Island. The raised welts from tribal initiation were still visible on the backs and chests of some male elders; however, their invisible mental scars ran much deeper. Apart from being on the island for reasons related to crime, poverty and health, many of the older generation were removed to Palm Island during the 1920s and 1930s for petty reasons such as being too lazy to work, being cheeky or immoral, frightening women, begging for food, engaging in prostitution, having an alcohol or opium addiction, having a low mentality, being insolent, trading lubras (colonial term for Aboriginal women) to the Japanese, and being eccentric and amorous toward white women.[58] By contrast, some of the newer generation who were born on Palm Island had committed no crime – but were delivered all the same into a captive and segregated environment.

I experienced huge culture shock on Palm. It took some time to adjust to being among a majority Aboriginal population. Some residents had really imaginative names, including Tommy Kangaroo,

Dick Wee Wee, Polly Inky, Dora Moonlight, Ziggy Sunlight, Dicky Blowhard, Mr Lefthand, Timmy Maverick and Billy Inkstone. There was also the highly respected elder and traditional owner, Mr Willie Palm Island. Local families included the Daylights, Starlights, Spiders, Bamboos and Chookies. The most intriguing name belonged to Mr Nandy Riflebutt N34. I was initially terrified of an elder, Mr Pompey Clumpoint; he fitted Mum's description of a cannibal to a tee, with his bright red lips and gums on account of his frequent chewing of *bunagi* (a narcotic chewable bush tobacco also known as *pituri*). The origin of many of these names remains unknown to me. Some may have been inherited, or represented associations with place, country or kin. Author Bruce Elder, in his book *Blood on the Wattle*, suggests the colonial inability and lazy refusal to pronounce Aboriginal names resulted in some of these names.[59]

Authority on Palm Island was concentrated in the power of the superintendent. There was minimal delegation of responsibility to other staff members, much less to the Aboriginal residents. The superintendent was able to exercise an extraordinary degree of control over daily life. Residents' behaviour was closely circumscribed by regulation and administrative fiat, and personal freedom was limited. According to academic J.P.M Long who visited Palm Island in the late 1960s, the Aboriginal people on Palm Island had 'no place at all in any class system but were an untouchable caste'. The aim of the new policy, as described by the Department of Native Affairs in 1958, was 'the ultimate assimilation of all Aboriginals and half bloods into the State's community life'. Life on Palm Island, Long wrote, had been so completely unlike life in ordinary Queensland communities, and so few of the freedoms and responsibilities of ordinary life were experienced, there had been no effective and useful preparation of residents for 'normal' living.[60]

This meant that all Aboriginal and Torres Strait Islander residents were required to live and work under Settlement rules. In addition to Protectionist legislation, Palm Island, like all other Aboriginal missions and settlements in Queensland at the time, was governed by the *Aboriginal Regulations (1945)*. These regulations were effectively the superintendent's instruction manual, through which he was able to manage residents in his charge. The regulations also ensured consistency in practice and operation among Queensland's Aboriginal Settlements, Reserves and Missions.[61]

Palm Island's Native Police Force, known as the Native Police, were tasked by the administration to uphold law and order. The Native Police comprised Indigenous male officers drawn from the local population. Although others may have a different memory, my recollection as a young girl was of the Native Police being upstanding men. During my time, some of the Native Police included Esrom Geia, Jim Stanley, Harry Daphne, Edwin Clarke, Jack Conway, Bernard Blanket, Tommy Dodd, Bamboo Friday, Bertie Massey, Harry Johnson and Ronnie Nemo. The role of the Native Police was to assist in the maintenance of good order and discipline, and supervision, as defined in Section 52 of the *Aboriginal Regulations (1945)*. On Palm, the Native Police were also charged with managing school truancy and enforcing school attendance by undertaking home visits to engage parents if their children were absent from school.

The first permanent, non-Indigenous members of the Queensland Police Service only arrived on Palm Island in 1971 as part of an 'immediate improvement.' program. The first deployment of non-Aboriginal police came at the behest of former Premier of Queensland Bjelke-Petersen and Aboriginal Affairs Minister Neville Hewitt following complaints from the local Anglican priest of widespread lesbianism, homosexuality, immorality, gambling and alcoholism.[62]

Before that, the Native Police on Palm had powers to arrest and detain residents for any breaches of the regulations. Sometimes referred to as trackers, the Native Police were largely a law unto themselves. Although my experience of them was different, some Palm Island residents thought of the Native Police as renegades who frequently engaged in unsanctioned acts of brutality and doled out harsh, arbitrary punishment for trivial offences.

Michael recalls meeting a young man who was transferred to Palm Island from another Aboriginal Settlement. Regarded as a troublemaker of sorts, on arrival he was allegedly driven to Butler's Bay. The man claimed the Native Police threw a hangman's noose over a tree, strung it around his neck, blindfolded him and forced him to stand on a makeshift platform. Traumatised, the man peed in his pants, much to the delight of the self-satisfied officers. The man was warned not to cause any strife on the island or he would meet his fate. Although he left Palm Island the year I arrived, Australia's first Aboriginal Senator, the late Neville Bonner AO, a member of the Liberal Party, lived and worked on Palm Island from 1946 to 1960. He held the position of Assistant Overseer with the Palm Island Administration, which was the most senior position, second-in-command to the superintendent, held by an Indigenous resident. Bonner recounted a similar story of witnessing four Native Police officers severely beating an Aboriginal resident with their batons; he said the resident was placed in gaol for six weeks while the officers were treated with impunity.[63]

Recent written accounts of Palm Island history have contained examples of residents who were unjustly arrested for laughing on the street, waving to their girlfriends or being late for the work line-up each morning. While there is no specific evidence of these offences in the Palm Island Court Records from 1964 to 1969, there are many disorderly conduct and antisocial behaviour charges, which were commonly written up as Section 70 breaches pertaining to 'conduct prejudicial to good order and discipline on the settlement'.[64] Section 70 charges included carrying tales so as to cause domestic troubles, evading work, creating a disturbance, breaking out of the Girls' Dormitory, rudeness to an officer, taking part in games of chance or prohibited games, gambling or congregating for the purposes of gambling, liquor possession, making fermented liquor, assault and being out of bounds after-hours.[65]

Black residents were heavily penalised for crossing into the whites-only Mango Avenue without authorisation. In the earlier days, female transgressors would have their heads shaved to the scalp, then be forced to sweep the streets wearing the dreaded hessian bag known as a sack dress. In those days, residents could not leave a mission without permission of the administration. Punitive measures also applied to individuals who failed to cease native practices such as traditional dancing. Failing to obey instructions could result in punishment. The regulations also governed marriages, wages, allocation of rations, employment, hours of work, punishment, and law and order, as well the establishment of Aboriginal Councils.[66]

Alcohol was banned on Palm and the yeast from the bakery was carefully controlled to prevent theft for its potential use in home-brews. Fermented coconut wine, known as *tuba*, was also prohibited. Of course, some people found a way to circumvent the system. And the anti-congregation rules, prohibiting groups of more than five people, did not really stop residents from indulging in vices like gambling and games of chance, which were also prohibited. Card games such as 'cut-tem', 'kuunkan' and 'sikai' were a serious social activity, with matches sometimes continuing for days on end. Although residents did not have much money, they gambled personal possessions, including their own or their children's clothing as wagering chips. It was not uncommon to see the same pretty party dress do the rounds among a few different girls in a week.

Mr Bartlam did not allow bitches on the island, fearing an escalation in the number of stray and mangy dogs. Firearms were regulated, with only .22 calibre rifles permitted, and those remained under lock and key at his office.

Palm Island operated according to a hierarchy of colour and privilege. The white residents were at the apex, enjoying preferential considerations including superior accommodation, the first choice of fresh food and meat, and freedom of movement. White students attended the Palm Island Provisional School; Aboriginal Students attended Palm Island Settlement State School. During my time on Palm, the non-Aboriginal residents, apart from the Bartlams, included the store manager, Mr Hoffman, and Mr Len Brandis. The Murphy, Krause, Fanning, Eleanor, Henry, Davidson, Pattison, Carey, Doolan, Greentrees, Spring, Hogbin, O'Brien, Whiting and Wilson families were long-established on the island. I also remember an American, Shelby Parsons, because of his loud, southern Yankee drawl. Nursing and teaching staff were among the transient service providers, along with a small contingent of Catholic missionaries including Sister Cortelle and Sister Michael, and the super-strict Father Edward Roper, who preceded Franciscan priest Father Cassian Double of the Order of Friars Minor (OFM), commonly known as Franciscans. Mr and Mrs Krause had oversight of worship within the AIM Ministry.

Palm Island was divided into three parts, also reflecting the racial and social strata – the white areas, the dormitories, and the Palm Island Settlement proper, known as the camp areas, where the Murri families resided (Murri is a name for Aboriginal people from Queensland). There was a bottom end and top end of the camp, where the various tribal groups were grouped. The Sundowner Camp was home to the Kalkadoon people from Cloncurry and Mount Isa and other tribes from throughout northwest Queensland and the Gulf of Carpentaria. The Lamalama Camp was home to Aboriginal people from the Cape York communities. The Cooktown Camp was home to people from east coast areas such as Mission Beach, Yarrabah and other locations. The Boys' Dormitory was located within the Lamalama Camp area.

Settlement houses were of a reasonable size and standard but were too small to contain large extended families. Formal inspections of residences were held and any deliberate damage to accommodation would be deducted from the residents' personal accounts. Dedicated teams of tradesmen, including plumbers, carpenters and electricians, undertook routine maintenance. Work teams were organised via the Administration Office. The Island's Hygiene Officer routinely inspected all dwellings for cleanliness, and assisted with the detection of preventable and treatable diseases as well as monitoring the regulatory building safety issues. The majority of Aboriginal employees either lived in the Settlement area or in separate accommodation near Casement Bay.

All the main stores and administration were on Main Street. Nobody paid much attention to the actual street names like Mango Avenue, Gribble Street, Beach Street or Clumpoint Road. There were no street addresses, house numbers or even post office boxes. People simply knew where one another lived.

Aboriginal and Torres Strait Islander residents were expected to work for 30 hours a week in exchange for accommodation and food rations, which usually included bread, tea, powdered milk, eggs, cheese, flour, salt, soap, baking soda and offcuts of meat. Tuesdays and Fridays were the meat and bread allocation days for families living in the camp areas. Meat portions were weighed and allocated according to the number of members per household. Michael reckons that the local butchers occasionally slipped choice cuts of meats to their families or friends in little white parcels while the supervisor was distracted. Meat from the mainland was supplemented with locally caught fish and seafood from the abundant supply in the island's waters.

Palm Island offered a virtual 'womb to tomb' existence for many of its Indigenous residents. Pre-natal care was provided to all expectant mothers. Children from the ages of one to five years old came under the control of the Infant Welfare Officer; at the clinic, weighing, vaccinations and health checks were undertaken weekly, and clothing and extra rations were provided if necessary. The female Welfare Officer monitored young girls of school age until they completed their primary education.

Parentcraft lessons on the care of three- to six-month-old babies were also provided at the Welfare Centre, after which young women were sent into the workforce with a view to becoming housewives upon meeting their future husbands. Nursing training was offered by the Townsville General Hospital. Other girls became domestic workers for the white employees on the island or were sent to remote cattle stations across northwest Queensland.

Only a portion of Palm's population was housed in the ill-reputed dormitories. The Women's Dormitory mainly comprised single mothers, many of whom were removed to Palm Island after having been left destitute and abandoned by their children's fathers. Their children, if under the age of five, were placed in the nursery. Children five years and older were placed in either the Girls' or Boys' Dormitory.

Wards of the State – like Terry, Michael and me – and other local children deemed to be at risk were also placed in the dormitories.

In December 1960, there were thirteen Wards of the State resident on Palm Island, including us; the eldest Ward was seventeen years old and the youngest was two.[67] Most of the other children had one parent or both living on the island, in addition to extended family or clan including cousins or family friends. Terry, Michael and I only had each other.

16

THE GIRLS' DORMITORY

The Girls' Dormitory was a rudimentary structure made from wood and corrugated-iron, and enclosed within a large, diamond-wire mesh fence. An enclosed veranda surrounded the building: the bottom half comprised wood panelling while wire mesh extended from the panels to the roof to form a 360-degree barricade. Long-term resident Jack Sibley was often taken aback by the sight of the dormitory girls peering out to the street from behind the wire netting. To him they resembled a 'mob of monkeys in a cage'.[68]

It was sweltering hot at all times. We dampened our sheets with water to escape the humid conditions. Linen was in short supply, with only one sheet per bed. The kapok mattresses and pillows were stuffed with coconut fibre and manufactured at the Home Training Centre. There were no fridges, air-conditioning, fans or internal showers to help us cool off. A series of eight small internal windows, four each side, provided the only source of ventilation in the sleeping quarters. The living quarters were dilapidated and inferior by comparison with the State Children's Home and, for that matter, our family home at White Rock.

It was overcrowded in the Girls' Dorm, with approximately 20 to 30 girls. Conditions generally were very spartan, with only two interior toilets and other ablutions amenities external to the building. Each dormitory contained a dining room with cooking and kitchen staff, in addition to separate laundry facilities. Residents were assigned routine kitchen, laundry and cleaning duties as a form of indenture. All our daily routines were governed by the clanging of the large mission bell that was near to the island's central business area. The bell tolled at 8am daily, heralding the start of the work and school day. The bell pealed again at lunch and dinner times, and again at 10pm, when it was time to be off the streets. Even so, the bell had minimal impact on the dormitories, and our evening curfew was very generous compared with our other restrictions.

During the day, out of school hours, we undertook our regularly allocated domestic chores, some of which were physically demanding. We worked like a team of little Cinderellas, or as we used to say 'Ginderellas'. My tasks included cooking, laundering and ironing school uniforms, scrubbing floors, stoking the big copper boiler and removing the wet, heavy sheets with a makeshift broomstick, and yard work.

Matron Bartlam was in attendance from around 9am to 5pm Monday to Friday and on weekend call, as required. The residential monitors were usually chosen from local families on the basis of their good reputations within the community. Matron Barnett, wife of Lionel Barnett, the garage mechanic and workshop manager, was the second-in-charge matron. She lived next door, in close proximity to both the Girls' and Women's Dormitories. Matron Barnett had regular oversight of domiciliary tasks allocated to the Aboriginal monitors and monitresses, including Moira Benn, Bill and Pat Seaton, Geraldine and

Roddy Geesu and Bernard and Beryl Castors, all long-term residents hand-picked from the Settlement Camp. Their role was to co-supervise and run the Girls' Dormitory around the clock. The monitors also meted out corporal punishment by disciplining children whom they perceived as wayward. Bad behaviours were not tolerated; the Girls' Dorm was certainly no place for belligerent young women.

Moira Benn (née Murgha) initially transferred to Palm Island from Yarrabah Mission. She was a domineering, short, round woman of mixed-race ancestry. She had several tattoos on both arms, including a heart-shaped one that encircled the initials of her two children, George Jnr and Diane, whom she doted on; those kids were spoilt rotten. Moira's husband, George, was absent from her life and she, like many other women resident in the Women's Dormitory, was left to fend for herself and her children.

Geraldine, or Gerry as she was known, was a mixed-race woman with long, flaming, Rita Hayworth locks resembling those of the goddess, Diana the Huntress, in Roman mythology. She was statuesque, a strikingly beautiful lady, particularly in her young years. Men were infatuated by Geraldine's presence, including her husband, Roddy, who often competed with his wife's many admirers for her attention. On rare occasions, Gerry confided in me about her upbringing, yet another story of dislocation and removal. Her family were from the Cherbourg/Woorabinda area of Queensland. Gerry was also a victim of violence on Palm Island; she'd survived an axe attack on Palm Island on Christmas Day 1954 at the hands of fellow resident Herbert Tanner. She spent nine days in hospital and came close to having her arm amputated.[69]

Apart from approved official inspections and visits, the dormitories were strictly out of bounds. Dormitory children led a cloistered existence. Locked away, most of us rarely entered the other parts of the Settlement. For individual – as well as group – security and protection, we were confined to quarters; the duty Native Police Officer secured all doors with heavy chains and locks from 6pm until 6am daily. It was always lights-out by 9.30pm. We led silent lives. There was no talking in class unless we asked questions. Conversation was not encouraged inside the dormitories when the matrons or monitresses were present. We never spoke unless spoken to.

Being locked up each night was hard to cope with. On reflection, I understand this rule was in place to protect us girls against predatory conduct. Aboriginal leader and former Commonwealth Department of Native Affairs advisor, Charles Perkins, expressed his concern in an internal note to Departmental management:

> *There were white workmen brought in from the outside to erect the new school building. It seems some of these white men have interfered with the Aboriginal girls and women and this has done little to ease relationships between Aborigines and – white management. Two fourteen-year-old Aboriginal girls have given birth to babies – it was not indicated whether the fathers were white or Aboriginal. Whatever, this situation is most unacceptable.*[70]

Sometimes peeping toms (male prowlers) would disturb one of the girls and we'd wake in fright to an almighty scream. 'Man! Man!' would echo throughout the building, causing us to rise as one and run frantically about the place. The prowlers had often escaped by the time our screams alerted police. Several times, men were found hiding inside the dormitory cupboards; the unmistakeable sight of a pair of male feet protruding from under the hanging clothes was always a dead giveaway. The intruders rarely returned after being set upon and roughed up by a large group of angry girls.

The girls sleeping in the middle section of the dormitory and those sleeping on the veranda area often swapped places as they ran about, panic-stricken. Sometimes you just had to laugh, it was such a funny sight. With every 'prowler attack', the same practice would prevail. After every incident, our reactions would become a standard joke as we likened our startled screams to shark attack alerts: 'Shark! Shark!'

There was a permanent supervisory Native Police presence and escort whenever dormitory girls and women attended social or recreational activities outside of the dorms. During my time on Palm, the Women's Dormitory was co-managed by Native Police Senior Sergeant Esrom Geia and his wife, Eva. Native Policeman Tommy Dodd and his wife, Beatrice, also had some association with the Girls' and the Women's Dormitories. The Native Police officers' quarters comprised a dilapidated shack at the rear of the Girls' Dormitory, and the police kept a close eye on it and its surrounds 24 hours a day. From time to time, accusations were also levelled about inappropriate conduct because of their close liaison with the dormitory girls. But the Native Policemen stationed did not provide escort services; their duties were restricted to the provision of dormitory security and the enforcement of in-house rules and regulations.

There were regular social and recreational activities held outside the dormitories. Most of these recreational activities were staged indoors at the Social Welfare Hall. The seating arrangements were segregated, with white residents in the upstairs section, and community residents and residents from the Boys', Women's and Girls' dormitories sharing the downstairs space, which was cordoned off. At the island's one and only picture theatre, white patrons sat upstairs and blacks sat downstairs.

The movies were mostly American Westerns and newsreels. Native Policemen, like modern-day usherettes, stood at the front and back of the black section, monitoring everyone's behaviour

Amateur boxing tournaments were also staged, a popular way for some participants to let off steam. Jim Daisy usually refereed, kitted out in immaculate attire: a blindingly white shirt, white trousers and tie. Lots of girls watched the boxing as we usually had family members, boyfriends or friends competing. Dances were held on occasion, usually on Friday evenings, and residents danced to the tunes of a local band under the watchful eye of the Native Police. English dances like the Military Two Step, Gypsy Tap, Rotational Barn Dance and Pride of Erin were popular, along with traditional Island dances. Young and old residents alike, male and female, from the bottom end and top end camp areas, always participated. The administration organised monthly corroborees too, and dancing competitions where rival teams would compete for the best in show.

If any of the Big Girls' Dormitory women fell in love or began courting, they would have to sit outside to conduct their romance, in full view of everyone, on the notorious spot called 'the green'. The green was a patch of turf, which stretched across the outskirts of the white picket fencing of the Women's Dormitory. It was wide-open, a very public space, primarily reserved for dating couples but to respect the privacy of other dormitory residents, often family visits were held there.

Those engaged in the practice of 'green sitting' were under the surveillance of overly observant Native Policemen. Matron Barnett also took random peeks through the front window of her house, which was directly opposite. Any overt displays of affection were discouraged by a prod from a Native Policeman's baton, as I can attest to. Physical

Me on Palm Island with Girls' Dormitory residents Fay (Patsy) Thimble and Rosina Norman. *Pic courtesy Fay Thimble*

My younger brother Michael.

My brother Michael was billeted by the Modic family (pictured) in Melbourne during holidays arranged through the *Harold Blair Aboriginal Children's Holiday Project* which brought groups of children from Queensland settlements to Victoria, for up to three months. Michael described this experience as a highlight of his life despite claims by others that the Project had ulterior motives.

My younger sister Johanne proudly displaying her catch.

Sister Johanne exhibiting miniature smooth-haired dachshunds at local dog show in Townsville.

Palm Island girls mixed netball team with me in the back row (second from left) with my arm around life-long friend Irene Doyle (née Simpson). *Pic courtesy Alison Bendall*

Me in netball uniform on Palm Island. *Pic courtesy Alison Bendall*

Me, back right, with Theresa Anderson holding baby John Anderson Jnr, Ellen Anderson (L) and Dulcie Anderson, front. *Pic courtesy Theresa Anderson*

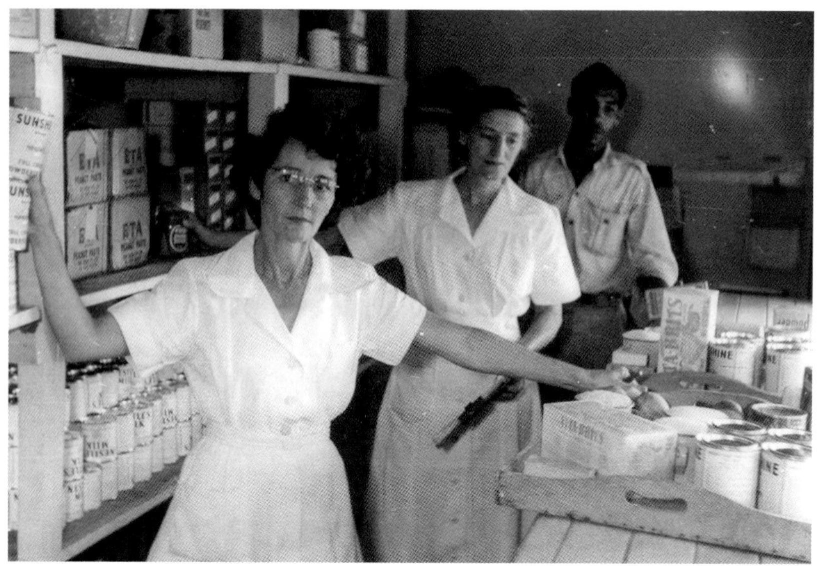

Food parcels and rations being prepared at the Palm Island store.
Pic courtesy Queensland State Library

Sewing class on Palm Island designed to teach young women life skills. Girls' Dormitory friend Marie Saylor is seated first on the left. *Pic courtesy Queensland State Library*

Children playing on swings at the Palm Island nursery.
Pic courtesy Queensland State Library

Aunty Iris and Uncle Fred Clay were among my mentors and supporters on Palm Island.
Pic courtesy National Archives of Australia

Domestic training. *Pic courtesy Queensland State Library*

Me with the Bartlam family.

Father Cassian on his Honda.
Pic courtesy of Carmel McMahon

Father Cassian in his robes.

Me with Father Cassian in Townsville circa 1969.

Palm Island from the Lookout. Panorama of Orpheus Island. *Pic courtesy of Alison Bendall*

Palm Island Settlement from a distance. *Pic courtesy of Alison Bendall*

contact was restricted to restrained gestures such as holding hands, an arm draped around each other's shoulder and a brief peck on the cheek at the beginning and end of the green encounter.

Like at the Townsville orphanage, personal correspondence continued to be vetted and withheld if the content was deemed by management to be unsettling. We were never told about this, merely left to wonder why we never received any replies to our letters. Bag searches were routine, particularly for prohibited items like alcohol that could be carried in personal belongings. Understandably, some residents saw this as an invasion of privacy.

There was no escaping the dreaded, mandatory head lice inspections. Kerosene was combed through our hair, killing the offending critters within hours. The younger girls, myself included, were then forced to wear male handkerchiefs on our heads with a knot tied in the corners to absorb the liquid and to catch the dying nits. This practice did nothing for our diminished self-esteem; it reduced us to feeling ugly and androgynous. In the event of a major lice outbreak, any final trace of feminine beauty and self-esteem disappeared when Matron Bartlam and Matron Barnet shaved our heads.

The women in the camp did not have to endure such a hideous ritual and, thus, had a far greater advantage when it came to competing for male attention. In the handkerchief headwear, I took to slipping into the picture theatre under cover of darkness, covered from head to toe in a big blanket. Today, as I listen to the debates around Islamic women's dress code, I cannot refrain from thinking, that, albeit unknowingly, I may have worn the first ever burqa in an Aboriginal community.

Sometimes I heard reports about previous dormitory residents having their genitals and skin scrubbed with carbolic soap, which has a strong phenol smell and was used in many institutional environments to disinfect women in the event they might have been sexually active. Such practices, the tough physical conditions and the isolation on Palm were, however, minimal compared with the taunting and teasing I received on account of my fair skin.

17

THE FAIREST ONES OF ALL

The history of Palm Island invariably involves some reference to the landmark 'Strike of 57', when a group of disaffected Palm Islanders actively protested against the rule of white administration, the oppressive conditions on the island and life under the Act. The uprising culminated in seven families being dramatically exiled from Palm under police escort. Former Olympic athlete Cathy Freeman's mother, Cecelia Barber, was one of many children uprooted with their parents from the island following that chain of events.

By 1960, Palm's racial melting pot was quietly bubbling away with under-the-surface, well-hidden hatred and contempt for whites. Although the State regarded my siblings and me as Aboriginal, the predominantly black population perceived us as white, and we were caught in a backwash of animosity. We were not the only mixed-race children on Palm Island; however, Michael and I did have the unfortunate distinction of being much fairer than the others.

For several weeks after I arrived on Palm, none of the girls wanted to be anywhere near me. They pulled their beds away from mine at night and rejected my attempts to befriend them in the hope I would be able to join in their chatter and games. I ate alone at meal times and during other group gatherings. I was often pushed away with hurtful words, called a *migloo*, told I didn't belong on Palm Island or in the dormitory because I was not one of 'them'. Some girls would pack up their music and move away or turn it off when I tried to be part of the group. There were secret whispers, gossiping and frequent taunts.

'You're not black,' some would say. 'Go back to where you come from! White slut!'

The first time I heard the 'c' word was when I was called a white one during a stoush with another girl. Some mistook my shyness for being stuck-up. Although I also owned two pairs of shoes when I arrived at the dormitory, in an early attempt to fit in, I mostly walked about barefoot like the other girls. The frequent bullying and harassment made my situation intolerable, and Michael experienced the same treatment in the Boys' Dormitory.

The dormitory was a dog-eat-dog environment: personal disputes were settled either by verbal or physical confrontation, or in some cases, by both. One thing was certain, as sure as night followed day, irrespective of effort, the weak rarely survived such encounters. Some of the older girls resorted to physical aggression, pushing and shoving and other intimidating behaviours. I could not run home to tell my mother, nor could I escape the shared dormitory. Mum was always with me in spirit and I often wistfully thought of her telling me to take care of Michael and willing me to be strong. But worrying about Michael continued to be a way to deflect my own feelings of inadequacy and hopelessness in the challenging dorm environment. I had no choice but to buckle up for the long ride ahead.

Ultimately, my acceptance on Palm was subject to the girls being convinced that I was a 'proper blackfella'. My competitive hackle was raised as I realised that everything they did, I had to do better. Any sign of weakness or faltering would not help my cause. If they scrubbed a floor, I scrubbed it twice as hard.

A few of the senior residents, including Stella Bell, Queenie Burton and Daphne Hooligan, felt sorry for me after a while and acted as mentors and protectors. I revelled in their interest and caring concern. I especially loved the way Daphne combed my hair and powdered me up for school.

Stella was one of the darkest girls among the coloured contingent. Her influence over the others, young and old alike, was something to be reckoned with. I was grateful that she chose to be for me and not against me. After witnessing the bullying and rejection I was subjected to upon my initial arrival, Stella became an unexpected source of support with her nurturing care. She was instrumental in finding novel ways to counteract the distress I suffered as a consequence of my constant rejection for being fair-skinned. One day, Stella took it upon herself to take me down to the huge copper boiler that sat above a furnace. Stella reached into the furnace and scraped some soot from the interior wall.

'This will make you darker,' she whispered, before 'sooting me up'. 'Now there'll be no more trouble for you. You'll be the same colour as the rest of us.' She gently smudged the soot all over my face, arms and legs. Abracadabra! Stella's instant suntan worked. Miraculously, the girls began to befriend me.

Marie Saylor (1944–2016) remembers befriending me in those days on Palm Island when I was so often sadder than sad:

The woman's gaol was one side of the dormitory, the other side was the toilet that was a thunderbox, and then there was a big open paddock area.

> *Bush lemon was growing on one side. The other side had coconut trees and we were picking up coconuts. Pattie picked up this coconut and she looked around. I never forget that Pattie had the saddest look on her face, so sad. All the girls like Evelyn Palmer and Joycie Wyles. We all noticed. Look at that girl there. She is so sad! She looks like she is scared of us. Why don't we go and make friends with her? So there was Evelyn Palmer, Joycie Wyles, Ethel Robinson and myself. We all went over to her and she started mixing with us then.*[71]

The first sign of acceptance came when I was given the nickname Casper in honour of the 'friendly ghost', a white character who featured in the cartoons we watched weekly at the picture theatre. However, in spite of my newfound dark skin, I still needed to prove myself by undergoing lengthy and varied rites of passage.

The only respite we ever had from the omnipresent Native Police and the boredom of confinement was when Superintendent Bartlam arranged truck rides around the island. A few of us were transported on the back of his truck to Butler's Bay, on the other side of the island, with the feted 'Kingy' James being the truck driver. Mr Bartlam also organised excursions to the outer islands of the Great Palm Island group. Esk, Possum and Havana were popular and safe; we fished, cooked on an open campfire, swam, ran amok over the reef beds and freely explored the island habitat.

We spent time walking on the beach. Usually someone would light a fire, boil a billy, and spear some fish for lunch. Some weekends we would go fishing or play on the beach. I became the fastest girl to run out to the reef, often sprinting while piggybacking some of the junior girls.

Irene remembers these days of carefree, lighthearted fun:

> *On day trips we'd swim all day while the senior girls fished in a flat bottom, mail boat. By the end of the day, Janke became as red as a beetroot. The brown- and black-skinned girls were sunburnt too. Their skin became dark brown, super black, tight and shiny. It didn't matter then whether we were black or white. We all felt sore.*[72]

It was during one of these outings when several girls including Theresa, her sister Linda Anderson, Irene Olive Bonner (née Phillips), Marie Pryor, Cynthia Tyson (née King), Erica Burton and Penny Seaton all gathered around a campfire one evening on Esk Island. We were yarning up, having spent the afternoon frolicking over the reef bed while the tide was out. Linda had shown me how to collect spider and clam shells, and how to detect the poisonous stonefish camouflaged amid the coral in the murky seawater. Ashore, she would throw the clam and spider shells holus-bolus into the smouldering hot coals of the campfire. All of the girls except me loved eating them.

In a scene reminiscent of *Lord of the Flies,* one of the girls pulled a charcoal-roasted possum out of the embers. It looked like a big dead rat, except its gizzards had been partly removed and the cavity stuffed with grass. All eyes fell upon me as Theresa handed the possum over to me to take the first bite. This was the moment of truth. The silence was interrupted only by the crackle of wood on the campfire coals. All eyes maintained their focus on me. I knew my misery would continue if I baulked. After all, this was what 'real' blackfellas ate.

I wanted to throw up. This was no task for the faint-hearted. Pretending it was nothing more than a roast chicken and taking a deep breath, I bit into the possum, slowly looking around at each of the girls with a challenging smirk while I chewed and swallowed every mouthful. Succulent? It was not. I could see the nods of approval, especially from Olive and Irene, whose loyal friendship has endured throughout the years. I wanted to be victorious for their sakes as much as my own. After all, nobody wanted to befriend a loser.

Campfire antics like this initially started as a prank but morphed into an informal teenage tribal council whose agenda was to exert tribal peer pressure for the sole purpose of confirming my Aboriginality and worthiness to be a member of their group. It seems ludicrous when I look back on it, but in a way, it is essentially no different from today's stringent Confirmation of Aboriginality criteria used by government agencies and some community organisations to determine an applicant's eligibility for services and programs earmarked for Aboriginal people and Torres Strait Islanders.

It is impossible to fully convey the pain of my initial non-acceptance on Palm. It was like solitary confinement without the walls. I felt as if I were a ghost walking among the living, desperate to be seen, heard and acknowledged. At times, I inspected my skin, pinching it, rubbing it. I looked at myself in the mirror, wondering if I truly was white as the other girls claimed. Or was it just that they were so black? Fleeting memories of Mrs Barnard's rejection of me because I was 'coloured' only added to my confusion. On occasion, overcome by despair and loneliness, I prayed to be a bit blacker just so the other girls would accept me. I just wanted to fit in and belong.

Assimilation? Identity? Where did we belong? We were sent to Palm Island by ignorant government officials who determined, in our best interests, that we would be more settled among persons of our 'own colour and kind', only to be told by people of our 'own colour and kind' that we belonged back on the mainland with people of 'our own colour and kind'. Often we were shunned in the most impolite terms.

While the ostracisation continued until I left Palm Island, it became less pronounced over time, and the bullying did not affect me so much once I found my own group friends and developed a bit more resilience. People who were central to my life on Palm Island ultimately became lifelong friends. I also came to appreciate and understand their personal circumstances. Irene's mother, 'Kippy' Simpson, was a monitress in the Boys' Dormitory where her stepfather, 'Mackie' Simpson, was also stationed as a Native Policeman. Theresa Anderson was born on Palm Island. Her family had lived on the island for several generations before I arrived. Olive was also raised on Palm Island. Marie Saylor was removed to Palm as a child with her mother and siblings from a pastoral station in northwest Queensland.

Being friends helped us all to cope with the strict rules that applied inside the dormitory. We entertained ourselves with music, either listening to the radio or playing records on a sound system donated by Australian singer and entertainer Shirley Abicair during her visit to Palm in 1960. It meant the world to us to be able to listen to music, dance, laugh and chatter, as teenage girls tend to do. Cliff Richard was my favourite at the time. Often we would be happy just to sit with the older girls as they sang and played guitars. Gospel songs, Connie Francis, the Everly Brothers and Elvis Presley were popular.

—

Whenever tourist boats arrived on Palm Island, we girls were obliged to engage in ceremonial dancing and singing performances. Sometimes the island would be inundated, with hundreds of visitors each week, a motley mix of international tourists and mainland Australians who always made a beeline for the blackest children to star in their photos. Light-skinned children like myself were overlooked, relegated to the side, as the tourists traipsed about in eager pursuit of an 'authentic'

Aborigine. Unfortunately, like many of today's fair-skinned Aboriginal children, we were not considered 'the real deal' and failed to make the cut.

Being both self-conscious and camera-shy, I was grateful to escape the camera lens. Irene reckons she did not get a look in either. She wore glasses and visitors did not regard spectacles as traditional attire. The tourists used to throw lollies and coins to us as if they were hand-feeding chooks, but it was fun scrambling to grab our share of this booty.

Perhaps due to the cultural restrictions imposed by the *Aboriginal Regulations (1945)*, Palm Island assumed something of a manufactured 'tropical island' identity. Lyrics for well-known Torres Strait Islander songs such as 'Old TI' (Thursday Island) were changed to 'Old PI' (Palm Island). Melodic Torres Strait Islander 'sailing songs' also became a big part of Palm's musical fabric. It didn't take long for 'When the *Saraband* Sails Away' to become 'When the *Irex* Sails Away'. The *Irex* was a Palm Island launch, while the *Saraband* was a Thursday Island-based ketch-rigged pearling boat (with thanks to Professor Karl Neuenfeldt and Henry 'Seaman' Dan).

Other Torres Strait Islander language songs like 'The Black Swana' were also taught at school. Us kids were all required to learn and perform Torres Strait Islander dancing, while hula dancing became a popular pastime among some of the women.

Somehow one of the Palm's renowned dance instructors, Roy Wilson, heard that Granddad Victor had danced before King George VI in 1941. He encouraged my participation in his dancing sessions and must have been bitterly disappointed when he discovered that a talent for dancing was not hereditary in my family. I moved with all the clumsy grace of a hatchling chicken, performing traditional Torres Strait Islander dances like 'Tamini' as if I had two left feet.

How I wished I could dance and do the hula as assuredly as Bethel Conway, Oriel Wilson and Moira 'Golly' Sibley. Bethel was the Island's standout with her stunning, artistic performances. On one memorable occasion, she emerged from a massive artificial clamshell to ecstatic applause.

—

Built in the 1940s, the Boys' Dormitory was, like the Girls' Dormitory, a basic wooden structure with thin galvanised-iron sheeting on the roof, but it had only canvas flaps for windows. The weathered, splintered wooden floors were riddled with gaping cracks and holes, and the building was in such a dilapidated state that the shift from these Dickensian-like conditions to the newer 40-bed Boys' Dormitory, completed in 1962 was, in Michael's words, like moving into a five-star hotel.

Michael and Terry both experienced rough times in the Boys' Dormitory. Terry has told me how many of the young inmates were hauled out of their beds in the middle of the night and sodomised by some of the older boys. He's spoken too of when he first arrived at Palm and would hear the young boys crying and fighting back, only to be overwhelmed by the stronger, bigger boys. He'd lie in bed traumatised, wondering when he would suffer the same fate. His brutalisation started within a month of his transfer from the State Children's Home in Townsville in January 1959. Upon resisting, he was beaten, received a black eye and was then set upon and sodomised. This treatment continued. At that time, he was twelve years old. Some picnic that turned out to be!

The cycle of abuse and violence continued over many years. As they grew older, some of the younger victims later became perpetrators themselves. Unfortunately, the shame and denial associated with these incidents have prohibited full disclosure of the extent and duration of this sexual abuse in the Boys' Dormitory and, as a consequence, the number of victims will probably never be known.

—

Dormitory children of both sexes were also 'loaned out' as a form of labour to support other Aboriginal residents in the camp and assist with household chores. Michael was plucked out of the Boys' Dormitory at the age of fourteen and billeted to Malcolm and Marcia Ross. Marcia, a small, frail woman, needed help looking after her three children, as well as general support around the house. Michael chopped the firewood and became a male *au pair* while still attending school. Although the arrangement started smoothly, Michael rebelled after Malcolm, under the influence of home-brew, repeatedly referred to him as his 'little white houseboy'. Although there was no physical punishment or beatings, Michael felt belittled, and his already fragile self-esteem and efforts to gain group acceptance were crushed even further.

Upon returning to the Boys' Dormitory, Michael experienced further harassment, including being flogged by the monitors and detained in a cell for no reason other than his fair skin:

> *Everybody got flogged. See the nature of the place was that if anybody done anything wrong, everybody was flogged … So that that was part and parcel of being in a boys' home. Now this term 'physically abused' you know, never heard of the word back then … that was our life to be flogged every day or every second day … we were physically abused on a regular basis … but other fellows were singled out for special punishment …*

> *I met up with a few of my cronies or my peers from that Boys' Home and they bray … and boast, 'Oh Palm Island never broke me, the Palm Island Boys' Home never broke me.' You hear a lot of fellows saying that. But when you look at their life and how they spent it and they're in and out of gaol, they're broken men all right but they just don't see it.*[73]

Michael recalls seeing boys whacked across the face and flogged full force with a skipping rope several days a week. In fact, Terry, then fourteen, was hospitalised following a brutal bashing by my friend Irene's stepfather, Mackie Simpson. He was beaten within an inch of his life because Mackie resented Terry developing a teenage crush on Irene. Because of the seriousness of the beating, Mrs Bartlam organised for me to visit Terry in hospital, albeit accompanied by a police escort. Terry was busted up, bandaged and bruised beyond recognition. No action whatsoever was taken against Mackie, and, if anything, the impunity set the standard for his continued violent abuse of other boys in his charge, as well as members of his immediate family.

The prevailing 'turn a blind eye', shirk responsibility attitude enabled such violence to continue. Indeed, Martin Luther King's words ring true amid today's inquiries into institutional abuse:

> *When the evil deeds of men stand trial, the silence of good men stands equally condemned. For they knew, yet did nothing.' Despite this incident and others like it, Terry thrived on Palm Island much more than either Michael or I did. Being much darker, he was readily accepted, particularly by the Torres Strait Islanders.*

In 1962, Terry was indentured by the Department of Native Affairs as part of a six-man canecutting crew to work in the sugarcane fields at

Moresby and Feluga outside Innisfail on the mainland. Only fifteen years old at the time, he was the youngest member in the gang. Along with fellow Palm Islanders Tommy Geia, Harry Johnson, Wilgie Thimbley and Alec Morgan, he worked long hours from sun up until sun down, cutting cane for Italo-Australian farmers Tony Stella and Leo Torrisi.

I remained on Palm Island with Michael.

18

A HELPING HAND

Queenie Burton was the cook at the Girls' Dormitory and I became her offsider. Her interest and support of me was similar to that shown by Mrs Anderson, the laundress at the Home in Townsville. I enjoyed helping out in the kitchen and in particular liked lending a hand to Queenie, who was not too sprightly when it came to clearing up and cleaning the cooking utensils. Most girls did not relish the prospect of my being Queenie's long-term cooking offsider. I couldn't understand what their griping was about, much less understand why they didn't want me anywhere near the kitchen.

Queenie was always kind to me, no doubt partly due to my befriending her daughter, Erica, who also lived in the Girls' Dormitory. I often helped Erica with homework in exchange for her letting me watch while she applied her lipstick. It reminded me of the times I watched Mum. I was also a friend of Robert and Willie, Queenie's sons. Willie lived in the Boys' Dormitory with Terry and Michael. Robert lived in the camp area. Erica, Robert and Willie were several years older than me but Queenie simply doted on her family. In her own quiet way, she used to care for me too.

I loved cooking, and Queenie delegated to me a fair portion of it. I sometimes thought of the kitchen advice once given to Mum by Mrs Hickey at the Glasgow Boarding House in Cairns. She believed there are only two sorts of cooking tragedies: the first occurs when one who cannot cook insists upon cooking; and the second when one who can cook refuses to. The cooking ingredients we used were often 'exotic'. I discovered that fish eyes were more flavoursome and much fresher than some of the rancid meat delivered from the island butcher. I irritated several dormitory girls when I delighted in sucking the jelly from the fish eyes, chewing it, then spitting the white eyeballs onto the ground. Palm Island is where I also learned to eat offal, including brains, tripe, sweetbread, kidneys, heart, livers and ox tongue.

Queenie possessed culinary *savoir-faire*. She was an imaginative cook and tested new recipes on me. I loved the way she pickled the ox tongue, cooked tripe in white sauce and prepared brains fried in fresh breadcrumbs. Mum would have been proud of my 'having-a-go' attitude, although she'd always dissuaded me from eating offal by referring to the cuts as 'awful offal'. Admittedly, de-veining the brains and livers was the most repulsive of cooking chores, but the delicious lamb's fry and bacon meal made all the odious preparation well worthwhile. Other staple foods included bully beef (tinned corned beef) with cabbage stew and chicken with an abundance of rice. We even had crispy grilled lamb cutlets with mashed potato from time to time. It's hard to believe that in the 1960s lamb cutlets were considered a pauper's meal whereas now they're considered gourmet fare, with prices well out of reach of struggling families.

Dessert comprised apples, often in rare supply, and mangos dipped in soy sauce. Spongy, tangy bush lemons dipped in a cereal bowl full of white sugar and salt were another sweet'n'sour treat, as well as Burdekin plums. Other fresh fruit was scarce. We had a good supply of tapioca and sago if the weevils left anything behind for us. Poor man's cakes or fried scones, just like the ones Mum used to make, were a popular and frequent treat.

Marie Saylor remembers that a certain level of etiquette was expected during meal times:

We were only allowed to speak three times at the dining table. 'Pass the salt please'. 'Pass the pepper please'. 'Pass the sugar please'. One day Ethel Daley was sitting next to me. She didn't hear me. I whispered a little louder in our local language for her to give me the salt. Matron Christie heard and she said she ordered for the monitor, Bulla Cootes, to pull me out.

Bulla Cootes pulled me out from my chair. When he used to flog us, Matron used to tell him to strip us naked. He hit us with a pure leather cattle whip. I would have been about nine years old. He would keep going till he made big welts in our backs. I don't think Pattie would have been there at the time because we were a little bit older when she came. And then I put my dress back on me, my uniform that was a white blouse and navy blue pinafore. I could hardly walk. I wasn't allowed to go to the hospital. The blood stuck to the blouse and the kids used to carry me and piggyback me. They would take me around. They flogged Betty Sailor too.

Even the young teenagers when they got their menstrual period used to get flogged with all that muck running down from their legs. It was very embarrassing. We would stand up and had to hold ourselves there. They had no consideration that we were human beings who were created by the same God as them. Because we were black women I think. They used to tell us we were stupid.

We were all skinny because we were starving in the dormitory. If we didn't eat our weevilly porridge (there were more weevils than the porridge itself), well we didn't get a half a slice of mildew bread. There were no proper cups in them days. Then the jam tin was used for drinking tea. We would get a small bit of tea. They had one big teapot that had to do the 95 girls. It didn't. So when it ran out instead of putting more tea leaves in it. They just put more hot water in it and we were just drinking more of the water.

An Aboriginal monitor was in charge. He would whack us for any other thing. Then when another couple came they would do the same. Another female supervisor was cruel. She used to put our hands flat on the table. She had a big cane and she used to hit us. She came down hard six times. She was not the only Aboriginal manager who did that to us. We couldn't do anything. We had no help. We just had to suffer the consequences. It's left us with a lot of bitter memories.[74]

Irene has her own memories of Palm Island's epicurean delights:

Overall the food we were given was mostly good but not enough of it. We ate bush tucker in between meals like bush lemons (skin and all), green Burdekin plums (they never had a chance to ripen), custard apple, soursop, mangoes (green & ripe) etc. One food we disliked in the dormitory was cooked rolled oats full of weevils or grubs. Another food cooked was flyblown mince. Some girls separated the grubs or weevils from the oats, others were turned off, while one or two girls ate the grubs and all.

We didn't know at the time about flyblown meat but we always wondered why the meat stunk. Some of us found out later when we were big enough to help in the kitchen that if meat weren't covered properly, the flies would get into the meat and lay their eggs. It was their cooked eggs we were trying to eat – no wonder. Whether we ate or not would depend on who was a monitress at the time and how strict she was. Whether she'd be easy on us or demand loudly that if we didn't eat our breakfast we would get 'this' as she banged the table with a switch (leather strap).[75]

Fresh milk was provided each morning courtesy of the island's own dairy cows. We also had small bottles of milk shipped from Townsville, provided daily at school. Bread, if one could call it that – there was no yeast in the bread-making mix – came fresh from the island's bakery each day: Mr Ernest 'Wanga' Puttaburra was the local baker. The weevils in the flour gave the bread the appearance of raisin toast.

Cutlery and china dinnerware were in scarce supply so we ate off chipped and stained enamel plates. There were barely any knives and forks. A few pannikin-style metal cups were made at the local workshops from Sunshine powdered-milk tins. When official visitors came to the island, the best linen and finest crockery would be rolled out, only to be promptly packed away in secure storage no sooner had the guests left the building. Appearances, it seemed, were everything.

—

If I was not cooking at the dormitory, I'd be looking after, attending to, showering, dressing, grooming and feeding the smaller girls whose care I was charged with. There were three: Alice 'Bunter' Meeks, Cecilina Mow and Carol Doomadgee. Looking after them was a minor guardianship position, which I inherited upon being considered responsible enough to take care of my own needs.

My friend, Olive Bonner, remembers a tragic incident involving another of the young Palm Island girls:

It was a Sunday. Everyone finished cleaning. It must have been around 8am. We never had much to do on Sundays. Pattie and Marie Pryor were somewhere, near the stairs in the kitchen. They looked around and saw a little girl on fire. She must have gotten too close to the flames downstairs in the laundry where the copper boiler was lit. People sometimes sat beside the flames to warm up. The young girl must have stepped too close to the fire. Dear little thing. I think she was about eight or nine years old. Pattie and Marie grabbed a blanket and rolled her on the floor to stop the flames. It was sad. She was wearing a light nylon dress that must have stuck to her after she got burned. I could hear the screaming. I am glad Marie and Pat were there. They flew her to Townsville Hospital. She died eventually. Pattie and Marie were real upset. It would have been very upsetting.[76]

Henrietta Doomadgee was her name. She was Carol's younger sister, and the daughter of Arthur and Doris Doomadgee (née Diamond). Although Marie may have come along soon after, from memory I was the first person on the scene, and tragically Henrietta succumbed to her injuries nearly two days after the incident; she died on 5 August 1965 after receiving 40 per cent burns to her body. Nobody knew Henrietta was downstairs at the time. Only six years old, she'd been playing in a little princess dress and clutching a long thin stick that presumably she was using as a magic wand. I can only assume Henrietta prodded the embers, causing a spark to fly out from under the copper boiler, setting her highly flammable nylon garment alight. I grabbed a heavy blanket from the laundry and did my best to smother the flames as we rolled her on the ground.

Henrietta and Carol Doomadgee were elder sisters to Cameron 'Mulrunji' Doomadgee, whose high-profile death in police custody on Palm Island in 2004 and the associated chain of events came to national attention. My family were stunned when I told them about

Henrietta's terrible accident; I have never said much about it, preferring to block it out. But I went into a state of shock that day, as did the others who arrived on the scene soon after. I was only sixteen at the time; Henrietta died two weeks before my seventeenth birthday.

In her award-winning book *The Tall Man* (2008), Chloe Hooper provided a different version of Henrietta's accident, claiming that Henrietta was making a cubby house outside when a 'white man', not realising she was there, poured petrol near some long grass and set it alight.[77] I was there that day, and respectfully challenge Chloe Hooper's version of events. There was certainly no 'white man' associated with that tragic accident.

—

I started to earn some pocket money when Mrs Davidson, Superintendent Bartlam's personal assistant, offered me the chance to clean her family's home on Saturday mornings; Mr Davidson was the Social Welfare Association Hall Manager. I used this money to buy Michael lollies or other treats from the local store or the canteen that operated whenever the pictures were screened in the Social Welfare Hall; Olive and I did casual work in the canteen and often bought lollies from there. Neither of us received any special privileges for doing this work. We were escorted to and from work by the Native Police and still subject to dormitory rules.

Barry and Dawn Davidson and their children, Peter and Jenny, were friendly folk. The family were kind to me while I cleaned their house. Mrs Davidson reminded me of Mrs Harding, my former neighbour in Hartley Street, Cairns. Like Mrs Harding, Mrs Davidson cooked a lot and would bake cookies for my morning tea break. At the time, I did not understand the servant–mistress protocol that prevented me from eating inside with the Davidson family: she placed the cookies on the back stairs with a glass of milk or cordial so I could eat outside.

In response to Mrs Davidson's unexpected kindnesses, I worked as hard as I could to maintain a high standard of cleanliness in the household. I also realised what a trustworthy position I had been given, as Mr and Mrs Davidson often left me alone in their house, disappearing for several hours while I did the cleaning. Unfortunately, it was on some of those occasions that I started stealing from them. Not stealing in the criminal sense, but rather stealing time to browse through books of interest in the family library. There was no library on Palm Island, or even at the school, let alone in the dormitory, and I was very keen to read some of their books.

Judging by the book titles in the Davidson library, I assumed Mr Davidson was into astronomy, yachting and building gadgetry, while Mrs Davidson's interests were cookery, suspense and drama as well as the *Reader's Digest*. I settled for Charles Dickens' *A Tale of Two Cities* and *Great Expectations* and Herman Melville's *Moby Dick*. To this day, I liken a book to having a friend. The fact that you can put one down and pick it up again at your leisure with no complaint is an added attraction.

Meanwhile I immersed myself in reading. Books! An invitation into a brighter domain of escaping, exploring, discovering, imagining and fantasising. I ploughed through the pages of written words, gaining new vistas of knowledge, wisdom and enjoyment. I could hide away in a book and be transported to other worlds without taking my feet off the ground, paying for a fare or asking permission. I became so engrossed in books that Theresa began to call me 'the professor'.

Irene recalls our shared love of reading:

> *Janke loved to read and write letters and Matron Bartlam would order extra magazines for 'us' to read. Teachers knowing her love for books would give her romance book from their private collections. These things probably helped her to survive. I received a book from Janke once called* Doctor Paradise *and I was caught reading it after lunch at school. Sister Cortelle disposed of the book and gave me six cuts.*[78]

As birthdays or special events were rarely celebrated on Palm, I often used the pocket money I earned to buy presents for my friends, including pens, writing pads, small pendants, Lily of the Valley talcum powder, handkerchiefs and small sample-sized bottles of Imprevu perfume. Irene says she has fond memories of my small thoughtful gifts and neat wrapping of them.

My path to belonging often felt akin to walking the razor-thin tightrope that connected the black and white realms on the island. I could never be too complacent for fear of falling out of favour with either group, and remaining neutral to preserve your own hide is never easy. Some of the white residents, including Father Cassian, Mrs Bartlam and my teachers, Mrs Beryl Hogbin and Miss Elaine Alexander, took pity on me. They took me under their wings, nurturing and guiding me, not realising that often made matters worse. I was perceived among some of the dorm girls and my classmates as a snob, a 'white man's crawler'. But having a foot in both camps sometimes had its advantages. Much in the way Mum exacted her wit and talents to drink in segregated bars, I too was able to enter areas designated 'whites only'.

Theresa Illin (née Anderson) remembers:

> *When Pattie first arrived we all said she looks like a* migloo. *But she was a breath of fresh air. We were* myall *(pejorative word for unsophisticated*

> *or a fool) and she was totally different. She was always happy and very caring for someone who got stuck over there with us. We pushed her up for everything. Pattie was a gang leader and a real ratbag. We were frightened to step out of line but she used to steal fruit from the stores. We used to say 'Janke steal fruit for us'. We used to all wear Bombay Bloomers made out of material with elastic in the legs and in the waist. We were so hungry to eat that fruit we never asked how she got it or what she had underneath. We didn't care. But she wore two sets of pants. Then we were more worried how she came to have two sets of pants. 'Where did you get the second pants?' We were flat out having one pair of pants. She was very caring and that was her attitude toward anyone. She would do anything for everyone. She had a real* migloo *style.*[79]

The Palm Island Administration allowed dormitory girls to partake in sponsored outings where, upon invitation from a reputable family and subject to Matron Bartlam's approval, we would be allowed to spend an unfettered day in the camp area. I was fortunate enough to have experienced several such opportunities. As much as Mum was not around, other people unknowingly carried her baton and, in their own way, assumed a quasi-parenting role. I was very fortunate to have had the intervention of these individuals who influenced my life for the better.

My regular sponsors were long-term residents. Auntie Ivy Sam (née Clay) and Uncle Assan Sam, a Torres Strait Islander, and Auntie Iris Clay (née Mapoon) and Uncle Fred Clay provided immeasurable comfort and support during my times of alienation and isolation in the dormitory. I met the Clays and the Sams through Terry's established networks. Auntie Iris and Auntie Ivy were sisters-in-law. Auntie Ivy would always send fried scones, rice and bully beef to supplement our at times indigestible dormitory diet. Auntie Mona Wyles, a resident of the Women's Dormitory when she was not working on cattle properties around Julia Creek, and Nonda and Maxwelton in northwest Queensland also played a key role in my life.

Irene remembers my association with Auntie Mona:

> *We did discover that Janke's mother was black but she got on the defensive if we asked her too many questions about her mother. We wondered why she formed such a close bond with Mona Wyles. It was because Aunty Mona looked like Janke's mother. If we said: 'How come your mother is that dark and you're so white?' Janke would want to knock our blocks off. She was always loyal and protective of her mother, just like she was with her younger brother Michael.*[80]

Every so often I would rail against the absence of God's mercy. Why had God abandoned me when, in the Scriptures, he gave a promise that in troubling times he would not leave people without comfort and support. Considering my circumstances, this promise seemed futile. I shared my disillusionment with Father Cassian, and he did his best to reassure me.

'Sometimes God can send you an intervention to help in your life. It can come in the form of a person, a movie, a song or even a book,' he told me. 'But you must also be prepared to recognise and choose what is good for you.'

19

THE GODSEND

Palm Island's resident Franciscan friar, Father Cassian (Mervyn) Double (1925–2009), was unorthodox in every way. Throughout his life, he ran marathons, rode a motorcycle as his preferred mode of transport, and was more comfortable in safari suits than his brown religious tunic. Father Cassian had a full set of hair and did not wear a tonsure, the round, bald patch on the head often associated with friars. Unlike the characters Meggie Cleary and Father Ralph in Colleen McCullough's novel *The Thornbirds,* there was nothing inappropriate about the nature of my relationship with him. Father Ralph was fictitious but Father Cassian was real, even if they exuded some similar qualities. Father Cassian had a square jaw, a solid build and dark features offset by his smiling eyes, a generous heart and an abundance of kindness and compassion.

I'd been introduced to Bible stories and books with biblical themes when I met Father Cassian the year he arrived on Palm Island in 1962. I was fourteen, and church and Sunday School attendance were compulsory. I attended the AIM services delivered by the pastors Mr Tresize, Mr Hallett and Miss Stephenson, but met Father Cassian through his pastoral work on the island. Irene, who was Catholic, asked me to accompany her on a visit to the presbytery one Sunday. I went with her, and occasionally after that Father Cassian would lend me some of his books.

During my adolescence, Father Cassian helped me with all the sorts of things a mother usually would. He bought me my first bra, taught me how to shave my legs and under my armpits, and educated me about all matters female. I thought I was dying of an internal haemorrhage when my first menstrual period occurred, but Father Cassian took me into his confidence and told me it was a normal female bodily function. I'd been naïve about any hormonal and bodily changes prior to this. Before I met Father Cassian, I remember feeling perplexed in the dorm one evening when a monitress called all the girls together for an urgent meeting 30 minutes before the weekly senior dance. The senior girls were all tarted up as they shuffled forward. Us juniors splayed to the side. The monitress stood at the front of the room and held up a filthy sanitary napkin skewered on a stick. She began to sweep the evidence around in a semi-circle.

'Nobody is going anywhere until the person who owns this and did not dispose of it properly owns up to it,' she declared, still exhibiting the offensive item in question.

The outraged seniors broke into small groups, determined to identify the culprit who had jammed the soiled napkin down the toilet. None of the girls confessed and we were all punished. I was mystified about why the item on the end of the stick had caused such a commotion. It seemed to possess a powerful magic, given the way it intruded on our social privileges.

Sanitary napkins were controlled through the inventory and were as good as rationed. A signature was required and sometimes girls' motives were questioned as to why they required so many. Upon reflection, the rationing was perhaps a strategy to identify whether a girl was pregnant.

Father Cassian advised about sex too, although not in so many words. He told me to sleep with my hands across my chest to prevent any fidgeting. He gave me the pep talk about relationships after I told him that one of the boys had expressed interest in me being his girlfriend. Much to Terry and Michael's chagrin, I had a brief association with a keen fisherman who had a boat, which he named *Miss Pat* in my honour. Although neither of my brothers will confess to it, someone decided to graffiti the *Miss Pat*, crudely renaming it the *Piss Pot*.

'Sex and love are not like a shoe shop,' Father told me when he got wind of this suitor. 'You don't try and buy,' he added, handing me four books about chastity and the sacrosanctity of sex.

Father Cassian was like a guiding force during those dark times. He became father, friend, confidante and teacher merged into one. I truly believed, and still do, that a Divine Intervention enabled his arrival in my life. He helped build my strength so I could endure the pain and anxiety of being separated from Mum. I was eager for his companionship. I listened attentively to his weekly sermons and homilies, and endeavoured to be in his presence on social occasions. He often reminded me that I would not be on Palm Island forever, encouraging me to make the most of my education and treat life's lessons as opportunities.

Father Cassian also spoilt me with an array of special treats. He prepared homemade ice-cream and even brought special strawberry milkshakes for me on the four-hour ferry ride from Townsville; he poured them into a thermos flask to keep them freshly chilled. For all his generosity, Father Cassian had a stubborn streak. Relying on God to provide, Father Cassian stuck by his vows of poverty, living a frugal existence and not buying any clothes or worldly goods for himself. He was bequeathed reading glasses and shoes by people whom he supported through pastoral care.[81]

Irene has her own memories of Father Cassian:

> *Fr. Cassian had a way of making certain girls feel special. Just one or two girls at a time would receive a writing case every year. Maybe it was Christmas? I know Fay Thimble, Janke, Teresa Stanley and I received one. He also liked Florence Conway. Before three of us went to boarding school, he offered to pay for my Art and Tennis classes. Mr Bartlam only let him pay the Tennis. He used to buy Teresa lipstick.*
>
> *Janke became so close to him, she used to openly shave her legs in front of him and use his aftershave. He also bought her personal things that only a father would buy for a daughter. 'Cassian', as he encouraged us to call him, used to write to us on a weekly basis when we were away. He'd even send money.*
>
> *Cassian used to tell Janke over and over again:*
>
> *You shouldn't be here on the island living with Aboriginals, you don't belong here. You should be living on the mainland.*
>
> *Janke would repeatedly relay this to me.*[82]

The nature of my relationship with Father Cassian was misunderstood in some sectors of the small Palm Island community. Terry and Michael rebelled against taunts from others that Father Cassian was my boyfriend. Wanting to be spared the shame, they asked me to disassociate myself from Father Cassian. I refused. And a young man I briefly dated expressed frustration with Father Cassian's advice.

'What's the matter with you? Are you frigid? Why are you listening to Father Cassian's relationship advice? Perhaps he wants to have you for himself.'

Father Cassian hosted many people from assorted backgrounds who travelled from the mainland just to visit him.

'I want you to meet someone special!' was his catchcry whenever he wanted me to meet certain visitors.

One time I met an international journalist who had just returned from being a war correspondent in Vietnam. She regaled us with stories of interviewing celebrities, including one with Sean Connery while he was in a bathtub. She was very impressive and inspirational, so much so that for a while I entertained the prospect of being a journalist.

Another time Father invited me to the presbytery to meet someone else who was special. Upon arrival, he gave me a cupcake and a glass of orange cordial. He was assembling a long, tubular contraption out of bamboo and crepe paper. I pestered him, curious about who the special person was and when they would arrive. He told me to be patient. At last he turned to me, after adding the final touches to his creation.

'Pat, would you crawl through this caterpillar?' he asked.

I crawled through the tube-like structure. At the end was an oval-shaped, full-length mirror. I had to reverse to get back out.

'How was it? Anything special you encountered in there?' he asked

'The only thing I saw was my reflection in the mirror?' I told him.

'Well, don't you think that was special?'

'Not really.'

'God thinks you're special,' he said. 'I think you are special. I wanted you to think you were special. The special person you met today was you.'

It was an enduring lesson, and many times since I have reflected upon what I learnt that day and shared it with others who have struggled with their sense of self-worth and identity.

Father Cassian provided most of my religious education. It took me a long time to come to grips with the passage in Luke 18:16 that said 'Suffer little children to come unto me, and forbid them not, for of such is the kingdom of God.'

'What kind of compassionate God thinks it's okay for innocent children to suffer?' I asked Father Cassian.

He explained that the term suffer, in Old English, means to allow or to permit, so in this instance Jesus was asking the children to come to him.

—

Palm Island buzzed with superstition and talk of black magic or *puripuri*. There were tales of the *Kadaicha* man, magic men and witchdoctors, little hairy men and tall, lithe spirits with beady eyes, much like the *quinkans* made famous by Queensland Aboriginal author, Dick Roughsey. All the dormitory inmates believed the old magic men had special powers to make young girls fall in love with them through a ritual called 'singing' or 'mussing', which acted like a love potion. The only thing the magic men needed to cast a spell was a lock of their victim's hair, a photo or other personal memento. We learned to routinely sweep up and burn our own hair after the monitresses shaved us, and we watched our personal belongings like hawks. The fear was very real for us at the time, as Marie Saylor remembers:

> *The puripuri men get dead people's bodies and scrape the fat off it. Then they put it in a milk tin and bury it. When they want to kill someone with*

> *puripuri, they'd strip themselves naked, paint themselves with traditional male marks and patterns and rub themselves with that stinking fat. You can smell it before you see it. It's all the work of the devil and the devil puts it in their mind to kill people. If those magic men can't catch you by puripuri then they murder you leaving no trace of who has done it.*[83]

Irene also recalls all the talk on the island about magic:

> *As children we were aware of 'quinkan' spirits. The locals use to call them 'guingans'. Nola Archie used to have a 'dibble dibble' stone – a black, smooth, shiny stone. She used to keep it wrapped in a hanky and treated it as if it could give you good luck or bad. We were afraid of it. There was also a story that went with a rock shaped in the form of a boat. The rock boat is on Doctors' Point.*[84]

Father Cassian gave me a crucifix and a picture of Jesus surrounded by children to place under my pillow for spiritual protection. He said it was a powerful amulet to protect me from any imaginary dark forces, a far better alternative to the circle of salt I'd placed around my bed to keep the evil spirits away. A crucifix certainly seemed much safer than the knives and other sharp objects like forks and scissors that some girls kept under their pillows as they slept.

20

SCHOOL DAYS

The schoolmaster, Fred Krause (1902–1973), was also a leader in the Aboriginal Inland Ministry (AIM) Church, which fiercely competed against the Catholic Church in a battle for parishioners and their finances. Mr Krause resented me wearing a crucifix. He named me on parade and called me to his office. Being a man of small stature, he worked out that climbing onto a small raised platform was more effective when it came to delivering his cuts with maximum force. He ordered me to stick out my hand and jumped down, applying his full fury with each blow of the cane. He repeated this action twice more. Mr Krause also gave me the cuts if I did not show up at the AIM Sunday school. In order to lessen the sting, Father Cassian told me to wear California Poppy or Brylcreem in my hair. He told me to rub my hands through my hair before extending my hand for Mr Krause's cuts. The cane would slide off on contact with my oily palm.

Michael also incurred Mr Krause's wrath following a conversation in which Michael told his classmate not to kowtow to teachers just because they were white:

> *I remember Mr Krause's hot, stinking breath on my face as he screamed at me 'How dare I say such a thing being white yourself?' Mr Krause regarded us as white children. When we arrived on Palm Island we spoke good English but then our speech changed and we started sounding like all the other blackfellas. He knocked me to the ground that day and ordered me not to talk or sound like 'them'. The thought of us as white children developing habits and becoming just like the Aboriginal people turned him into an instant maniac.*[85]

Every school day started with a mandatory parade, the raising of the flag and assembly, during which we all sang 'God Save the Queen'. Mr Krause addressed the students through his office window atop a two-storey building, after which we all marched off into class like military cadets. Our school uniform was a plain blue pinafore and a set of unsightly navy blue Bombay bloomers (long knee-length undergarments).

Children in Grades 1 and 2 participated in the school-feeding program, receiving midday meals at the Home Training Centre. Education was provided from Grades 1 to 7. A Grade 8 class was offered in 1965. A scholarship system applied for students who passed the State scholarship examinations, with further education being provided on the mainland in Townsville or Charters Towers. Upon completing their primary education, young Aboriginal girls were enrolled in a compulsory one-year home-training and domestic science class, where lessons included housekeeping, cooking, cleaning and sewing.

Boys were enrolled in manual arts classes and required to do courses in the joinery shop in their final two years of school. A rare apprenticeship opportunity on the mainland was highly coveted. Some boys were sent to work with Queensland Rail as porters while others were sent to cattle stations around the state.

The Queensland Education Department assumed responsibility for the two schools on the island from 1 July 1962. At that time, there was some disparity in conditions between the segregated schools. In 1962, there were 274 students enrolled in Grades 1 to 7 at the rudimentary and cramped Palm Island State School, with pupil numbers expanding to nearly 300 by 1965. The number of male and female students was almost equal.[86] The 'White School' – or Provisional School, as it was known – had no more than fifteen students at any one time throughout the 1960s. The school appeared to desegregate in 1967 with the enrolment of the Fourmile and Condren children, whose Aboriginal parents were employed in the Palm Island Administration. But attendance dropped to just eight students by 1970, presumably after the withdrawal of families and in response to the gradual decline of State Government management of the island.[87]

In later years, the learning and curriculum modules at the Provisional School included projector shows and filmstrips such as *Aborigines – A Different Way of Life* and *Aborigine – Dependence on the Environments.* You'd have thought that being on an island full of Aboriginal people might have lent itself to a few practical, first-hand learning opportunities.

I was drawn to one teacher, Miss Alexander (1906–1989), who reminded me of Miss Havisham in Charles Dickens' *Great Expectations*. She lived a partly reclusive lifestyle with only her beloved dog, Patch, for company. A mature woman in her late fifties, Miss Alexander was a dedicated teacher and visionary in pursuit of educational excellence for her students. She plied me with home-baked orange cakes, my love for which continues. Miss Alexander was also an outcast because of her choice to remain single. In the 1950s and 1960s, a single woman was something of a pariah. I remember thinking it grossly unfair that unmarried women were slighted with the term 'spinster', while the word 'bachelor', which applied to single men, carried far less of a social stigma.

Irene recalls our escapades while cleaning for Miss Alexander.

Patsy and I used to work as housekeepers for Miss Alexander for £2 per week. Janke was always picked to steam the vegetables. Miss Alexander instructed her how to use the stove, how to prepare the vegies and how long to cook them for. I used to think to myself Patsy must have been picked because she was considered 'white' and therefore had more brains then I did. I secretly disagreed with this attitude.

Patsy certainly did have more knowledge when it came to recognising a bottle of Barossa Pearl sparkling wine.

'White people drink this,' she'd say to me.

'True!' I said.

'Want to try some?' she asked.

'No, we might get into trouble,' I answered.

'Nah, no one here. We'll only take a little bit ah?' she said.

We shared some of the wine in a cup, just tasting it a sip at a time.

'We might get drunk,' we laughed.

When we finished our cup, Janke cunningly replaced the wine with water. This absolutely amazed me.

Patsy proceeded to have a stickybeak around the house and I followed her. In the bathroom she pulled out a packet of Meds.

'What's that?' I asked.

Patsy studied it while she pulled out a tampon and looked at it.

'This is what white people stick up their asses when they go swimming,' she said.

'What they do that for?' I asked.

'When they got their periods,' she replied.[88]

One day Irene and I walked into Miss Alexander's house to discover Patch dead on the porch with ants crawling over his ears and protruding tongue. I was not sure how to react or feel. I'd never seen a dead dog before. We ran inside and told Miss Alexander. She was utterly devastated, wailing and crying as if she had lost her only child. In a way, she had. That little animal was her baby, a substitute for family. My initial derision of her grief turned to concern; Miss Alexander's anguish made me understand how and why some people invest so much in their pets. Over time, I lost contact with Miss Alexander but my memories of her endure.

Mrs Beryl Hogbin (1928–2014) was my domestic science teacher at the Palm Island State School. I fondly remember both her educational and personal guidance, and the support she gave me throughout my formative years on Palm Island. Her influence sustained me on many occasions after the dormitory doors were padlocked each night. Mrs Hogbin recognised the difficulties Michael and I encountered on Palm, the way we were considered misfits, and has her own memories of us being bullied during an oral history interview for the National Library of Australia:

> *To look at them they were white children ... we felt they shouldn't have been there. The children didn't treat them very well. They had their class distinction. I mean, they had 'yellow bellies' and 'Murris' and they called each other some dreadful names amongst themselves. They used to call them 'whitefellas', 'white bellies' and all this sort of thing, roughed them up a bit and gave them a bit of a hard time and I felt sorry for them. That's the main thing and secretly I think just about everyone on the island felt sorry for them, all the white staff, but there was nothing they could do, they weren't the government.*[89]

Both Mrs Hogbin and Miss Alexander realised the best way to support me under these circumstances was to actively support my learning and academic development. Mrs Hogbin also sought my assistance in helping the younger students to read, using the *Happy Venture Playbooks* for children, featuring the characters Dick and Dora. I spent four afternoons a week after school helping a group of five younger girls to improve their literacy and numeracy. Among these students was Carol Doomadgee, the sister of Henrietta, who died after the fire incident at the dorm. I was twelve, maybe a little older, when Carol was in Grade 1 at Palm Island State School. After spending several afternoons with her, I noticed she was tongue-tied. I informed Matron Bartlam and Miss Alexander of Carol's speech difficulties and eventually she was taken away to the mainland for medical treatment.

Perhaps with Mrs Hogbin and Mrs Davidson's cultivation, after a while, a mutual friendship developed between their daughters, Sandra Hogbin and Jenny Davidson, and me. We played in netball, basketball and other sporting tournaments arranged on the island. Because of my competitive nature, I loved participating in any organised sporting activities. As a result of my association with some of the white teenagers in these teams, I came to realise that we were all restricted by circumstances. As far as I could see, many of the white families and staff on Palm, drawn to the island out of occupational and financial necessity, had also become misfits of a sort as a result of the segregated lifestyle, which limited their interactions with others.

Mr Greentree, the island's finance officer-cum-clerk, also empathised with my predicament. He and Mrs Greentree sought official approval to host me at their home. The Greentrees were elderly compared to others on the island; they kept to themselves and lived a frugal existence, which was reflected in their diet. Dinner was always the same: canned sardines mixed with onions, butter and Holbrook sauce on toast.

An Aboriginal teachers' aide at the school, Mrs Monica Willis (1930–2010), proudly proclaimed me to be her protégé. Like many other students, I really enjoyed her company; her sense of humour brought many fun-filled moments and certainly plenty of laughter. Monica assumed more of a supervisory, life-skills role in my life. She was very kind to me and, I believe, was another who sympathised with my situation. Although she too was powerless to change the circumstances surrounding my placement on Palm Island, her kindness and attention were welcome points of relief.

Matron Noela Bartlam (1918–1986) became my 'behind the scenes' confidante and mentor. She arranged for me to spend extra time at her house studying, reading and playing with her daughter, Allison. Matron also invited other dormitory girls over to her house under the pretext of study so I wouldn't be singled out as receiving any special treatment. Mrs Bartlam was very much a maternal figure – loving, warm and nurturing, if in a somewhat constrained way. Given our segregated lifestyle, I found it difficult to fully reciprocate her depth of feeling for me. In that regard, our relationship always remained conditional. But despite my insecurities and vulnerabilities, I loved her as much as I could love anybody at that time.

Mrs Bartlam also encouraged me to work hard at my studies, reaffirming that education was beneficial to my securing future employment on the mainland. Unlike most Palm Island residents and other dormitory girls, my visits to the Bartlam home also afforded me rare opportunities to see the more personal side of Mr Bartlam as a father and husband, not just his official superintendent persona. During one visit, I was confident enough to ask Matron why places like Palm Island existed for blacks only. She suggested it was a way of assimilating, preparing people to integrate into mainland lifestyle.

'Well, if we are supposed to be assimilating, why is it that white people and black people live in separate parts of the island?' I asked her.

At the time, life on Palm Island was like living in a bubble. We were ensconced in our own world, free of many perceived external negative influences. Because of our isolated existence, I remained unaware of the groundswell of support for the black civil rights movement in the United States during the 1950s and 1960s, and the ripple effect this had on Australia.

'Now, Patsy Janke, we will have to leave this conversation for another day,' Mrs Bartlam replied.

She could be quite firm in her manner when necessary. There were no 'if or buts' and no further discussion entered into. She had little hesitation cutting me off mid-sentence or directing me to leave. I can still hear her saying, 'Patsy Janke. No. Go away!' whenever I tried to alert her to Carol Doomadgee's speech and reading difficulties. For a while she thought I had concocted the story to evade taking afternoon lessons.

Mrs Bartlam and Mrs Hogbin were the architects of my academic advancement. They identified an opportunity for me to apply for a scholarship to continue my secondary education, and chose Blackheath College on the mainland in Charters Towers.

—

Education support schemes like Austudy or Abstudy did not exist at this time. You had to gain a scholarship in order to advance beyond Grade 8. It was a merit-based system, which enabled entry to boarding school, unlike the identified Indigenous positions that are common today. Initially, a hurdle was encountered. Mrs Hogbin fixed the problem after consultation with her peers. I was automatically promoted from Grade 6 to Grade 8, which enabled me to sit for the scholarship examination. Unfazed, I sat for the test and promptly forgot about it.

By this time, another teacher, Don McAdam, had also noticed my scholastic progress. Some fellow students were peeved by my eagerness, believing I was a 'smarty-pants'. His solution was to move my desk to the side of the class, which excluded me from normal classroom activities. I was restricted to revision work, but much to my detriment, Mr McAdam's plan backfired. I was teased and ostracised by fellow classmates for receiving special treatment. Upset, I shared my grievance with Matron Bartlam. I felt it unfair that Mr McAdam expected my education to stagnate until the other students caught up. Without fuss, the situation was resolved and I resumed my regular place in the classroom.

One January afternoon in 1962, Matron Bartlam came running down to the Girls' Dormitory, jubilantly waving a piece of paper above her head. Visibly elated, she revealed I'd achieved a 52 per cent pass mark for the scholarship examination, which meant I would attend boarding school in Charters Towers. My initial surprise and sense of achievement were intermingled with anxiety and worrying thoughts about Michael's welfare. How he would cope during my absence at boarding school?

21

YOU SILLY GIRL

I was fourteen years old when I commenced boarding school. I felt no sense of emancipation after arriving in Townsville. Nor did the town seem any different through my teenage eyes since our transfer to Palm Island two years before. I barely had time to savour the fact I was no longer on Palm before boarding a train for Charters Towers.

Located 140 kilometres west of Townsville, Blackheath and Thornburgh Colleges were founded in 1919, initially as a Methodist and Presbyterian boarding school. It was yet another change of church for me! God was the destination but the journey to him assumed many denominations. Along with All Souls, St Gabriel's College, Mt Carmel and St Mary's, Blackheath hosted a number of students from the Aboriginal Presbyterian missions around Cape York Peninsula and North Queensland. Students from Papua New Guinea also boarded at the college. I was among a handful of students from Palm Island to attend Blackheath College, including Dorothy 'Dotty' Dalton and Pat Seaton. Fellow resident Noreen Baira was a student at nearby St Gabriel's.

Blackheath College was where the female students boarded, with co-educational classes held at Thornburgh. The college offered a non-segregated environment and staff worked hard to make every student feel welcome. The most difficult and confronting aspect of life at college was taking my place alongside the majority white students. Once again I had to adjust to the challenges of living in a new environment. It reminded me of when we arrived at the Receiving Depot. But Jenny Davidson's presence provided a welcome measure of familiarity. Even so, I contemplated my existence without Michael. While Terry was capable of looking after himself, I constantly worried about how Michael would fare. But I reverted to survival mode, which stopped me from mulling too long over matters beyond my control.

I had gone from a racially segregated community to a freer, de-segregated college environment. Suddenly I was sharing the same facilities as white students, including the dining room during meal times, sleeping quarters, showers, and recreational areas. It was a bizarre experience, feeling juxtaposed between two opposing worlds, and I had difficulty seeing myself as equal to the white students. There was also the matter of free and full participation in church, shopping, school and other activities outside college. Overall, it was an awkward reintroduction to the daily mingling that living in a free society involved, and there'd been no preparation to assist me with this.

The Aboriginal male students seemed to fare much better at college life than girls, mainly because of the extensive sporting interests, including football, and School Cadets, which kept the boys motivated and engaged. Many of these Aboriginal students were older than their non-Indigenous classmates because of the disparities in the learning environments. It was not unusual for a fifteen- to seventeen-year-old Indigenous student to be placed in the same class as the thirteen- and fourteen-year-olds in Form 8.

Miss Jessie Landsberg was the most memorable of my teachers at Blackheath College. Her friendly, challenging and encouraging manner whetted my appetite for learning. She was pivotal just at the time when I craved a role model. Miss Landsberg, now in her late seventies and still volunteering at the college, remembers me as a bright, well-behaved but very spirited student.[90] She also describes herself as spirited.

Miss Landsberg insisted that I join her Junior Latin class. Perhaps she had to maintain minimum class attendance quotas. In any case, believing Latin would be unbearable, I resisted. I failed to see the benefit of learning a 'dead' language, especially as I aspired to be a clerk or secretary. Latin seemed much more useful to students wanting to pursue professional careers in law and medicine.

As luck would have it, Miss Landsberg intimated I had no choice but to accept enrolment in her class. I was not particularly good at Latin – and, by her own admission, neither was Miss Landsberg. She was more competent than me, though. I struggled to keep pace. One day, feeling completely exasperated, I scribbled a note to myself during her class:

I hate Latin, I hate Latin, First it killed the Romans, Now it's killing me!

I was also enrolled in Science with Mr Beasley, and in English, Commercial Studies and Maths. I settled in well after a while, helped by my involvement in non-academic pursuits such as swimming, basketball and athletics. I competed successfully in inter-house and inter-school sporting carnivals. I can still recall the anxiety of the opposing basketball team from St Mary's who believed their chances of winning were enhanced by the power of prayer. Mid-match I heard one of them whisper an incantation to the Virgin Mary: 'Hail Mary, full of grace, please let this ball fall into place.'

I also participated in speech and drama productions, including *The Pirates of Penzance*. But my 'yin-yang' co-existence with white students was rudely interrupted by the mandatory return to segregated life on Palm Island during the school holidays. Jenny reverted to her usual family life in the white section of the Island and I to the black side in the dormitory. I continued cleaning the Davidsons' house, albeit experiencing a mixture of shame and humiliation because of my continuing friendship with Jenny. I was her schoolmate and equal in Charters Towers, but the family housemaid back on Palm Island. Nonetheless, I cast aside any feelings of shame and subservience in order to earn that much-needed pocket money.

In my spare time, I hung out with Irene, who was a boarder at St Patrick's College on The Strand in Townsville. Our tree-top retreat high in the branches of the Burdekin plum tree offered not only an escape but a way to shirk work. From our cubby perched on high, we could see local residents darting about, doing their daily activities and performing their chores.

—

My education at Blackheath ended abruptly following an incident involving the College Principal, Mrs 'Flossy' Byres. I was sitting under a tree reading during my free time over the weekend. I stood up and lazily tossed my book over to the neighbouring tree where I had decided to move in search of more shade. Unbeknownst to me, Mrs Byres, a short, dowdy sexagenarian, had been watching.

'You, Patricia Janke. Come over here! What do you think you are doing? Pick up that book and bring it over at once,' she commanded curtly.

I handed her the book.

'Are you crazy? What a stupid thing to do!' she said.

Grabbing the heavy textbook from my hand, she began to beat me about the head with it.

'Patricia Janke, you are a silly, silly, silly girl,' she said, a painful thumping blow following each utterance of the word 'silly'.

I still do not know what happened next. Reflex action kicked in as I retaliated by striking Mrs Byres on the chin. Stunned, she stumbled backwards and uttered a faint 'Oh'. Such was the shocked look on her face that I believe she wanted to say, 'You hit me!' But the words would not come out. Instead, she dropped to the floor like a sack of potatoes.

Knowing there would be serious repercussions, I ran to my room, gathered what personal possessions I could and absconded over the hill. I took refuge at Mr George Reid's house. Fellow student Dotty Dalton was related to the Reid family. George and his daughter Patsy occasionally came to Blackheath for day visits. Mr Reid was a former Native Police officer who was well respected on Palm Island. He'd moved back to Charters Towers with his family some years earlier and I'd stayed with the Reid family for two nights. Now, taking the initiative, Mr Reid acted as an intermediary. He advocated on my behalf with Thornburgh Principal, Mr Graeme Thomsen, and Mr Bartlam, while I deliberated the outcome of my actions. The incident would be a permanent stain on my character, I was sure. And I knew my chances of returning to college were zilch.

Although I was not expelled and no official punishment was applied, of my own volition I wrote to Mr Thomsen to apologise for my retaliatory conduct. Principal Thomsen was gracious in his reply, thanked me for my courtesy and wished me all the best with my future education. I never returned to Blackheath.

Most people, including my children, laugh whenever I recount this story, believing Mrs Flossy Byres received her comeuppance as she provoked the assault. But the incident remains one of the most shameful moments of my life and I have carried the guilt of my reprisal against Mrs Byres ever since.

The burden of expectation was heavy so I knew Mrs Hogbin and Mrs Bartlam would be disappointed in me. I was disappointed in myself. I had wanted to make Mum proud of my educational success. Since she'd been unable to complete her own secondary education, I had hoped she might be able to achieve some of her aspirations vicariously through me.

—

On the way back to Palm Island, I was obliged by Father Cassian to call into St Patrick's Catholic College in Townsville. He thought he could advocate on my behalf and so had arranged this visit. Again George Reid was the intermediary, facilitating the necessary contact.

Irene and Francis Corporal were boarding there at the time but I don't recall seeing either of them. Instead, an obliging but officious Catholic sister escorted me on a tour of the school facilities. She commented on my long fingers and suggested I might be interested in piano lessons. On the walk she guided me to a piano, inviting me to have a test play. For a brief moment the misery of Blackheath was put aside – until the keyboard cover 'fell' heavily on my fingers. I winced in pain, unsure if it was an accident or deliberate on the part of the Sister. Either way, perhaps it was an omen. I thanked the Sister for her generosity and left. As a Ward of the State, I had no option but to return to Palm Island.

22

RETURN TO PALM ISLAND

After the peaks and troughs of my fleeting secondary schooling on the mainland, I returned to Palm Island as a fifteen-year-old – straight back into a restricted lifestyle of the dormitory. I felt the full weight of failure, all the missed opportunities, and assumed my place among the six other dormitory girls employed at the Palm Island Home Training Centre. My reunion with Michael restored some calm to my battered spirit; Terry was still seconded with the Palm Island canecutting crew on the mainland.

Father Cassian was disappointed I had returned to Palm Island and believed my prospects of leaving Palm again anytime soon were doomed. I blithely accepted my penance by undertaking domestic chores, scrubbing floors under the watchful eye of the Centre supervisor, Mrs Eleanor. Mrs Henry, the Centre's seamstress, allowed me to participate in sewing classes, where we made the free-issue clothing. This hard, physical work became my path to atonement, a distraction from my profound regret. I also helped prepare lunches for the state school children in addition to other general duties. My work ethic did not go unnoticed, and a few months later, I was transferred to start administrative work with the Social Welfare Association. Mrs Davidson and Mrs Myrna Doolan were the senior Administration Officers. Both played a pivotal role in my training.

Under Mr Davidson's guidance, I supervised the island's curio sales section; at the time, this was a critical component of the Palm Island Administration's Social Welfare and Enterprise Strategy. Mr Davis and Mr Bartlam championed the burgeoning arts and crafts industry on the island, believing it was a sustainable model to generate revenue while at the same time preserving and promoting the island's rich and diverse Aboriginal and Torres Strait Islander cultures.

The Social Welfare Association purchased craft products and hand-made items from Palm Island residents. The colourful curios made of coral, feather, beads, sea and turtle shell, pandanus leaves, coconut and wood from native trees were sold to tourists and official visitors. The solid wooden boomerangs, coolamons, clap sticks, woven baskets and coral ornaments were always popular. The Welfare Association operated on a commission basis, with the bulk of revenue returned to the individual artists and craftspeople. The sales commission retained by the Association helped fund the island's diverse recreational and sporting activities.

I was eventually promoted to a clerical role in the Palm Island Main Office. I enjoyed the occasions when Mr Jack Doolan, the Finance Overseer, invited me to accompany him on trips to the old people's home. One of my duties was to assist him in obtaining the thumb-prints from elders who were receiving social benefits. Mr Doolan was a real knockabout bloke whose jovial demeanour endeared him to most of the locals, black and white alike. He later became the elected Labor Member for Victoria River, which has a large Indigenous population.

It was a joyous moment when I read in 1977 of his entry to the Northern Territory Parliament, where he served until 1983.

In the course of my work, I gained access to the 'Native Files'. Because of the personal and confidential information they contained, these files were held in a restricted area of the office, reserved for senior white staff. The files could only be accessed under strict supervision; it was as 'rare as hen's teeth' for native staff like Olive and me to even be allowed into the restricted area.

During my time, there were seven full-time staff, five white and two black. Evelyn Greenwood (née Palmer) and Pat Conway had worked in the office before Olive and me. I performed minor clerical tasks, including switchboard duties, handling accounts with the 'adding machine' and managing purchases for local residents. We all occupied the Main Office, which was not as spacious. Most times, the cramped working conditions made staff keen to grab any opportunity to do fieldwork.

The meticulously ordered Native Files contained detailed information on the circumstances leading to individuals or families being removed to Palm Island. They included social history cards, personal accounts and official correspondence from the Department of Native Affairs. One day at work, a fortuitous opportunity presented itself to me in the form of a white administration officer employed in the Palm Island office. He was most empathetic about the plight of 'downtrodden blackfellas', myself included, and allowed me to peruse my own official records while he dutifully stood guard. Glimpsing inquisitively through the official documents in my personal file provided some invaluable insight. At last I had a comprehensive understanding of the conditions attached to being a Ward of the State.

The next time I saw him, I shared some of this information with

Father Cassian, whom I trusted completely. He interpreted the complex terms used in the legal documents, but I was still unclear about the process I was supposed to follow when at eighteen I was no longer a Ward of the State and my moment of 'freedom' arrived. Given the strict controls in place, the notion of any Aboriginal resident simply upping and leaving Palm seemed audacious.

—

Life continued for me as though I had never left Palm Island in the first place. I slotted straight back into dormitory life. Although I was employed at the Main Office, I was still expected to do my share of chores, including cleaning, washing and cooking again with Queenie. And with my return I was exposed once again to the harsher aspects of confined living. As time went by, I copped my share of both corporal punishment and psychological abuse. The latter is harder to endure, in my opinion. Broken bones and bruises heal with time, but mental scars never go away.

Mum had raised me to never speak ill of the dead. But I am going to make an exception with regard to one of the Aboriginal monitresses, whom I wish to remain anonymous. For reasons unknown, but no doubt embittered by her own life experiences, this woman singled me out for her own brand of punishment. She took such a dislike to me; I do not think 'despise' would be too harsh a description. At every opportunity she would repeatedly flog me with a cane, whip, cord or belt, although the cane was her preferred choice of weapon, as I used to jokingly say after she had whacked me about. Some of the girls – Linda, Theresa, Olive and Irene in particular – thought I was crazy to shrug off my beatings in such a way. She broke my skin several times, resulting in bruises. But I resolved never to spill one tear as she laid into me.

Theresa and her sister, Linda, were witnesses to one particularly nasty encounter. They were so traumatised by her brutality that they cried on my behalf, hoping that seeing them cry, I would in turn cry too. The monitress was relentless in her assault, but I was determined to not give her the satisfaction of my tears. As she kept flogging me, Theresa and Linda pleaded.

'Please cry! Just pretend. You won't get flogged anymore!'

Never!

Later on I told them she might bruise and bust me up but she would never break my spirit. Eventually her tenure as monitress ended. Without excusing her abuse of me, I still believe that her anger and rage were symptoms of other things happening in her life at the time. Nonetheless, her behaviour spawned some awful demons for those in her care and certainly made me question how the State and the Palm Island Aboriginal Settlement Administration could place broken, angry people in charge of young children. And there were other people to contend with. Like in prisons, the dormitory environment was dominated by a strict pecking order. Every novel or movie about a harsh prison environment invariably contains one domineering character who rules the roost. In my case, it was Sophie Butler.

Sophie lived in the dormitory because her mother worked as a domestic on cattle stations and she made my life hell during my first few years on Palm. Her behaviour and physique were intimidating in every way. She was tall and built like an Amazon warrior – and when one is victimised, the bully becomes twice the size. Sophie's true power base was her large extended family on the island. Anyone who messed with her had to contend with her gaggle of siblings, cousins, aunts and uncles.

Sophie took my plate and food away before I had finished eating. Other times she would push me against the wall and put her hands around my throat while threatening to beat me. And there was the verbal abuse, taunts and insults about my fair skin. Her intimidation was unrelenting. I believe Sylvia was threatened by my popularity among the other girls. Nobody did anything to stop her – myself included.

Sophie's bullying ended one day when I was on the roster to share cooking chores with Queenie. I walked into the kitchen and asked Queenie for her advice on how to defend myself. Without hesitation, she responded to my call for help. She pulled a big carving knife out of the kitchen drawer and, placing it in my hand, said, 'Go now! Sort that Sophie out once and for all!'

I knew what needed to be done, but I could not find Sophie anywhere. I returned to the kitchen where Queenie was slicing pieces of meat. Suddenly, I felt strong. Perhaps it had something to do with her belief in my being able to take care of myself. She reassuringly tapped me on the forearm as we continued with the food preparation. Then Sophie appeared. I caught a glimpse of her through the kitchen window. She was strolling towards the small bridge that was adjacent to the kitchen, en route to the Girls' Dormitory. Throwing my apron aside, I hurried down the kitchen stairs. My gaze fixed on her. I do not know how I summoned the courage to pounce on her in the manner I did. It happened so quickly; I was more surprised than Sophie.

No planning had gone into any of this. It was instinctive. I had to win this fight; otherwise, I risked becoming Sophie's lapdog – or a lapdog for anybody else who badly needed someone else to put down. I felt cloaked in Mum's indomitable spirit that afternoon. It was as though I was caught in a revolving door, drawn back to the Depot in Townsville when I fought the big boys bullying Michael. I psyched myself up with Mum's words to Dad reverberating within me: 'If you can't be the lead dog in the pack, then you might as well bugger off!

Because if you aren't the lead dog, all you've got to look at are the other dogs' arseholes!'

It sounds weird to say that I went straight for the jugular, but that is precisely what I did. I shoved Sophie against the stairs and raised the carving knife to her throat.

'If you know what's good for you, back off,' I said. 'Leave me alone!'

The dormitory girls who witnessed the scene could not contain their jubilation and pride as they nudged me back and forth. Queenie winked at me. In the wash-up, my ferocious attack had me tagged an unpredictable crazy, someone not to be messed with. I didn't mind. At least Sophie never bothered me again. And neither did any of the other girls.

Still, my deed did not go unpunished. Although I was only fifteen, I was placed in solitary confinement in the Women's Dormitory cell. That section of the dormitory was dark and almost airless, with just one window and no inside lighting. I can't recall any proper ablutions facilities, let alone any accessible water tap for drinking water. I felt desolate, not only on account of the awful confinement but also because I was missing out on seeing Theresa make her debut that evening. She was judged the Belle of the Ball. I could hear the goings-on, the excited announcements and the music. It was a form of torture not being there and knowing that everyone else was having fun.

I admired Theresa and her fighting spirit. I was perhaps sixteen years old when our head shaving and delousing ritual abruptly ceased. Theresa decided she had had enough and in a stroke of defiance whisked the clippers right out of Matron Barnett's hand. Strewth! That was akin to snatching the strap out of the principal's hand.

A mini-rebellion of sorts, erupted as the eight of us lined up for shearing broke ranks and fled, leaving Matron Barnett shaken and astonished. Theresa had not only saved the day but also spared us the shame and embarrassment of having our heads shaved ever again. There was no retribution for any of us.

On another 'round for a pound' occasion, it was Theresa's turn to cop it. Another monitress was lashing into her and by now I was fed up with the mistreatment of us from those who were supposed to be responsible for our care. I snatched the strap and retaliated, telling the monitress it was wrong for her to attack Theresa for no good reason. Emboldened by my defence of her, Theresa suddenly became embroiled in the dispute, and between us, we gave the monitress a taste of her own medicine – a touch-up with her own strap. Such was the camaraderie between the dormitory girls: you fought one of us, and you fought all of us. There was never any half measure in that regard. It was – and still is – all in or all out.

—

Still aged fifteen, I decided to run away and so set about organising the great escape. Several other girls were also desirous of some temporary freedom. We hatched a fanciful plan, which included leaving our school uniforms hanging on the clothesline. It did not take long though for the shrill, clear blows from the Native Police whistles to herald our absence from the dormitory. I scaled the closest tree, 200 metres away, and was the last to be found. At the time, we thought we were being daring, flexing our teenage muscle. We thought we had a great impact but were left to make the 'walk of shame' back to quarters. I don't recall Mr Bartlam or any of the monitors punishing us for our Clayton's escape. In all honesty, it probably gave them a good laugh.

Like caged birds, many Palm Island residents became psychologically conditioned to living in a captive environment; they grew accustomed to the government-imposed constraints and regulations, and accepting of a servile, segregated lifestyle. Some, including the late activist, Pastor Don Brady (Qwaanji), believed some Islanders were 'too afraid to be free'.[91] It suited some people, including the State bureaucracy, for residents to remain unaware of their legal rights in order to preserve white domination and social control. Living under the constant threat of punishment certainly quashed any ambition to challenge the norm. And some people did not know how to respond when the door to freedom was opened.

Around July 1963, some of us dormitory girls were taken to Townsville to attend the annual Townsville Agricultural Show and enter our garden vegetables, arts and crafts, and haberdashery in the competitions. The logistics resembled a paramilitary exercise. Upon arriving on the mainland, we were ushered into a large, army-style troop-carrier truck, complete with canvas flaps and seats along the sides. Once in the back, the canvas was zipped up and we had no idea where we were going.

We arrived at Aitkenvale Reserve to be met by former Palm Island Native Police officer Tommy Dodd, who had previously foiled our 'escape' from the Girls' Dormitory. Tommy and his wife, Beatrice, with their daughter, Alison, had transferred to Townsville to take up resident caretaker roles at the Aitkenvale Hostel. Mr Spencer, a white administrator employed by the State Department of Native Affairs, had overall management of the hostel. He, his wife and family lived in a spacious modern house on the hostel property. Mrs Toohey's store was across the road. I spotted some people nearby and as I walked over to introduce myself, some of the hostel girls came rushing over to warn me.

'No, you can't talk to those people. It's not allowed. You will get into trouble,' they said.

'Where do the rules say that we can't talk to other people?' I asked.

Such was the type of fear under which some people lived – being too scared to even make friendly conversation for fear of the consequences.

—

I thought of Mum often, especially during the difficult times. Sometimes my emotions collided with each other: love, sadness, anger, resentment, regret. It was easy to rush to judgment when there was complete silence and loss of all contact since our removal from the Home in Townsville. It hurt to think that Mum's frequent declarations of love for us were now questionable; no wonder her silence gave way to the feeling that she had abandoned us. There was no contact with Johanne or Uncle Kaj either, and I remained indifferent toward Dad given that he'd made no effort to contact us since our departure from Cairns. I assumed he was settled in his marriage to Eileen.

I wrote several letters to Mum. After receiving no response, I decided, for the benefit of my unsettled mind, not to write anymore; however, having made that decision, I came to realise that there is a vast difference between the decision that your mind makes as opposed to that of your heart. I tried hard to erase all thoughts of Mum.

Surprise! Out of the blue, around Christmas, I received two bags of Chinese salty plums in the mail. My mouth watered at the prospect of opening the packet. I assumed Mum had sent these as a Christmas gift, but I was more excited that it confirmed that Mum had at last found us. Mind, the only clue that the package was indeed from Mum was her beautiful handwriting. Nothing else. I thought it unusual that there was no note or card, but my flickering hope that our family would one day be reunited suddenly reignited.

23

LEAVING PALM ISLAND

Terry was the first to leave Palm Island. Upon expiry of his canecutting labour contract in 1964, Terry was expected to return to Palm Island. However, he decided to remain on the mainland. The Department of Native Affairs declared him an absconder and an arrest warrant was issued. At that time, he was one year short of his release as a Ward of the State. Terry evaded the authorities for six months. He found casual work canecutting and tobacco picking for Mr Tony Greco, a tobacco farmer at Biboohra, before finding full-time employment with Collins Cordial factory in Innisfail, where he promptly established himself as an industrious, reliable worker.

The Queensland police finally located Terry. Mr Bartlam was informed of his whereabouts and he arranged for Terry's return to Palm Island. But upon hearing of this development, Terry's employer, Mr Len Collins, personally intervened. He took the unprecedented step of guaranteeing he would personally supervise Terry and take an active interest in his welfare. Mr Collins said Terry had proven himself to be one of the best workers he had ever employed.

Satisfied Terry could live independently and responsibly, Mr Bartlam requested the police revoke the arrest warrant. The Innisfail police and the local Protector of Aboriginals in Innisfail continued to monitor Terry's conduct, even threatening his immediate repatriation to Palm Island if he caused any trouble.

Although Terry was no longer resident on Palm Island, he was still required to pay five per cent of his salary into the notorious Queensland State Government Welfare Fund. From 1904 to 1972, the State controlled the wages and savings of Aboriginal and Torres Strait Islander workers, some who commenced work as young as ten, living under Protection Acts. By the late 1960s, the Queensland Government retained controlled over 10,450 personal savings accounts of Indigenous Queenslanders, Terry, Michael's and mine included. These funds were supposed to be held in 'trust' but many workers found that after decades without access to their funds very little remained in their accounts.[92]

Terry secured his 'freedom' in April 1965 when he became an adult. Michael and I had had minimal contact with him in the meantime, but Terry did not forget us while he was gone; he gave approval for Mr Bartlam to deduct money from his savings account to buy us clothes, to give us some pocket money at Christmas, and for Michael and me to attend the Townsville Show. At some point I also took Michael to see singers Dinah Lee, Brian Hyland, Laurel Lea and Judy Stone in concert. I have never forgotten Terry's generosity to us at that time, or the maturity he demonstrated. He was barely an adult but he was prepared to support us financially. Ironically, his direct contributions to the Welfare Fund subsidised, in turn, our welfare. Although I missed him dreadfully, I was so thankful he was no longer on Palm but enjoying the fruits of his labour on the mainland.

Terry's liberation, coupled with my own impending discharge as a Ward of State, encouraged me to plan for my future beyond Palm Island. This included attempts to re-establish contact with Johanne. Six years had elapsed since I had any contact with my sister, so I wrote to the State Children's Department seeking their assistance to help me locate her.

—

Palm Island
Via Townsville
8th April, 1965

Dear Sir,

I would like some information regarding my little sister who was an inmate of your Home some years back.

I also was there, during which time my little sister was adopted out and taken away. The lady who had taken her lived in Townsville at one stage, but has now moved to another area. Her birthday will be coming up within the next month and I would like to remember her on this occasion. Johanne was only six or seven at that time of her adoption, if I can remember. I would appreciate it very much if you could help with this matter. If under any circumstances you are unable to supply me with the above, would it be possible for you to find out how she is and let me know?

Thanking you.

Yours faithfully
Patricia Janke

—

28 April 1965
Miss Patricia Janke
PALM ISLAND
Via Townsville

Dear Patricia

I thank you for your letter concerning your sister Johanne and wish to advise that she is living c/- Mrs A.R Stephenson of 127 Sturt Street, Townsville.

I have had a conversation with Mrs Stephenson and have informed her you may be writing to Johanne.

Yours faithfully,
District Officer

—

Michael was next to leave Palm Island, albeit temporarily. He was enrolled in secondary school at Thornburgh College in 1964. Under the Harold Blair Scheme, he spent a month with a white family in Melbourne to prepare him for desegregated college life and support his gradual assimilation into a predominantly white Australian society. He recalls details from the journey:

> *There were Murris from Yarrabah, Palm Island, Cherbourg, Woorabinda and we all gathered in Brisbane and we flew by plane from Brisbane to Melbourne. It was a big plane. It was just full of Murri kids and I had the distinction of being the fairest. I was sent to Melbourne to live with the white family. They had three boys roughly around my age … They were getting me used to white people. When I came back to Palm I was sent virtually to an all-white boys' college.*[93]

Resisting the requirement to return to Palm Island during school holidays, Michael ran away from Thornburgh College three times in his first year. Each time, he headed for Innisfail, where Terry was living. On his third attempt, the police apprehended him en route. Despite being only fourteen, he was handcuffed and returned to Palm Island. Michael remains emphatic that he was not running away from Boarding School or his formal education, but from Palm Island.

He has some positive memories of his time in Charters Towers. Aside from his studies, he participated in the cadets and won prize money for his entry in a drawing competition. Michael also remembers Miss Landsberg fondly, after an encounter with her on the last day of school before the Christmas break. Michael was waiting to board a bus as it stopped by Blackheath College to collect female students before heading to the railway station. Miss Landsberg was standing on the footpath outside the college, farewelling her students. She looked up, saw him and uttered three words that he has never forgotten.

'Merry Christmas, Michael!'

At that point in his life, she was the only white person who had ever wished him a Merry Christmas. The memory endured for him even 50 years later.

Once back on Palm, although a minor, Michael became part of the adult carpentry gang that repaired and maintained the housing on the island. Five per cent of his low income was also deducted for the Welfare Fund. In 1966, Michael left Palm Island. He remembers it was the same year decimal currency was introduced. Sensing his reluctance to remain there, Mr Bartlam arranged for Michael to work on a cattle station near Mount Surprise, 320 kilometres west of Cairns. Michael mustered steers, herded and dipped livestock as part of his daily duties. This work was instrumental in helping him to establish independence.

—

One afternoon in 1966, I found a copy of the *Australasian Post* magazine, which one of the senior girls had brought over from the mainland; she loved doing crosswords. A full-page recruitment advertisement for the Royal Australian Navy (RAN) caught my interest. While the invitation to 'Come See the World' seemed too hard to resist, I was more interested in securing full-time work. I showed the advertisement to a few of the girls. All of us longed for the same opportunities as other Australians; each of us harboured dreams of life on the mainland because of the limited employment opportunities on Palm Island. Employment in the Navy could be the panacea for my situation. I had no interest in working as a jillaroo or an *au pair* on remote cattle stations, which seemed to be the norm for most women on the island. I wanted to roam and explore at will. But to realise my ambitions I needed a job and money.

Without telegraphing my intentions to Mr Davidson, I surreptitiously printed copies of a generic cover letter on the Social Welfare Office's Gestetner Roneo machine, and a group of fifteen of us, some eager, some hesitant, completed applications for the Navy. As our mail continued to be vetted and censored, I befriended a nurse at the Palm Island Hospital who undertook the task of smuggling the applications to the mainland and posting them on our behalf. Many months passed without any acknowledgment or response, so I assumed we had been unsuccessful and moved on.

My final departure as a Palm Island resident was unceremonious. I left on 6 September 1966, just two weeks after my eighteenth birthday.

I was granted annual leave from my clerical role at the Administration Office, receiving a salary advance of $15.63 (about $192.23 today) to pay for my return train fare between Townsville and Cairns and for incidentals. I had intended to return to Palm Island, but once on the mainland, I decided to take my chances and stay.

I cannot recall resigning from my office position, and although I had legally ceased being a Ward of the State, I still feared I might be declared an absconder. There was no confirmation or official a 'Deed of Release' from the State Children's Department confirming I was no longer under their care.

Not long after this, Johanne and I reconnected. I walked into David Jones Department store in Townsville, where Johanne's foster brother, Allan, a store employee, recognised me. Allan also entered dachshunds ('sausage dogs') in local dog shows and told me Johanne would be helping him to prepare the dogs for display at an upcoming local competition. He invited me to come along and see her. I accepted.

It was an emotional reunion. Our meeting, in part, was chaperoned by Mrs Stephenson, Johanne's stepmother. There was no privacy. By this time I felt Johanne had been completely absorbed into the Stephenson family as her remembrances of our family life together had blurred with the passage of time. Johanne recalls:

> *It was my foster brother Allan who bred miniature smooth-haired dachshunds. That's when Pattie came around. She gave me a nice little gold cross to wear around my neck. Probably from my perspective it was more emotional for her than it was for me. I would have only been about twelve or thirteen then. It was at the Townsville Dog Show. I had seen Terry in Townsville at West End because we used to live next to a car sales yard,*

> *McKillops, and they used to sell Mini Minors. Terry came down in a little Mini Minor. I can vividly remember him in his blue overalls.*[94]

Mr Oswald Stephenson was not there during our reunion, which was awkward and uncomfortable. Johanne and I had no recent, shared experiences in common and little to talk about. Busy and distracted, she seemed more interested in the dogs than me as she primed and groomed them for show. My sister felt like a stranger. Not only did I feel that she had moved on without us but I was hurt that she had become fully absorbed into the Stephenson family.

It was so painful that I decided to sever all contact with Johanne. I felt she was better left alone. This was a difficult decision, one not prompted by my no longer loving her, but taken as a consequence of separation and loss. The absence and silence of the intervening years had displaced our familial bond, leaving no vestige of the family togetherness we had shared before our separation in October 1958. Battle weary, I no longer had the emotional resilience to compete with the Stephensons for the restoration of our family's place in Johanne's life.

The reunion with Johanne really put a dampener on my mood, and I decided to lift my spirits by meeting up with a group of former Palm Island girls who were either visiting Townsville or working on the mainland. Over time, Townsville, the largest and closest regional town to Palm Island, had become an unofficial hub, a meeting and transit point for former island residents. Most Palm Islanders developed ongoing family connections in Townsville, and indeed these linkages continue today. It was never difficult to find someone from Palm Island on the mainland. Before Facebook, email, mobiles, even telegrams, Telecom and Telstra, there was 'Tell-a-Murri'. The informal but highly effective social, news and gossip network had been perfected over many years. Based on the 'all blackfellas are related' principle, the 'Tell-a-Murri' system operated through word of mouth. Although not foolproof, news usually travelled fast because there were fewer degrees of social separation. Everyone knew someone or was related in some way. To 'send word' to another Murri, all you needed to do was speak to other Murris, who'd pass on the message. This process continued until the intended recipient was reached. It worked brilliantly!

Matron Bruce from the Receiving Depot in Townsville often passed messages to me through the 'Tell-a-Murri' grapevine. When she happened upon Palm Islanders around Townsville, she asked them to convey her greetings to me, and I always received them.

Eva (Evie) Geia was a Palm Island stalwart and respected elder, known for her formidable activism and leadership. Evie was the main 'go to' person when Palm Islanders needed support on the mainland. Her generous deeds were renowned. Evie's house at 32 Hale Street was near a church on a hill; the large neon cross was powered 24/7 – a perpetual beacon that helped guide the weary and needy to her house. Evie offered a sanctuary from strife and loss. She offered me non-judgmental advice and temporary accommodation without charge. I have no idea how she survived as most who stayed with her paid no rent or electricity.

On the mainland, my salary advance quickly disappeared. Having no permanent abode and little money, I relied on the goodwill of others, namely dormitory family, including Theresa and Linda Anderson and Marie Pryor, who all had jobs on the mainland by now. I moved like a refugee between the Anderson family's Walker Street residence and Evie's home. Marie Pryor in particular was 'cashed up', about to return home to Palm Island after a long stint working on a pastoral property out west. She was generous and kind enough to support me when I needed assistance.

In the meantime, I maintained intermittent contact with the Bartlam family. In an unofficial reunion, Mr Bartlam accepted my reasons for not returning Palm Island and arranged for some money held in my savings account to be released at the Townsville Court House. Matron Bartlam was beside herself with concern for my welfare as a single woman on the mainland and begged me to return to the safety and security of Palm Island.

In 1966, Mr Bartlam was transferred to the Department of Native Affairs Townsville office after accepting a promotion as Regional Manager. He offered to help me find work. Although Mr Bartlam was continually reasserting the need for me to find work, I knew this time it was a 'do or die' situation. I did not want to return to Palm Island. Mr Bartlam agreed to provide a reference if required. Father Cassian was due to leave Palm Island in 1967 following the completion of his five-year term and, as always, he offered whatever support he could.

Marie's persuasive encouragement to reconnect with Mum touched my emotions. Marie lost her mother at an early age and was keen to do her best to reunite me with Mum. She was a sentimental benefactor, paying for my train fare to Cairns and accompanying me on the trip. Marie was two years my senior and also considered herself a protective travelling companion. So began our journey.

24

FINDING MUM

In 1966, almost eight years after my removal to Townsville and Palm Island, I returned to Cairns. Now eighteen, it had been six years since I had seen Mum and Uncle Kaj, and eight years since I had any contact with Dad. The events in between made this seem an eternity.

One day, a year earlier, in the course of his employment with Collins Cordial, Terry was making soft drink deliveries throughout the Tableland region and had a chance encounter on the Kuranda Range with our elder brother, Kevon Glendon, from Dad and Emma's marriage. By Kevon's account, Dad had not only hit rock bottom but had also hit the bottle. Kevon told Terry that Mum, Dad and Uncle Hans were now all living together at Dad's house on Spence Street in Cairns.

Dad's second marriage to Eileen had ended after she deserted him for a Luftwaffe pilot whom she later married. Eileen spent several years in Germany before returning to Australia in the late 1970s to live in Cairns. As a consequence of her desertion and ultimate betrayal, Dad suffered a nervous breakdown, which resulted in his seeking refuge in the bottle. It seems karma repaid Dad in kind for all the misery he had wrought in other people's lives, including Mum's and Emma's.

Terry was the first to be reunited with Mum. It was not the joyous homecoming he anticipated. He recalls meeting Mum and Dad again after seven years of separation in 1965:

> *When I saw Mum she looked like she didn't have pride in the way she dressed. They were all living in squalor and were dirt poor. I felt sorry for them. They were so poor they said they couldn't afford their electricity bill. They claimed they had no money. I gave them the money to pay the electricity account. I was angry when I found out later that they used the money to buy alcohol. I did not feel like she was my mother. I was stand-offish. I remember what she had done to me when I was young. I had never forgiven her for the abuse. I kept that grudge between myself, Mum and Dad. Uncle Hans was a gentle man. He had always been with Mum for a long time. It is a wonder they never got married because they were so close.*[95]

By the time I arrived in Cairns the following year, Mum and Uncle Hans had moved on. It was unclear as to what happened to Uncle Kaj. Terry suggested that I visit Hubbard's Store on Sheridan Street, which was owned and operated by our sister, Glenda. He thought she might be able to help me locate Mum through Dad.

Cautiously optimistic, Marie and I called on Glenda at the store. Although I had no memory of Glenda, eleven years my senior, she clearly remembered me as she recalled carrying me around on her hips as a baby at the Daintree farm. Glenda offered immediate hospitality. She was actively supporting Dad and helping him to get his life back on track. Dad was employed as a general roustabout to help Glenda with chores at the store.

That afternoon Glenda took Marie and me to visit Dad who was by now living with my other sister, Megsy (Margaret). Dad occupied a small room attached to her house. Megsy also offered Marie and me accommodation until we settled. I found immediate comfort in Glenda and Megsy's welcoming ways, but I felt no strong sense of attachment to Dad after our lengthy separation. There were no outward displays of affection between us as I remained emotionally guarded. I resented Dad for the years of silence and lack of contact during our time in Townsville and on Palm Island. I also continued to hold him responsible for his part in our removal and his antipathy toward Mum.

Initially, Dad was not forthcoming about Mum's whereabouts, unwilling to give me any contact information. Instead he sought to monopolise my time, endeavouring to make amends for his absence over the years. I eventually gleaned from him that Uncle Hans had taken Mum into his care and they had relocated to Bloomfield River, 170 kilometres north of Cairns.

Uncle Hans was transferred from the Foxwood Timber and Truss Company in Cairns back to Patterson's Plymill in Bloomfield, where he worked when he first arrived in Australia. Concerned by Mum's chronic drinking, he hoped moving to a quieter environment might provide some much needed respite and offer her better opportunities for sobriety. Mum and Uncle Hans were now living in a de facto relationship since Mum had become a widow.

Uncle Kaj had died in Cairns a few years back, in August 1961, less than a year after Michael and I were sent to Palm Island. He was only 38. We were never informed of his death. Uncle Kaj died from a combination of barbiturate and alcohol poisoning. He overdosed on about 30 sleeping tablets, washing them down with copious amounts of beer. His Blood Alcohol Concentration (BAC) at the time of his post mortem was 0.26 – more than five times the current acceptable legal limit of 0.05 BAC in Queensland.[96]

Mum and Dad appeared before the coronial inquest along with four other witnesses. At the time of his death, Mum, Dad and Uncle Kaj had all been living together at Progress Road, White Rock, Dad having moved there at some stage after his marriage to Eileen ended. Both Mum and Dad had been asleep in the house when Uncle Kaj died following a prolonged drinking session that afternoon. Dad was also considered a person of interest at the inquest: Uncle Kaj had overdosed on Dad's sleeping tablets, which had been prescribed for his nervous condition.[97]

Uncle Kaj's death was determined accidental. It was impossible, the coroner maintained, for the pentobarbitone tablets to have been administered by force without visible injury. Deliberate poisoning was also excluded as a cause of death. The coroner further determined that such a large number of tablets could not have been dissolved in a glass of beer without Uncle Kaj's knowledge; he considered that Uncle Kaj took the tablets in a drunken stupor, either intentionally or accidentally, without realising how many tablets he had taken. No motive for foul play or murder could be established, particularly in view of the fact that Uncle Kaj had held no cash, assets or insurance.[98]

—

Marie accepted an offer of work as a domestic helper with Glenda's family. Meanwhile, I was still looking for employment in Cairns and called into the local Navy Office one day to check on the status of the job application I had lodged months before on Palm Island. There was no news. I updated my contact details, providing them with Glenda's address and phone number.

Being in unfamiliar surrounds, Marie became dependent on my

company and was anxious that I'd leave Cairns to look for Mum. Although deeply appreciative of the support I had received from her, Glenda and Megsy, I was torn between my emotional indebtedness and my growing impatience to find Mum and be reunited with her. One morning I made an impulsive decision to leave for Bloomfield River via Cooktown. With minimal funds and a small bag of clothing, I headed to the Cairns Marina. After a few enquiries, I found myself on a boat headed for Cooktown with no idea or expectations of what lay before me. The boat was not long out to sea when the ship's steward came around to check tickets. I did not have enough money to pay for the fare, but the crew struck a generous compromise after I explained my predicament and the reason for my journey. An understanding captain's mate, Derek Scott, devised an arrangement that allowed me to work for my fare by preparing meals and helping with the catering service. I was travelling not only on the smell of an oily rag but also on a wing and a prayer.

The boat arrived into Cooktown at nightfall. Empathising with my situation, the captain took me to the Sovereign Hotel, where he 'shouted' me a meal. The crew asked the publican and some of the patrons about the prospects of my making the journey between Cooktown and Bloomfield River. I learnt that the storekeeper, Mr Olsen, from the nearby community of Ayton, would be arriving in Cooktown the next day to collect his supplies from the boat. His general store serviced Bloomfield and the surrounding communities, including Wujal Wujal, the former Bloomfield River Aboriginal Mission.

I was heartened when the Aboriginal barmaid, Isobel Harrigan, who hailed from a prominent family in the Bloomfield River area, confirmed that Mum and Uncle Hans were living at Bloomfield River. Hans was working at the plymill, she said, as were several of her family members.

'I know them,' Isobel said enthusiastically. 'They are a lovely couple.'

I returned with the crew to spend the night on board the boat and await Mr Olsen's arrival the following day. The captain offered me his quarters, located above deck, but at some time in the early hours of the morning, he returned. His body pressing against mine woke me. There was no pillow talk, no seduction or foreplay. Any of the captain's inhibitions during our dinner at the pub some hours before were cast aside.

'Are you awake?' the captain asked as he began to smooth his hands over my body and under my clothes.

Frightened, I repelled his advances. My response was stern.

'Fuck off! Don't spoil a good night.'

I knew how to handle myself, having on occasion received unwanted attention on Palm Island, but the captain's behaviour was most distasteful. How could I have been so gullible to place myself in such a dicey situation? My neediness to see Mum was making me stupid. In that moment, I recalled Mum's warning about never accepting gifts from strangers. There's usually an obligation attached, she'd say. Now I felt I might have to pay my way in kind.

Perhaps through Divine Intervention once again, however, my guardian angel, Derek Scott, appeared in the cabin, saving me from this awful situation. He berated the captain for taking advantage of someone who was young enough to be his own daughter. Ashamed, the captain skulked away. I offered yet another grateful prayer.

'Please forgive the captain for his indiscretion. It must have been the alcohol,' Derek said. 'This is very out of character for him.'

—

Next morning I put the incident behind me. My single focus was on finding Mum and nothing could distract me from that objective.

While waiting at the wharf for Mr Olsen, I had become the topic of conversation among some of the locals who were curious about my being the only woman on board. Some people approved, I could tell; others were judgmental. When Mr Olsen arrived at the wharf in his pick-up truck to collect his supplies, I helped him to load the goods despite his objection. But I was determined not to hitch a free ride. Mr Olsen confirmed that Mum and Uncle Hans were at Bloomfield River; he knew both of them personally. My expectations of meeting up with Mum soon made all my worries from the previous night disappear.

It was a bumpy journey through the Black Mountain terrain but my soaring spirits and natural high lessened the discomfort. We passed through Helensvale, stopping at the Lions Den Hotel on the way. The people at the pub also knew Mum and Uncle Hans. My elation evolved into uncertainty with the passing of each kilometre. I began to steel myself as we approached Bloomfield River. Maybe I'd built up my hopes only to have them dashed. My mind shifted into fifth gear as Mr Olsen moved into second to avoid becoming bogged. What if Mum did not remember me? Worse yet, what if she wasn't at home? My tears welled silently.

Upon arrival into Bloomfield River, Mr Olsen pulled up on the verge near a ramshackle houseboat on the edge of the Bloomfield River. I assumed this accommodation belonged to Patterson's Plymill. There was a little jetty at the back that seemed perfect for fishing. I could see the faint figure of a woman in the distance.

'I think that's Aggie down there,' Mr Olsen said, pointing out the window.

I thanked him for the ride, hopped out of the vehicle and began making my way down the path. Mum was crouched over a wood-fired copper boiler doing the washing. As I approached, she stood and hoisted some steaming clothes onto a long, thick stick, preparing to hang the items on a makeshift clothesline.

'Mum!' I called out to her.

She looked at me, startled. The moment she recognised me, she tossed the boiler stick and clothes aside and ran towards me calling my name, her arms outstretched.

'Patsy!' she exclaimed. I caught the familiar scent of her hair and body as I nuzzled into her embrace; all the old memories of Mum came back.

'Mum! Mum! I have come home!' I cried.

As I hugged her, I knew I had come home spiritually, physically and emotionally. Tears flowed from a deep reservoir of pent-up emotions. Our years apart, the hurt, the pain, the loneliness endured without her, my sheer hunger for her presence all collided in that single moment.

—

Based on Terry's encounter with Mum the previous year, I expected the worst but she was in better shape than I had imagined. My only disappointment was that she had continued drinking. I did not judge her; time was too precious to waste doing that. Mum somehow appeared settled. Although still drinking, she seemed content in her relationship with Uncle Hans, whom I had not seen since 1958.

Life had been bitterly unkind to Mum, but much kinder than she had been to herself. Her broken spirit was visible. She had never come to terms with Dad's rejection, or with our removal. She continued to rely heavily on alcohol as a preferred painkiller. Her face was more weathered than I remembered. Her once immaculately coiffed hair was replaced by a bushy, silver afro. The spot on her lip, which I had always assumed was a facial mole, had increased in size. There were still the familiar flickers of brilliance in her witty conversations and retorts, but Uncle Kaj was never mentioned in our conversation, and any mention of Elin was also met with a reflective silence.

Regret was cast aside as we tried to recapture the lost years. We whiled away the weeks fishing off the jetty or along the river, cramming endless conversations into the passing hours and days. Sometimes we would huddle around the radio listening to radio series like *Blue Hills, Portia Faces Life* and *Dr Turner's Family* drama series on the ABC. Somehow, the world felt safe again.

In spite of these close times, Mum, like many of her generation, remained deeply guarded about her emotions, selective as to what she chose to reveal to me, her eldest daughter. There was no Hollywood screen moment in which Mum admitted remorse or responsibility for our removal; nor were there any deep and meaningful mother–daughter conversations where she tearfully professed how much she had missed me over the years and wished she could start over again. But Mum did not have to say anything, and I did not expect her to. I intuitively knew how she felt.

Mum filled me in on some things, though. She told me my godmother, Mrs Nakamura, had passed away while I was on Palm Island. She died from heart disease and diabetes-related complications in July 1962, aged 50. Two daughters survived her.

Like Uncle Hans, Mum too had found casual employment at Patterson's Plymill, the main industry in the community at that time. She helped to sectionalise the timber while Uncle Hans was a general labourer. Mum had a faithful, four-legged companion too, and Leo followed her everywhere and rarely left her side. Mum always subscribed to the theory that dogs make better friends than people because they wag their tails and not their tongues.

As an eponymous tribute, Uncle Hans had lovingly crafted Mum a small scull: a tiny one-seat rowboat with oars. He named it the *Timena*, a variation of Mum's birth name, Temana. I was in the *Timena* when she capsized and sank after a mishap in the crocodile-infested waters. Mum's refusal to let go of two of the heavy wine flagons she was holding on to did not assist my attempts to salvage the dinghy.

'I don't think this boat can carry all this plonk,' I told her.

'Let go and let God, Patsy,' Mum uttered, or words to that effect.

Squeezing one of us onto the boat let alone two along with at least four litres of wine was wishful thinking. The boat went down but the flagons survived. We sank like a ship out of *Moby Dick*, all because Mum refused to let go of the grog. Thankfully the tender boat was close to the makeshift jetty Uncle Hans had built. After that mishap, Uncle Hans constructed the *Timena Too* and Mum often paddled to a secluded section of the river where she fished in the nude. She loved the exhilarating freedom and quiet anonymity of Bloomfield River.

Mum's lethargy and impatience sometimes caused her to improvise when gathering bait. She'd grab a double-barrelled shotgun, fire it into the water, then scoop up the stunned garfish when they floated to the surface. Sticks of gelignite, given to her by fellow employees at the Plymill, delivered the same outcome when she ran out of ammunition and needed a fast catch.

I stayed in Bloomfield River for several months. In trying to make up for lost time, I actually lost track of time. In the meantime, I remained in touch with Michael, Terry, Glenda and Marie. Mum proudly paraded me around and introduced me to local families. She had continued her friendship with her old schoolmate Auntie Marie Swindley, whose mother, Granny Sim, was a long-term resident in the Bloomfield River area. One day I realised in the midst of some introductions that I had been to Bloomfield River before. Mum had taken us there when we were younger to meet the Swindleys. Granny Sim made the best toffee I had ever tasted.

It was also on that earlier visit to the Bloomfield River, despite Mum's stern cautioning, that Terry loaded myself, Johanne and Michael into a small dinghy and decided to take us for a row. Mum noticed that Terry had lost control of the rowboat. Upon seeing a couple of shark fins in the water, she beckoned him to come ashore immediately. Terry panicked and jumped overboard, leaving us to drift in the currents. But Super Mum came to the rescue; she swam out and took control of the dinghy, despite the presence of sharks, and returned us safely to shore.

Bloomfield River at that time was a tight-knit community with Aboriginal and non-Aboriginal families living and working together harmoniously. Everyone was genuinely happy about Mum and me reuniting. The celebrations, the welcomes and the generosity of strangers continued throughout my stay. I spent time with some local Indigenous families, including the Swindleys, Harrigans and the Doughboys as well as Vivian Harlow.

There were many carefree days on Bloomfield River reminiscent of my childhood antics. I especially loved spending time with the Swindley family. Auntie Marie's husband, Uncle Clarrie Swindley, was a rugged 'salt of the earth' character. He and Uncle Hans became father figures for me at Bloomfield. Dependable and strong, Uncle Clarrie made his living from tin mining. He would be away for weeks at a time but return to sell his tin for a good price. He regaled me with stories of what a beautiful baby I was and how he first taught me to walk on a pub bar counter. He was so proud of the fact he guided me to take my first steps.

Uncle Clarrie was a true bushman. Terry remembers one encounter with him:

> *Uncle Clarrie was slicing a fresh damper on the table with a big sharp knife. Next thing a green snake came up and into the house through a gap in the wooden floorboards. It wasn't a venomous type. Uncle Clarrie grabbed the snake and cut its head off using the same knife. There was blood on the floor and snake blood on the knife. Uncle Clarrie came back to the table and just kept cutting the damper. He didn't even rinse or wipe the knife clean. Then he offered me a slice of the damper. I didn't want to eat it but I couldn't refuse.*[99]

I also went pig hunting with the Swindley children: Ernest, Gerald, William, Marie Justina, Vincent and Coral. The Swindleys had a ritual of tying a feral pig in the mangroves to lure the crocs during our spotlighting on the river at nights. The boys also attached a torch to a spear and caught fish as we waited for the crocodiles to appear. We didn't starve. Other days, I rode about on an old horse named Pawpaw.

It was wonderful to feel sheltered and connected and to have a sense of family after so many years of loneliness and isolation. As the months drifted by, the hardships of the Receiving Depot and Palm Island dissipated. I was surrounded by the love of family and caring people again.

—

The communications system in those days was a common exchange known as a party line, which comprised a single line telephone network. If the phone rang, anyone who had a telephone could listen in on other people's conversations. Mum took tremendous delight in eavesdropping, as did many other residents who considered the party line to be a regular source of gossip and entertainment. At times Mum unknowingly interrupted callers and participated in their conversations, providing advice once the callers became aware she was on the line.

News came via the party line that the Navy wanted to schedule me for a first stage recruitment interview, fitness test and medical assessment. They had tracked me down via the Bloomfield River telephone exchange with Glenda's assistance. The Navy officer advised that the recruitment and enlistment process was time-consuming. I would need to be patient.

I decided to return south to Cairns for the mandatory medical assessment and then travel on to Innisfail to prepare for the interview. Uncle Hans and Mum took me across to Port Douglas on a larger, sturdier boat Uncle Hans had built. It was seaworthy, a testament to his boatbuilding skills. A storm brewed. The seas became incredibly turbulent, forcing us to find sanctuary at Cedar Bay inlet. The angry waters tossed the boat; we bobbed up and down. At one point, the waves rose so high that I feared we would sink when they came crashing down on the bow. Poor Mum was so seasick she sought refuge in the quarters below deck.

Uncle Hans's nautical skills came to the fore. I took hold of the rudder while he battened down the hatches. Together we navigated the stormy waters to safety. Uncle Hans was so proud. He said he would take me to sea any day as his shipmate because of my calmness and commonsense.

It was a tearful separation from Mum. I knew that I would see her again; I just wasn't sure when. This time, adapting a quote from American poet Oliver Wendell-Holmes, Mum reminded me that although our feet may wander and leave many places, home is where we love and leave our hearts.

25

THE VISITOR

I returned to Cairns with a renewed sense of purpose and an overwhelming inner peace born of being reunited with Mum. Upon learning that Michael was now staying with Terry in Innisfail, I decided to join them while awaiting my naval call-up. I provided the Navy with Terry's forwarding address and hoped for the best. As Marie also had close family ties in Innisfail, she decided to come with me.

The Navy selection process took longer than anticipated. With a sense of shame, I registered for Social Security, receiving three weeks of unemployment benefits, which tied me over while job hunting. It was important for me to be independent. The challenge was to find employment quickly so as to avoid relying on family and friends for social and financial support. Michael was also unemployed at this time but eventually found work as a carpet layer at See Poy's & Sons Department Store in Innisfail.

Meanwhile, Dad had tried hard to make up for lost time by trying to restore our splintered relationship. He regularly drove from Cairns in his miniature Austin vehicle to visit me. Other times he caught the rail motor. He stayed at Miriwinni outside Innisfail with family friends Kaj and Del Pedersen, who were part of Mum's Hartley Street clique. Because of Dad's efforts to re-establish ties, I decided to let bygones be bygones. Now on his own, he'd become a forlorn figure, living a solitary existence. I began to enjoy spending time with him and appreciated his attempts to reconcile.

Marie, Michael and I all squatted temporarily with Terry and his then partner, Esther Andy, and baby, Terri-Lee, at their place on Rankine Street. Although conditions in the two-bedroom unit were cramped, I welcomed Terry and Esther's hospitality. As each of us – Michael, Marie and myself – found our own bearings and gained employment, we left Terry and his family to enjoy their own space and privacy.

When Marie began training as a nursing aide, I accepted an offer to stay with Rosie and Johnny Jose, a well-respected Aboriginal family. Johnny was a technician in the Postmaster General's (PMG) office, now Australia Post. The Joses were a supportive family. Johnny and Rosie's values had a stabilising influence. I dated their son Bertie for a brief while, and much to his dismay, our friendship became strictly platonic once I moved into their family home.

One day, an advertisement for a position of postal officer with PMG's telegram and delivery section caught my interest, even though they preferred a man for the job. When the supervisor, Mr Les Scheu, who eventually became the Mayor of Innisfail, gave me the job, I became the first female postal delivery officer to be employed by the Innisfail PMG.

Having achieved my goal of financial independence, feeling uncomfortable about receiving unemployment benefits and wanting to assuage my guilt, I paid in full back to the government what I considered to be a debt. The PMG job proved physically demanding although it was mind-numbing in its repetitiveness. The bulk of my workday was spent pedalling about on a pushbike, delivering letters and telegrams to residents in the regional communities of Mourilyan to the south and Goondi Bend to the north. The steep inclines and declines along the route from Innisfail to Goondi Hill and Goondi provided a daily speed and time challenge.

Working for the PMG helped me to find my place in a world well beyond the lifestyle of Palm Island. For the first time I allowed myself to be content with my daily life; I'd attained a measure of success and felt a sense of fulfilment. After all the years of grief and uncertainty, my life seemed to be going right at last. On occasion, self-doubt undermined my happiness; I'd believe I was unworthy of such personal contentment and prosperity. Like the story character Chicken Little, there were days when I too wondered if the sky was falling in, whether misfortune was looming.

Several months after I settled in Innisfail, I received a letter from Johanne's foster father, Oswald Stephenson. He told me he had important news to share about my sister. He asked if he could visit me in Innisfail. Mr Stephenson worked as a ticket inspector for Queensland Rail and made frequent trips between Townsville and Cairns. He also worked day trips between Townsville and Ingham and further north to Innisfail. With the ongoing silence between Johanne and me, I was anxious to hear the news about her so agreed to meet. He reassured me there was nothing to worry about in terms of Johanne's health or welfare.

I have thought about it many times over the years but remain baffled as to how Mr Stephenson knew my postal address. I was not in contact with Johanne at the time and can only assume he made enquiries through the State Children's Department or Department of Native Affairs, who provided Terry's forwarding address. I barely knew Mr Stephenson. The only time I saw him was in the background when I was having my usual 'set-tos' with Mrs Stephenson while visiting Johanne.

I met Mr Stephenson at a small café opposite the Goondi Hill railway station. The meeting started uncomfortably when he presented me with a bunch of flowers and a box of chocolates. I was surprised by this gesture. Then Mr Stephenson began to question me about my private life.

'What are you doing with yourself these days? Are you dating anyone? Do you hope to be married some day?'

As much as I expected him to share his news about Johanne, he procrastinated and continued to quiz me about my love life, career and general aspirations. It became apparent that he was more interested in me than he was about conveying the news about my sister. His conduct was unusual. I became impatient with his stalling and intervened.

'Why are you here? What is the news about Johanne?' I asked him.

At that moment, Mr Stephenson professed his desire for me.

'I want to take care of you and look after you. I will send you money. You won't have to go without,' he declared.

Mr Stephenson had an air of superiority; it was as if he was an adult talking down to a child. But I was streetwise by now. He made the mistake of assuming that I was as fragile and vulnerable as Johanne. A gut feeling – call it a sixth-sense or sibling intuition – suddenly kicked in.

'Have you been interfering with my sister?' I asked him angrily.

Mr Stephenson was stunned.

'Now, you listen here,' I continued. 'If I find out you have touched Johanne in any way, I'll come find you myself and cut your fucking balls off!'

Our meeting did not end very agreeably. Mr Stephenson knew I meant business. I told him not to contact me again and left his gift on the table.

It took several decades for the truth to surface. Mr Stephenson had begun to sexually abuse Johanne within the first two weeks of her placement in foster care with the Stephensons. She was six years old at the time and the abuse continued unabated for ten years.

Johanne recollects this time:

Dad Stephenson didn't make any more advances after Pattie threatened him. He backed off completely. I did not know he saw her in Innisfail. She told me about it years later. His behaviour stopped around that same time though.

Having foster-brother Allan around me also helped end my abuse. Allan has always been there for me. He was the one who first sensed that I was being interfered with. He was concerned that if he made too much of a fuss earlier on that I would have been removed from the family and had no other place to go to.

Allan and I spoke openly about my abuse for the first time a few years ago.

'I couldn't leave home because I wanted to protect you!' he said.

During our conversation Allan explained that not long after I came to live with the Stephenson family in 1958, he walked in to find Mum Stephenson crying.

'Mum why are you crying?' he asked her.

'I think your father's fallen in love with Johanne!' Mum Stephenson said.

God, I was only a kid. Mum Stephenson must have been aware of something going on. I wondered why didn't anything happen and why Mum Stephenson didn't do anything about it. I wrote to the other Stephenson children and let them know what had happened. They were supportive. Allan has always had my best interests at heart. Out of all of the Stephenson children Pattie had the best relationship with him.

Dad Stephenson died of bowel cancer in 1981. Mum Stephenson died a few years after that.

I have been following the hearings and media coverage associated with the Royal Commission into Institutional Responses to Child Sexual Abuse. I have listened to the stories of abuse that took place at Neerkol Orphanage in Rockhampton – that could have been us too. The State Children's Department wanted to send us to Rockhampton instead of keeping us in Townsville. It's been quite upsetting hearing all the stories from Royal Commission proceedings around Australia.[100]

I was not in contact with Johanne during any of this time. Although I could not be certain that Mr Stephenson had been sexually abusing her, I knew he would be terrified at the thought of someone knowing his secret if it were true. Sunlight is the best form of disinfectant.

In 1967, Father Cassian also moved to Townsville and took up a position at St Mary's Parish Catholic Parish, West End. The Stephensons lived in the same suburb and Johanne's high school was across the road from St Mary's on Ingham Road. Such close proximity allowed Father Cassian discreet access to Johanne without the Stephensons' knowledge and he was able to counsel her. Sometimes after school Johanne walked alongside Father Cassian while he pushed his bicycle along the road and they'd talk. As Johanne turned the corner to the block on which she lived, Father Cassian continued down the main street toward town.

Yet another Divine Intervention by Father Cassian.

26

THE NAVY

Distracted by the busyness of work and life in general, I lost track of time and, in the process, the status of my naval application. After eight months' employment with the PMG, I was thrust into a quandary of indecision when I received official notification of my acceptance into the Women's Royal Australian Naval Service (WRANS). When I tendered my resignation, Mr Scheu's genuine reluctance to see me leave was such a morale boost that I was tempted to retract it. He was disappointed I was going, he said, as I could have had a rewarding career in the postal service.

I left Innisfail after a farewell party organised by the Jose family and several friends. Dad drove down from Cairns and gave me a banking bag filled with 50-cent pieces. Among his many entrepreneurial and financial interests, Dad was a coin collector and proud of his gold sovereigns and large silver coin collection.

'I didn't know what to give you. Make sure you hang on to these. One day these coins will be worth far more than their weight in silver,' he said.

Dad was right. The original round 50-cent coins were 80 per cent silver and 20 per cent copper; the modern-day dodecagonal coins are made with cupro-nickel. But I did not have the same attachment to the coins and spent Dad's gift almost straightaway on items for the Navy. I light-heartedly considered his bag of silver coins a belated part-payment for the maintenance he should have paid throughout the years.

I enlisted in the WRAN three days before my nineteenth birthday, on 18 August 1967: this was the same year as the landmark referendum held on 27 May in which Australians voted in favour of changing the Constitution to make special laws relating to Aboriginal people. The referendum was an empowering and vital precursor to increased rights and recognition for Indigenous Australians at both State and Federal levels, so for me, 1967 was a significant year on more than one front.

My call up was a bittersweet affair. Of the fifteen girls from Palm Island who originally applied, I was the only successful applicant. It was disappointing, difficult to accept that other members of my dormitory family had missed their chance. My joining the WRANS was not motivated by any sense of patriotism. Irrespective of divided loyalties to those who missed out and my own beliefs, for me it was another 'do or die' moment and I determinedly seized this break with both hands. As I saw it, the prospect of being unemployed presented the risk of a return to Palm Island whereas the WRANS offered a mandatory four-year contract. Enlisting was a no-brainer. The Navy would be my passport to economic opportunity and, seemingly, deliverance to broader horizons and a secure future.

Much later in life, I learned that Mr Bartlam played a pivotal role in my selection into the Navy by providing a personal reference. He could have easily scuttled my aspirations but noted in his correspondence to the Naval Office that, while he rarely provided references, in my case he was willing to make an exception.

With a mixture of nervous trepidation and excited anticipation, I boarded the Sunlander train at Innisfail. Still bearing the emotional scars of my initial separation from Cairns in October 1958, my thoughts were dominated by the memories of the journey my siblings and I had made together as a family aboard this same train. There were numerous opportunities for reflection in the hours during the 3000-kilometre train trek from Innisfail to Melbourne. The previous journey was made with dread and pain, but on this trip I was full of optimism and a renewed sense of authority.

Fellow WRANS recruit Cornelia 'Nellie' van Maastrigt joined me during a transit stop in Townsville. A snowball effect ensued as six other WRANS recruits embarked along the way.

—

Anyone could smell the gum leaves on me as I wandered the city streets fresh from the country. Overwhelmed by the tall skyscrapers and cityscape, I developed a sore neck from walking down Pitt Street in Sydney and looking up, down and all around. The fast-paced, modern city and the affluence of mainstream life was almost unbelievable compared with the impoverished years I'd spent in the Girls' Dormitory.

I saw a film at Sydney's majestic State Theatre, an over-sized, opulent cinema adorned with chandeliers, regal curtains and plush velvet seats. The picture screen was enormous, the characters larger than life. This experience was a stark comparison with the hot, cramped, segregated indoor hall with insufficient seating on Palm Island. Having lived in the tropics all my life, I was unacclimatised to the cooler August weather. Caught between the extremes of a hot shower and the cold outside, I had a fainting spell. A self-diagnosed haemophobic, I already felt giddy after having blood taken at the doctor's that afternoon. Nellie's care effected an immediate mateship, particularly after she found me in the bathroom wearing nothing but my birthday suit. She wrapped me in her woolly cardigan and maintained a watchful eye over me for the rest of the trip.

My time in Sydney also opened my eyes to a new standard of living. A group of us WRANS went to dinner one evening in an upscale restaurant. I was unused to eating in fancy places and equally clueless about dining etiquette that included the use of silverware. The vast array of knives and forks and other cutlery was overwhelming. There were entrée knives, steak knives, fish knives, bread knives, wine glasses, water glasses, champagne glasses, decanters, napkin rings, bread roll plates, bowls and large china dinner plates – a far cry from chipped enamel. I was utterly perplexed as to what to use first. Not wanting to alert people to my ignorance, I watched and waited, figuring to take my lead from those more sophisticated than me.

As a self-reliant, no-fuss, no-frills type of person, I felt uncomfortable when the waiter pulled the chair out for me and placed a serviette onto my lap. Not knowing what a serviette was, I blew my nose into it. Nellie nudged me disapprovingly. Just when I thought the situation could not be any more embarrassing, the waiter selected me to be the official wine taster. Unfamiliar with wine-tasting conventions, I watched attentively as he poured a tiny sample of wine into the glass.

'Is this all I am getting?' I asked disbelievingly as the other WRANS chortled.

—

It was a bleak, blustery, wind-chilled day when we arrived in Melbourne. While filming *On the Beach* (1959) with Gregory Peck, Hollywood movie legend Ava Gardner reportedly described Melbourne as 'the perfect place to make a film about the end of the world'. I felt she was overly polite in her description. Although the quote attributed to her is supposedly a myth, these words hold true.

We were transferred by bus to Her Majesty's Australian Ship (HMAS) *Cerberus* on Western Port Bay, Frankston. *Cerberus*, named after the three-headed dog in Roman and Greek mythology that guarded the gates of hell, is a naval land base for training navy personnel of all ranks. Residential accommodation on the base was segregated by sex. Men slept in one area of the base, women in another. Commissioned officers lived in their own area.

I shared a cabin with Nellie and two other WRANS from a previous intake. No doubt due to my being conditioned to institutionalised living in the Receiving Depot, Palm Island Dormitory and Blackheath College, my settling in period was an uneventful and easy process. Several of my colleagues struggled, however, in making the transition from civilian to naval life, and sometimes they looked to me for guidance and support. I considered it part of the team-building process to reciprocate the kindness Nellie had shown me.

At induction I was kitted out with my naval uniform, which included an all-weather Burberry coat, gloves, blazers, skirts, shirts, hat, stockings and shoes. Three sets of uniforms were issued: daywear, nightwear and formal wear. Unused to wearing enclosed leather shoes – my work shoes at the PMG were soft canvas Dunlops – I developed severe blisters and became a regular at sickbay. I needed crutches for several weeks when my blisters became infected.

Our induction as recruits meant participation in mandatory

parades. Unbeknown to us, senior WRANS were given authority to test the mettle of the new recruits by undertaking a mock kit muster exercise. Three senior WRANS dressed in officer uniforms led the inspection, much to our bewilderment.

The seniors were deliberately over-zealous in their inspections and made caustic comments, conduct that would not be acceptable by today's standards. Several recruits were reduced to tears by their bullying tactics. Two members of my intake eventually left the Navy as a result of this intimidation. Many of us were aghast at the proceedings, feeling especially sorry for the recruits who emotionally caved in under the barrage. In another of those 'why me?' situations, a member of the inspection team, a Leading WRAN, singled me out for attention.

'Look at the state of your shoes,' she bellowed with an inflection of disgust in her voice. 'You should be ashamed to be parading yourself in those shoes.'

I tried to restrain my anger at being ridiculed in front of the other recruits. Her belittling behaviour deflated the great deal of effort and pride I had invested into spit-polishing my shoes. Then my eyes fell upon her shoes.

'How about taking a good look at your own shoes,' I retorted. 'They are nowhere near as clean as mine. In fact, I would say they are dirty.'

You could have heard the proverbial pin drop. The other recruits were shocked I had the temerity to defend myself. It was only at the end of the parade that we realised it was a mock procedure. Upon hearing of the incident, the officer in charge of the WRANS, First Officer Barbara McLeod, counselled me in confidence. Although it was acceptable to defend myself in a forthright manner, she said, I needed to become more measured in my response to discipline.

During the six-week orientation and training period, all recruits were assessed for their suitability to undertake various duties on base. My initial classification was a Sick Bay Attendant (SBA). This did not eventuate, however, and I asked to be considered for the option of WRAN Steward or WRAN Writer classification. As a steward, I undertook domestic duties about the 'Wranery', which included general waitressing in the mess hall and kitchen servery. Nellie was also a steward; together we revelled in the work and became inseparable as we conducted our chores. It was reminiscent of working in the dormitory kitchen with Queenie Burton and with Mrs Davidson in the Home Training Centre back on Palm Island. Recruits were also offered the opportunity to enhance their skills by enrolling in education and commercial classes.

During this induction period, I unwittingly provided moments of hilarity for the other recruits. The Quarter Master Gunner, our drill instructor, regularly made an example of my ungainly coordination. When he yelled the command 'right wheel', I would invariably take the left wheel. The rest of the recruits would march off in one direction while I marched off in another.

'Recruit WRAN Janke,' he beseeched me, 'if it is your intention to join us in this war, please fall into line.'

He also corrected our deportment.

'Those recruits standing with their legs apart need to bring them to attention. Don't be afraid. I can assure you that nothing is going to drop out if you do so.'

Upon the completion of one particularly arduous drill instruction session, he presented me with a small box of chocolates for persevering.

—

After leaving Palm Island, us dormitory girls were thrust out into the world with a tremendous naïveté about sex and relationships. Fortunately, Human Relationship Education (HRE) was also a part of the Navy induction training. The course provided another steep learning curve. I had never engaged in frank and open discussion around what I considered to be a taboo topic. Recruits were educated about safe sex, and warned against promiscuity and unplanned pregnancies. The class had some dumbfounded moments as I shared my interpretation of HRE and the associated phraseology.

'Can anyone here share an experience about their knowledge of oral sex?' the educator asked.

My hand shot straight up.

'Oral sex is when people talk about sex.'

The class erupted with laughter.

A discussion about 'wet dreams' was led by a recruit who was a sex worker in Kings Cross, Sydney, before she joined the Navy; she was confident in sharing her experiences in her previous occupation. In response to one of her questions, I offered my definition of wet dreams.

'A situation wherein one awakes abruptly from sleep out of fear of wetting the bed after having had a dream about going to the toilet,' I said awkwardly.

As word of my sexual naïvety travelled throughout the base, I was besieged with dating requests, receiving unwanted attention from unsavoury characters who mistook my naïveté for loose morals. But as Winston Churchill once said: 'A lie gets halfway around the world before the truth has a chance to get its pants on.' I was unfairly branded by some on the base as fair game.

Such conduct today would be regarded as sexual harassment. Until now, I always trusted Father Cassian's advice on such matters;

however, with contact being difficult, I needed to figure matters out for myself. I recalled his advice: tongue kissing could result in pregnancy; an aspirin or a coin held firmly between my knees was the best contraceptive.

As a result of ongoing sexual harassment, I developed a complex. In one instance I received an anonymous letter with an offer guaranteeing bigger breasts in ten days. Inside was a picture of a male hand – and a giant one at that. Nellie explained the inference of the letter. I also became aware of my 'shortcomings' when I saw larger bras hanging on the clothesline and in the laundry drying room. Mine seemed like a training bra in comparison.

Channelling Mum and drawing inspiration from comediennes Phyllis Diller and Joan Rivers, I deflected any humiliating comments about my physical appearance through self-deprecating humour. I often joked that I was the only woman in the world with two backs or that you did not have to be a pirate to have a sunken chest.

Breast implants were not an option for most women in the late 1960s, so I improvised by padding my training bra with tissues – lots of tissues, at times a whole box of tissues. This practice turned out to be another form of contraception of which Father Cassian would have been proud: in the heat of the moment, the rustling of tissues and a startled query from an excited suitor generally brought any petting to an abrupt end.

I minimised my dating activities, becoming more selective with the company I kept. This self-protective strategy earned me a reputation of being frigid, a lesbian or a prude. But if I had surrendered and given in, I would have been slut-shamed. Unfortunately such double standards are still applicable today. I often recalled Father Cassian's advice about chastity and knew I had made the right decisions.

'Sexual intimacy is a serious business and should be preserved for marriage,' he once told me. 'You need to save yourself for that very special person.'

—

In discussions with my fellow recruits, I realised most of them were unaware that places like Palm Island existed.

'Where are you from?' they often enquired.

'I was removed from my family and sent to Palm Island,' I would invariably reply.

Many colleagues had a concept that Palm Island was a paradise and believed I had lived some sort of idyllic, beachcomber existence; they considered me privileged to have lived in such a place. Although I was willing to talk about my ancestry, some colleagues refused to accept it. Their perception of an Aboriginal or Torres Strait Islander was of a 'full-blood'.

The further south I ventured, the more apparent it became that many people were ignorant about Aboriginal identity and associated issues. In my experience, many people struggled to understand Aboriginal issues and had little, if any, awareness about Torres Strait Islanders. Those I met off the naval base were mostly uninterested or lacked any cross-cultural awareness. Although the 1967 Referendum had placed a spotlight on Indigenous affairs, a rights agenda was still emerging around issues such as land rights, the right to equal pay, the right to self-determination and the right to be free from discrimination. Some people were threatened by such change and believed those who supported this agenda were angry radicals.

As I grappled with my own personal challenges about belonging and identity, it was both annoying and confronting to have my assertions

My stepfather 'Uncle Kaj' Eggertsen, with his first wife Selma and daughter Judy (Copenhagen, Denmark circa 1950). Uncle Kaj abandoned his family when he moved to Australia in June 1954. *Pic courtesy of Judy Nielsen*

My official Women's Royal Australian Naval Service (WRANS) portrait circa 1967. *Pic courtesy Royal Australian Navy*

Me with a fellow Women's Royal Australian Naval Service colleague. *Pic courtesy Irene Doyle*

Me with brother-in-law Reg Hubbard and my sister Glenda, from Dad's first marriage to Emma Glendon.

The Women's Royal Australian Naval Service (WRANS)Class 96/1967. I'm in the second row, fourth from the left. *Pic courtesy Royal Australian Navy Communications Branch Association and Jennifer Beazley*

My wedding to Terry in Queanbeyan (April 1969), with Terry's younger sister and my bridesmaid, Annette.

Guests gathering outside St Raphael's Church, Queanbeyan (April 1969). No family attended my wedding.

Me visiting Mum in Port Douglas in 1970 with my first-born child and eldest daughter Nyree.

Me with my eldest brother John. I was 28 when I discovered I had an older brother from Mum's first marriage to Jack Janke.

Me with sister Johanne and my niece Carissa (Mount Isa, 1978).

A family reunion during the *National Inquiry into the Separation of Aboriginal and Torres Strait Islander Children from Their Families* community hearing in Cairns, 1996. I was reunited with my youngest sister Elin after 38 years of separation. From left, brother Terry, me, sister Johanne, brother Michael (standing), and Elin with her son Michael.

Pictured with Palm Island Dormitory residents Marie Prior and Theresa Illin (née Anderson).

Me with brother Michael and fellow Palm Island dormitory girl Olive Bonner (née Phillips).

Me with my oldest living relative, Rusty Williams (Bamaga, 2015). I visited the Torres Strait and Cape York in search of family connections.

Pattie with Terry and grandchildren; Percy, Ebony, Isabella and Ranee.
Pic courtesy Anne Hartung Photography

My portrait by Melinda Mason for the 'Serving Country' Photographic Exhibition.
Pic courtesy Belinda Mason

of Aboriginality constantly countered by comments like 'you're not much darker than me'. Such comments struck me as curious given the prevalence of people wanting a tan and roasting themselves in the sun like chickens. I never quite came to terms with this contradiction. Nor can I understand the soaring use of skin whitening and bleaching creams among some women of colour. What a mixed-up world when consumers spend billions of dollars on tanning and skin bleaching products in the desire to become another's colour!

Unsure of my place in the cultural melting pot of the Navy, and lacking the necessary confidence to withstand the inquisitorial questioning, I busied myself in work. It was an exercise in futility trying to justify my ancestry. I simply wanted to be judged for my own values and standards – for who I was. I grew weary of educating the ignorant and the misinformed about colour bars and racial separatism which, unfortunately at the time, was the lived experiences of many Aboriginal and Torres Strait Islander people both in Queensland and nationally.

In 1968, I visited HMAS *Albatross* in Nowra, NSW. *Albatross* is the largest naval establishment in Australia and the Royal Australian Navy's only air station.[101] I attended a training camp with physical training instructors (PTIs) and other athletes. Unbeknown to me, there was an undercurrent of racial tension in Nowra at the time. Accompanied by several naval colleagues, we went to a local hotel. We were all surprised by the bartender's refusal to serve me at the public bar when I asked for a shandy. No explanation was offered for the refusal. Having come from Queensland where segregation and colour bars were the norm, the attendant's refusal seemed no big deal to me. We simply took our business to another establishment where we were welcomed. I had occasion to reflect upon that incident in July 1982 when the former

Mayor of Shoalhaven Shire made headline news when he burned the Aboriginal flag.[102] In December 2014, however, while participating in the *Defending Country Workshop* at the Australia National University in Canberra, I was heartened to hear of a positive Reconciliation initiative in Nowra. Traditional owner Margaret Simoes told of the Council's support for an exhibition acknowledging Shoalhaven's Aboriginal service men and women.

Being in the Navy unwittingly provided me with an opportunity to see the singer Dame Shirley Bassey performing in concert at a dinner show and cabaret at the popular entertainment venue Chequers nightclub in Sydney. To me, her show was an extravaganza beyond compare. Breathtakingly beautiful, she dressed resplendently in a stunning array of sequined, feathered costumes – all the glam and glitz for which she is acclaimed. I saw Shirley Bassey as a role model, admiring her ability and capacity. A talented woman of mixed black and white heritage, she transcended class, sex and race restrictions, as well as personal adversity, to become one of the most successful singers in the world.

27

FOR BETTER OR FOR WORSE

After four months at HMAS *Cerebrus*, I was promoted to working in the Ward Room, which involved looking after the officers in their quarters. I enjoyed the camaraderie of working with the cooks and other support staff. I became acquainted with some of the commissioned officers, both male and female. Second Officer Jan Slosar and I, despite rules forbidding fraternisation with commissioned officers, developed a friendship. Nellie was my true friend, as was Leading WRANS Writer Stenographer (WST) Jan Cox. By now, Irene had ventured from Palm Island and relocated to Melbourne. She contacted me via Father Cassian and we continued our friendship. It was a deeper, more mature bond now than the one we had enjoyed together as dormitory girls.

As much as I was catching up with old friends and making new ones, there was little contact with Mum, Terry, Michael and Johanne. I took the approach that no news was good news. A self-appointed loner in the Navy, I was conscious of not allowing anyone to become too close to me because of the excess baggage I carried from my formative years.

I retreated behind impenetrable barricades out of a fear of suffering further loss and separation.

This changed the day I was summoned by Commodore John Dowson, the highest-ranking officer on the base, who wanted to discuss a personal matter.

'You've been a very naughty girl,' he started in a firm, fatherly manner.

The commodore had received a letter from Johanne advising that she had not heard from me. She sought his assistance in re-establishing contact after obtaining my details from Father Cassian. Johanne was sixteen or seventeen at the time. I gave the commodore an overview of my personal and family situation. Being sympathetic, he undertook to support me with my response to Johanne's letter.

Gathering a pen and some foolscap paper, he set aside a chair and writing space in his office and directed me to respond to Johanne's letter while he watched. The commodore wished me well and committed to personally sending the letter after I had placed it in an envelope marked 'Private & Confidential'. Initially I resented his involvement in what I considered to be a personal matter but, upon reflection, I appreciated his intervention. Johanne and I have maintained strong family links ever since.

—

On completion of one year's service at HMAS *Cerberus*, I was given the opportunity of a three-month temporary placement at HMAS *Harman* in Canberra. Although I didn't want to leave yet another comfort zone or my friends, I accepted the transfer. During the settling in period at *Harman*, I remained a loner, enjoying my own company and returning to reading.

In another of those serendipitous encounters, I resumed my friendship with fellow Torres Strait Islander WRANS Writer (ST) Frances 'Fran' Loban; her familiar presence made the transition easier. Fran and I had met previously at *Cerberus* as members of the WRANS tennis club. Our relationship strengthened when we reconnected during our service together at *Harman.*

Jan Cox had generously provided me with a quaint letter of introduction to Leading WRANS Writer (ST) Pam Watts, hoping Pam would help me to settle in the base. Fran and Pam were both senior staff members based at the Defence Services sector in the Russell Hill offices in Melbourne. Pam was a commodore's personal secretary, an elite position, so I was chuffed when she took a positive interest in me, given my lower ranking and classification. It was unusual for naval personnel to fraternise outside their ranks but I managed to intermingle regardless.

—

Nellie and I returned to Townsville on two weeks' furlough after our first year of service in mid-1968. We travelled in our naval uniforms, and the railway staff allocated us a sleeping compartment in a males-only carriage from Melbourne to Brisbane. What a convivial time we had playing cards and socialising with servicemen from the Air Force, Army and Navy.

I spent some of my annual leave in Townsville with the Bartlam family in Pallarenda and also visited Father Cassian, who was still resident at St Mary's Parish, West End. I caught up with my dormitory friend Theresa Anderson, who told me there was going to be a social dance where several Palm Islanders and members of the local Aboriginal community gathered. The dance was held at the Waterside

Workers–Maritime Union Hall, South Townsville. Excited at the prospect of seeing some familiar faces, I decided to attend. Mr Bartlam drove me to the venue in his conspicuous green Jaguar. Unfortunately for me – big shame and embarrassment – Mr Bartlam pulled up at the entrance right in front of curious onlookers. It was an unsettling night. People were more interested in my relationship with the Bartlams than what I'd been doing.

—

Over the next year I travelled between naval bases in Canberra and Melbourne. In October 1968, I had returned from a weekend camping trip on Pine Island Reserve and was relaxing with friends at the club on base. Social activities, including dances, were often held on base, and members of the public, known as civilians or 'civvies', came as invited guests of service personnel. We were drinking and generally enjoying ourselves, when suddenly I was left alone when others got up to dance. I noticed a man with dark, thick-framed Clark Kent-style glasses ogling me. Self-conscious, I had a flashback to my brothers' taunting rhyme: 'Men don't make passes at girls who wear glasses.' I found myself in the reverse situation: this man in glasses was making a pass at me. His name was Terry Lees and he still recalls meeting me:

> *It was 1968 on a Sunday night and I was at the Rates Club at HMAS* Harman *in Canberra with my best mate, Laurie Scutts. We had been there for a while, playing darts, pool and having a few drinks, but with the usual Sunday night dance about to start we grabbed a couple of chairs at a long table.*
>
> *While we were talking a group of WRANS, dressed in civvies, came in with some Sailors and sat at our table. One WRAN caught my eye, as she*

seated herself at the end of the table, opposite me. She was striking and I found myself staring at her, smiling at her when she looked back – which happily she did a few times. She was in a simple sleeveless dress and I can recall thinking how exotic she looked. She was beautiful, even stunning! I couldn't take my eyes from her.

I asked Laurie who she was and he, in turn, asked around before telling me she was Pattie Janke, a WRANS Steward. The decision was made – I had to meet her and I figured the best way was to ask her for a dance. But, before I could move, a big tough looking guy (Tom) who was seated with her asked her to dance and they hit the dance floor. So, I asked another WRAN for a dance and we moved close to them on the dance floor. After a few dances, we all sat at the table again. When the music started again, I did not hesitate and moved to the end of the table to ask for a dance. I was rewarded. We even got a slow dance, so I was able to hold her. She had the smell of musk – it was terrific! We talked and danced and laughed. It was great! Pattie and her group of friends had spent the weekend camping out bush and enjoyed a series of adventures, including one where she put a hot toasting fork into her mouth!!!

That was the only dance bracket I had with her that night. Tom got her up for the next bracket he was quicker than me! Then, they decided to call it a night and Tom escorted her towards the door. Well, I gathered up my courage and chased after them to ask if I could call her during the week. I wasn't sure of Tom's part in her life but I wasn't going to let the opportunity slip by me. I was ecstatic when she said 'yes'. It was a memorable night – the night I met the woman of my dreams … and I just knew that she was the ONE![103]

Being a cliquey set, my social outings and dates at that stage were usually limited to service personnel from the Navy, Army and Air Force. It was rare for WRANS to date civvies. Invariably, because of the close-knit community and confinement of personnel, many available men had previously dated other WRANS – they were either recycled or on the rebound. Terry's arrival on my dating scene offered a gentler, more interesting association; I felt emotionally safe with him in view of other disappointing experiences and my background.

Terry exuded similar qualities to Father Cassian: he was compassionate, caring and considerate. I believe these values were a consequence of his five-year training at Bowral and Mittagong, NSW, to become a Marist Brother; a bout of rheumatic fever had ended this vocational aspiration. Terry was also raised within a devout Catholic family. Three of his great-aunts were Catholic nuns, and he is related to Saint Mary McKillop through his maternal family, the Duffys.

Before we met, Terry worked for the Australian Public Service. He was employed with the Prime Minister's Department as clerk in the gazette and personnel section. The prime minister at the time was Robert Menzies, and Terry was given the task of minding Menzies' bottle of Johnny Walker Black Label whisky during the first annual Prime Minister's Christmas Party he attended. He became the first staff clerk at the newly opened Royal Australian Mint in 1965, before moving to the Superannuation and Defence Forces Retirement Benefits Boards (DFRB), where he was involved in providing pensions and compensation payouts to the employees and families affected by the HMAS *Voyager* and HMAS *Melbourne* disaster of February 1964.

Terry's experience in processing compensation claims opened the door to work in the insurance industry. He was employed with Legal & General Assurance as a salesman when we began dating but later transferred to Royal Globe Life Insurance and Tukinya Marketing, where he worked as a sales supervisor.

Terry's demeanour was a stark contrast with the largely ocker, alpha male, chauvinistic behaviour displayed by many of the servicemen, some of whom were hardened after seeing active service in war zones such as Vietnam. Terry was accepting of my Indigenous heritage that I spoke about at the beginning of our relationship. Inter-racial relationships were still uncommon at the time. Terry's first personal association with Aboriginal people occurred in 1967 during a 2200-kilometre canoe trip along the Murrumbidgee and Murray rivers. He and his mate Tony Summerville met some Aboriginal people when they camped along the river. Terry and Tony became the dual Australian and world record holders for the world's longest downstream two-man canoeing journey, a record which appeared in the *Ampol Book of Australia Sporting Records* and the *Guinness Book of World Records*.

Terry and I were compatible social companions. Neither of us was seeking a long-term relationship at the time. We lived in the moment, enjoying each other's presence. While dating, we went camping with friends and participated in bush parties known as 'smokies'. Pine Island Reserve was a favourite spot, as was Kambah, bushland back then before it became part of suburbia. Our movie outings were always preceded by dinner at the Kangaroo Club. I remember watching *Cool Hand Luke* and *Barbarella*, both now considered cult classics. I found *Barbarella* confronting, quite an eye-opener; it was soft porn in its time. I wrote Father Cassian an eight-page letter with my views and observations.

In the meantime I formed a close bond with Terry's sisters, Carol, Claire and Annette, and their partners. After six months, during which our relationship had deepened, Terry came to the realisation that he wanted me in his life and asked me to marry him. I had my misgivings about the relationship's chances of longevity because of my own damaged upbringing. I was wary of commitment, feeling vulnerable, and fearing love and rejection again. But Terry assured me he had enough love for both of us; if I was willing to take a chance, he was sure my love for him would grow. I accepted his proposal.

To prepare his parents, Claire and Percy, and the rest of his family for the news of our engagement, Terry arranged for us to meet them for dinner at the family home in Queanbeyan. Conscious of the difficulties we might encounter with her son marrying an Aboriginal woman, Terry's lovingly protective Mum expressed her concerns. She cautioned him about the difficulties associated with inter-racial marriages and the rearing of mixed-race children. Wisely, Terry advised me of his mother's comments before the visit. On our arrival at his parents' place, Terry rang the bell and his mother opened the door. A look of surprise came over her face, replaced by one of sheer relief.

'You're not quite what I expected!' she quipped.

'Well, what were you expecting?' I quipped right back. 'Somebody with a bone through their nose?'

While my jovial retort broke the initial embarrassment, it would take several years before I stopped referring to my mother-in-law as Claire and accepted her offer to call her 'Mum'.

Terry is of English and Irish heritage, so our imminent marriage would add some diversity and 'colour' to his family tree. His maternal great-grandparents – from Fermanagh in Northern Ireland, County Kildare, County Cork and Sussex, England – were settlers in Yass, NSW. His paternal ancestors migrated from Cheshire and Lancashire, England. Terry's English ancestry can be traced to 1685.

—

Although no longer a Ward of the State in Queensland, I was uncertain if I was still subject to provisions of the *State Children Act (1911)* and the Queensland *Aborigines and Torres Strait Islander's Affairs Act (1965)*. The absence of any official letter from the State or 'deed of release' when I turned eighteen added to the confusion. Terry and I took a trip to Townsville to discuss my concerns with Mr Bartlam, whom I believed was still my registered guardian. We left Canberra on the Thursday and Terry promised to have me back at HMAS *Harman* by Tuesday morning. Mr Bartlam advised there was no legal impediment to our marriage and provided his unequivocal personal blessing to our union.

While in Townsville, I visited Father Cassian, whose opinion always mattered to me:

> *When she was in the Navy, she came to me for everything, everything. And she was so naïve, even about sex or anything like that … she come to me with these questions, and people were trying to seduce her and all … She was in another world. But when she finally got engaged, or was, you know a fellow proposed to her this Terry Lees in Canberra … When he proposed to her, you know what she did? She took five days leave, or she had five days leave. She got him into the car, and they drove all the way up to Townsville where I was … it took them two days to travel up, and she wanted to show him to me, did I approve of him? And she says to this day, if I had said no I don't, she would never have married him, ever … so they had the rest of the day in Townsville and took two days to go back. And she arrived a few hours late and she was charged with being away without leave. But she says to this day, she tells me 'I would never have married him if you said no.' Gosh!*[104]

Not only was I charged for being late, I was also penalised, and had to scrub the skirting boards with a toothbrush for an entire week. I did not speak to Terry for three weeks.

—

HMAS *Penguin* at Balmoral, Sydney, became the last naval base at which I worked; I was there from December 1968 to March 1969. By that time, I had spent about half my life in institutions. I often joked with friends and colleagues that I was about to surrender to the most daunting institution of all – marriage! In April 1969, I was officially discharged from the Navy. At the time, it was Naval policy that married women could not remain in the service.

The cliché 'love is blind' became a portent for the future when Terry married me without full knowledge of my family history. I rarely mentioned my parents and siblings so he was surprised to discover they were all living in North Queensland. I had always portrayed myself as a loner because adopting that persona enabled me to protect my privacy. At times, I still struggled under the weight of my early childhood experiences in Cairns, at the Receiving Depot and on Palm Island. In many ways, I resented being caught under the well-intentioned but prying eyes of others and having to explain my 'blackground'.

Despite sending wedding invitations to family and friends – including Father Cassian, Johanne and the Bartlams – I did not expect any acceptances because of the cost and travelling distance. Although I would have welcomed their presence, I accepted the fact I would walk down the aisle alone.

Terry and I married on Easter Sunday, 6 April 1969, at St Raphael's Catholic Church in Queanbeyan. I was 20 years old and Terry almost 25. The wedding was a simple affair with about 50 guests, mainly Terry's family and friends. The ceremony itself was beautiful, memorable on account of its simplicity. I hired my wedding dress for $60. Terry's sister Annette was bridesmaid and his younger sister Julie the flower girl. Nick, a pub acquaintance of Terry's whom I barely knew, walked me down the aisle and gave me away. Terry's sister Carol hosted the wedding reception in the backyard of her spacious home in Curtin; she worked so hard to organise a memorable day for us, and I appreciated the warm, loving welcome to my new family.

Several days after our wedding, we returned to Townsville for our honeymoon, with a stopover in Brisbane to visit Michael and Johanne. The first week was spent with the Bartlams at their home in Pallarenda by the beach. There was the occasional serious round of golf with Mr Bartlam and his daughter Allison at the Rowes Bay Golf Club. I hold fond memories of sharing such a significant, special time with the Bartlams. The warmth they extended was wonderful.

Our travels took us further north to Innisfail and Cairns, where we met up with Terry, Dad and my sisters Glenda, Megsy and Emma, and were introduced to some other family members. Sometimes it was difficult to distinguish between brother Terry and husband Terry during conversations. We solved the problem by calling them 'Terry B' and 'Terry W' – Terry 'Black' and Terry 'White'. This system remains in place today.

Our final honeymoon destination was Port Douglas, where Mum and Uncle Hans were now living following the closure of Patterson's Plymill at Bloomfield River. By chance, when we arrived Mum was drinking at the Central Hotel with Uncle Hans and some other companions. I had not seen Mum, nor heard much from her, since my departure from Port Douglas in 1967 en route to Innisfail and ultimately the Navy, and I was saddened to learn from her that her dearest friends, Auntie Marie and Uncle Clarrie Swindley, had both died within two years of my 1967 visit to Bloomfield River. Uncle Clarrie died at 54 from a heart attack in August 1967, followed by Auntie Marie, 46, in January 1968, who died as a result of a chronic kidney infection. Bloomfield River was not the same without Mum's faithful buddies. But despite the sad news, it was an exuberant reunion. I was full to the brim with joy as I introduced Terry to Mum.

'So, you married a white man! Did you know that your ancestors thought so much of them, they used to eat them?' she said, eyeing Terry for his reaction.

Terry was flabbergasted by the unconventional welcome. Then, turning to everyone in the bar, Mum cheerfully exclaimed, 'Hey, everybody! This is my new son-in-law and he's going to shout the bar.'

There was raucous applause as everybody lined up for their fair share of free booze.

Another memorable highlight of our time with Mum and Uncle Hans at Port Douglas was a Saturday afternoon euchre tournament conducted at the popular Courthouse Hotel. This pub was a family-managed enterprise with Mrs Betty Whiting, the pioneering doyenne-cum-hotelier of the region. Mrs Whiting's humour was revealed when a set of dentures was found on the bar. In her endeavours to locate the owner, she posted a flyer on the hotel's noticeboard: 'Found. One set of dentures. Owner without may apply within.'

The prize for winning each euchre round was a rotisserie-cooked chicken. Terry and I were a lucky pair, winning most rounds and collecting a grand total of eleven chooks. We were crowned overall champions of the day. Mum, delighted with our skill, claimed the birds on our behalf. Alas, under the influence of one too many celebratory drinks, her generosity got the better of her. She left the hotel before us with the intention of preparing a stir-fry version of *sabi sabi* chicken. We were impatient to return to Mum's house, our appetites whetted by the thought of feasting on the exotic dish. What a let-down to arrive to a bare table and, even worse, not a single chicken in sight. Mum had given all the chickens away on the way home.

28

STARTING OVER

After spending the first few months of our married life in a small unit in Queanbeyan, Terry and I invested in a modest three-bedroom 'spec built' house on the crest of Shackleton Circuit in Mawson, a newly developed suburb of Canberra. Our house was among four others under construction at the time. The property had a sprawling backyard and the nearby O'Malley Pine Forest provided a picturesque view from the back veranda. Within five years, our family had grown from two to six, with the pitter-patter of the little feet of four children under the age of five – and seemingly endless nappy washing and general mothering chores. This was my new full-time job. I had a busy schedule, and my brother Michael was like a fifth child as he followed us whenever we relocated.

Not long after we moved into our new house, Terry opened his own insurance brokerage, Terry Lees & Associates, and rented a shared office space at the Woden Plaza with two other independent brokers.

We welcomed our first child, Nyree Justine, in November 1969; followed by Cassandra Timena in June 1971; Adam Carter in

May 1972; and Matthew Aaron in July 1974. Cassandra, or Cassie as we affectionately call her, was named in honour of Father Cassian; she also has the same birthdate as my sister Elin.

Our family GP, Dr Carter, remarked on the eleven-month gap between Cassie and Adam's births.

'Most women have a break in between,' he said. 'There is a period in which women become very fertile not long after giving birth. Husbands are meant to be considerate. You, my dear, are so fertile that if your husband hung his trousers on the corner of the bed, you would fall pregnant.'

—

The arrival of grandchildren and great-grandchildren were not only pivotal to Terry's mother's acceptance of my ancestry but also to the longevity of my marriage to her son. Her frequent proclamations that her grandchildren and I were welcome additions to the Lees family enabled me to move beyond the comments she made at the time of my engagement to Terry. I accepted that Claire's views were a product of the era in which she was raised.

A telephone call in the early 1970s between Claire and her Aunt 'Meta' further strengthened our family ties. Aunt Meta was formally known as Mother Mary Athanasius and had served as Reverend Mother Superior at the Sacred Heart School on Thursday Island between 1938 and 1940. Aunt Meta had taught my Aunt Tina at the convent school and was well acquainted with Mum through church activities. Aunt Meta spoke glowingly of both Mum and her sister. She also said Mum was highly regarded by the school staff as a conscientious student.

Like Claire, I was surprised by this coincidence, which became a bridge across our cultural and racial divides. Claire's social consciousness was also sparked over time. In the 1980s, she spent several months volunteering with the Catholic sisters at the Warmun (Turkey Creek) Aboriginal community in the Kimberley region of Western Australia.

Motherhood was a blissful time but, once again, the negativity of self-doubt intruded, and I wondered what I had done to warrant such happiness. I was determined to be the best mother, giving with full measure my children the love, security and stability that I craved and was denied during my childhood because of my removal. Unconsciously, motherhood painfully reminded me all over again of the loss and grief I'd experienced through my separation from Mum. I was anxious to make up for the lost years and spend as much time with my family and friends as possible. It was important to me that my children be lovingly bonded with the whole family. Motherhood gave me a stake in the future and I embraced the challenge to create the best possible environment for my children.

My social life was limited once I became a full-time mother. All my time was spent with the children or on household chores. I seemed to be forever washing. Often we took the children to Tidbinbilla Park and Nature Reserve, where they could feed the kangaroos and emus. I bought a playpen and put it in the living room. Some days I closed myself away inside the pen and relaxed on the beanbag while the children played outside around me. They were easy to manage. If they weren't playing on the swings, they would be running around under the sprinkler in warmer weather.

We became very family-oriented in our social activities. Claire was a huge help and gave me lifts to do the weekly grocery shopping as I've never held a driver's licence. Terry purchased a clapped-out second-hand vehicle with faulty brakes that Claire and I used as a run-around car. I usually jumped out of the vehicle at the front of the shopping centre while it was still in motion and Claire drove laps looking for a car park.

I maintained contact with Mum, Dad and the Glendons during holidays and regular trips to North Queensland. Our home became a rallying point, with a mixture of new and old friends visiting often. Father Cassian was foremost among our guests, having become an Air Force Chaplain stationed at Richmond Base in Hawkesbury, NSW.

Fran Loban used to have sleepovers and would thoroughly spoil me with her Malay–Torres Strait Island cookery. She introduced me to delicacies including *sambal*, *belacan*, bamboo shoots, dried mushrooms and *simurr* chicken, a spiced dish mixed with vermicelli noodles. Fran, like Father Cassian, was perfectly at ease sleeping on a mattress on the floor in an unfurnished bedroom. I absolutely loved her company. Fran and Nellie were surprised I had settled into domestic life so quickly. They knew me as an independent, spirited, carefree woman and wondered if marriage and motherhood might 'cramp my style'.

The Bartlams were also guests, as were Palm Islanders Rachel Cummins (née Wilson) and Francine George. Most Palm Islanders remained in contact with one another through the grapevine or common acquaintances, including Father Cassian. My brother Michael stayed with us when he was employed as a labourer with Pearson & Bridge Construction Company, working on the Tuggeranong–Western Creek tunnel. Terry's elderly grandfather, Tom Wilmott, an octogenarian, lodged with us for seven months. His placement into a nursing home hastened his demise because he fretted for company.

—

No matter how hard I tried, I could not always outrun the past. Once the bureaucracy had me firmly in its grip, it would not easily let go.

Throughout 1970, I received several curt Letters of Demand from the Queensland Department of Aboriginal & Islander Affairs seeking repayment of an outstanding debt of $20.39 ($251), which I had accrued four years earlier in September 1966.

I was initially baffled as to how the Department of Native Affairs located me in Canberra. In a manner much like the 'Tell-a-Murri' network, the Department contacted the Townsville Court House, whose clerks contacted the Cairns police. The Cairns police contacted the Innisfail Court House, who referred them to Mrs Buller, a family friend and neighbour in Innisfail. She informed them that I had joined the Australian Navy.

I'd neglected to repay the Department for an advance I received while still on Palm Island for the purchase of a new dress, a pair of shoes, my train fare and some Kodak film when I was employed in the Palm Island Main Office. The Department erred in its calculations. My tally of the receipts they provided totalled $20.19, a 20c difference. I forwarded a cheque less the 20 cents and a covering letter explaining their error.

Thirteen months later, in September 1971, I received another letter seeking recovery of the 20 cents ($2.12), followed by a further reminder in January 1972. The Department insisted the 20-cent debt be repaid in stamps or cash. I later learned the Department actively pursued Michael in a similar manner for six years between 1966 and 1972 for a $5.44 ($66.90) debt.

—

In a clear separation of roles, Terry became the sole breadwinner and manager of our household finances. I played my role conscientiously as a dutiful housewife and devoted full-time mother. In those days, finances were not seen as a woman's domain, save for the glamorous secretaries many highflying executives surrounded themselves with. I often chided Terry about the constant praise he lavished upon his company's attractive secretary. Ingrid was tall, blonde, leggy and buxom. By comparison, I felt inferior. Ingrid's reminders to Terry about business were attributed to her 'efficiency', while my reminders about domestic chores, including taking out the rubbish, were considered nagging.

But I considered it a privilege to be a full-time mother without having to place the children into day care. Terry, meanwhile, assumed control of our financial matters. Essentially, I was relegated to the role of a silent partner in every aspect of his professional life and business affairs. Unaware of our pending financial collapse, family life continued as normal.

Unbeknown to me at the time, Terry's insurance brokerage was struggling. He found it difficult to make sales because of the difficult economic conditions at the time. People did not seem to favour buying insurance from the newer, smaller brokers, preferring the larger firms. As is standard with commission-based income, no sales mean no dollars. It got to the point where Terry was spending more than he earned while keeping up appearances that it was business as usual.

In late 1974 came an announcement that caught me by surprise but excited the children; Terry informed me that he was sending the children and me to Cairns for a holiday. At the time, Nyree was five, Cassie three, Adam two and Matthew a newborn. We had been married for about five years. I had no reason to assume there was a problem.

Several weeks later in the midst of enjoying our holiday and catching up with family and friends in Cairns, the exhilarating mood was shattered by a phone call. Terry's nervous monotone voice conveyed the bad news: we could not return to Canberra just yet. He was trying to settle some unforeseen business problems, he said, and reassured me he would join us in Cairns once he had sorted everything out.

I did not return to Canberra for at least five years, maybe ten. We lost everything when Terry's business collapsed. Our financial ruin resulted in catastrophic upheaval. While I was in Cairns, the bank foreclosed on our home; I was unaware it was happening. Terry was also forced to sell the contents of our home and dispose of other assets to finalise the debt. All that remained of my life in Canberra were the contents of the suitcases I'd taken on holiday and some precious family photos and other treasured belongings Terry had salvaged.

The news came as a shock but I could not entertain the luxury of just giving up. The very real fear of a welfare intervention simply made that 'non-negotiable'. I cloaked my little ones in love and affection, and at the earliest opportunity enlisted the support of family and friends as I tried to keep the routine of family life as normal as possible and find a roof over our heads. There was certainly nothing in our lifestyle that I considered to be lavish. We lived simply and frugally.

The disaster could not have happened at a worse time. Nyree was enrolled in her first year of school and Matthew was, at that stage, experiencing periods of hospitalisation with an undiagnosed medical condition. Our relationship with some of Terry's family was also tested after they lost a significant amount of money on an insurance policy that he had promoted. Although we were not declared bankrupt, we would have been had it not been for the support of family and friends.

It was disheartening many years later when we returned to Canberra for a visit and decided to drive past our old home in Shackleton Circuit. By chance, on that trip I bumped into our former neighbour, Margaret Wright, who was overcome with emotion when she saw me at Woden

Valley Shopping Centre. She'd wondered what had happened to us. Our departure and disappearance was so sudden that she genuinely believed we had been taken into a Witness Protection Program.

A dispirited Terry eventually joined us in Cairns. Being unemployed, he became deeply depressed. Family and friends rallied, providing us with unconditional personal and financial support, and we began the slow and painful process of rebuilding our lives. Terry could not readily find work, unfortunately, and struggled to regain his confidence. His pride would not allow him to register for unemployment benefits. Father Cassian became an unlikely benefactor, providing money from his own chaplaincy stipend, which assisted with car repayments. Father Cassian believed it was important to have a car to find work.

'The Lord will provide and "she" seems to work in mysterious ways,' was one of his well-known sayings.

Understanding our dire situation, Glenda and her husband, Reg, offered practical support. I accepted casual work at their booming small business, Hubbard's Corner Store. Working there enhanced family ties as my sister Megsy and Dad also worked at the store. The Hubbard offspring, 'Little Reggie', Russell and Jeanie, helped out with babysitting and took the children swimming and on picnics.

The support extended by Megsy and her partner, Joe Byers, was phenomenal in the light of their own 'struggle street' trials and tribulations. Their unconditional hospitality was most humbly received. She and partner Joe put on a sumptuous Christmas lunch and shared what little they had by inviting us for meals from time to time. We would reminisce over family history and folklore.

Our family stayed in a basic, self-contained apartment at the Cairns Hollywood Inn. It was a difficult time, and an exhausting one, motivating Terry to apply for work. His recovery from the loss of face and dramatic downward spiral was slow. Gone were the trappings enjoyed in his pursuit of the entrepreneurial life. It took him over twelve months to find his feet and a new direction. Securing intermittent work with real estate firm LJ Hooker, and compiling a weekly rugby league magazine and doing other printing jobs, gradually restored his confidence and helped him to recover from depression.

Our overall family wellbeing improved significantly when Terry secured full-time employment with Carlton & United Breweries (CUB) as a marketing executive based at the Cairns Brewery. It was a well-paid, coveted role. I considered it redemptive for his past professional and business failings. The job benefits included an accommodation allowance, a fully maintained motor vehicle and an incentive bonus, in addition to the practice where the company would provide all employees with a free glass of beer at lunchtime every day. The job involved frequent travel on a six-week cycle; Terry would spend one week at home working in the Cairns area, two weeks away south to Townsville and Mackay, and then go out west to Camooweal and Mount Isa.

One of the ironies of Terry's employment in the alcohol industry was the devastating impact alcohol had wrought in Mum's life as well as mine. But this job became my family's salvation and our chance at a new beginning.

29

A CHANCE ENCOUNTER

In 1976 when I was 28, another moment of serendipity presented itself when I discovered I had an older brother, John, from Mum's first marriage to Jack Janke. The revelation occurred when I was asked to provide identification to collect a registered parcel at the Cairns Post Office. Postal officer Mr Gary Maltby questioned me when he saw my maiden name on my official documentation.

'Do you have any family in Cairns? We have a Janke, a John Janke, working in the back room. Are you related to him?' he asked.

'Not that I am aware,' I said.

Gary returned to the back room and signalled for John to come and introduce himself. Understandably, it was awkward as we stood staring at each other. But the brief discussion between us provoked a curiosity that needed to be satisfied. We arranged to meet up at the Hollywood Inn after John finished work.

I soon established that John was my older brother from Mum's first marriage to Jack Janke. Born in 1943, John was raised by the Jankes after Mum walked out in the mid-1940s. Eventually Jack re-married after his divorce from Mum and had two more children. Jack had died from cancer in December 1961, aged 44. By the time we met, John was married and had a family of his own, including three children.

Although we were unable to develop the strong bonds that are forged by growing up together and having an early association, I still consider John and his family an important part of my life. I recall telling Terry about our meeting and that I'd felt an instant sense of attachment. Perhaps it had something to do with reaching out, yearning to know more about each other. In any case, with our immediate connection established, we steadily bonded. Initially we were inseparable in the impatience of getting to know each other better. I wanted to introduce news of Mum to gauge his feelings about meeting her, but for a long time it was a 'softly-softly' situation.

—

Our relocation to Cairns enabled ongoing contact with Mum and Uncle Hans, and we visited one another in Cairns and in Port Douglas. Mum's dog, Leo, often accompanied them. We shared Christmas festivities together and Mum doted on her grandchildren. I also took Father Cassian to meet Mum. As ridiculous as it sounds, he was surprised that Mum was so dark and yet I was so fair.

With these regular visits, over time I noticed a change in Mum. Her speech became slower and memory lapses peppered her quick, spiky wit and wordy brilliance. I still play 'pick a moment' recollecting that extraordinary time. I recall alighting from the bus on a visit to Port Douglas. It was Australia Day weekend, and I was dressed for the occasion in brightly coloured shorts adorned with an Australian flag design and an equally vibrant shirt.

'My Patsy. Such an ostentatious display of patriotism!' Mum declared.

While I knew that a stamp of approval had been given, I was clueless about the actual meaning of her words. Back in Cairns, I went to a bookstore, found a dictionary and deciphered what she'd said. Depending on the occasion, the audience or the conversation, Mum would often politely – or impolitely – surprise people with her off-the-cuff remarks. When queried about her birthplace or country of origin, she would invariably remind people that her ancestors were there to meet and greet the First Fleet. Taking a leaf out of Mum's book, whenever I'm asked the same question, my response is that 'one part of my mob were there to meet the other part of my other mob'.

With the passage of time, the alcoholism impacted on Mum's mental, emotional and physical health. She quickly deteriorated but rejected the seriousness of her situation, refusing to seek medical help, saying she was 'allergic to doctors'. Her continued decline meant supporting Uncle Hans in his caring for Mum. He was in casual employment at that time, undertaking carpentry, and boatbuilding and repair, which thankfully enabled him to monitor Mum's escapades to the pub. Conscious of time slipping away and with it Mum's cognitive capacity, I made it a priority to attend to any unfinished business of family reconciliation, restoration and forgiveness.

I accompanied Michael on his reunion with Mum. His last memory of her was a fleeting glance of her standing outside Central State School in Townsville in 1959. He was seven years old. Michael grappled with last-minute indecision about seeing Mum, and the reunion occurred amid high expectations and much tension. The conversation was stilted at times, and Michael was disappointed that Mum could not remember much. The door to the relationship he and Mum once had was now permanently closed. Only remnants of blurred memories remained. Mum's recollections were so impaired by her memory loss

I became the bridge for them, encouraging the conversation with 'remember when' questions.

Understandably, Michael considered me his mother figure. He could not relate to Mum. Perhaps he hoped for a warmer, more loving response, some recognition that Mum no longer had the capacity to provide. I was grateful that Michael had no memory of Mum's former beauty and vivaciousness. There was little trace left of the person she once was. If it is indeed true that 'people grow old on the battlefield of grief', this was true in Mum's case. Being a mother myself by now, I could empathise with the horrendous emptiness that would have accompanied the separation not from one child but all six. It was a difficult time for Michael. The woman standing before him was his mother but in many ways a total stranger.

Some time after this, I facilitated a reunion between John, his family and Mum. By this stage, Mum had moved again with Uncle Hans to Mossman to be closer to improved medical facilities. Johanne also travelled from Brisbane to meet Mum for the first time, a reunion that still evokes many raw memories for her:

> *I was with Terry and his wife Dalveen when we met Mum again after all those years of separation. It was a very emotional moment when I saw her under the tree. We hugged each other after all those years. She kept on saying 'my baby, my baby' as she hugged me. It was heart wrenching but also very heartening to be reunited with her.*[105]

—

Our near bankruptcy and time in Cairns offered many lessons in gratitude. Although we lost material wealth, including our home and a productive business, we gained so much more in the ways our family and friends came together to support us during this difficult time. Before leaving Canberra, our youngest child, Matthew, had a series of inexplicable bone fractures including of his thigh bone (femur), shinbone and outer ankle area (tibia and fibula). These breaks became more frequent after we moved to Cairns. Not even one year old at the time, Matthew was often hospitalised for up to six weeks, particularly when his fractured femur required traction. His periods of isolation from our family compounded an already traumatic situation. It was an all-round awful time, with Terry travelling for work and there being no public transport where we lived on the outskirts of Cairns.

By the time Matthew was five years old, he had already sustained 23 fractures to various parts of his body. Unfortunately, the general practitioners in Canberra failed to diagnose his illness earlier, his broken bones often arousing suspicion that Matthew was an abused and neglected child. The congenital birthmarks on Matthew's body, known as 'Mongolian spots' (bluish coloured congenital birthmarks common among Asian, Oceanic, Caribbean, Latin American and Indigenous children in Australia), were also mistaken for bruises by ignorant of medical staff. Because of their concerns, the Canberra Hospital reported the matter to the police. Following up on the report, a police officer visited Terry and me and questioned us about Matthew's care at home. While they found no evidence that his injuries were inflicted as a result of abuse, the suspicions caused tremendous anxiety.

Matthew's illness added another layer of stress to our existing woes, but fortuitously, the move to Cairns resulted in him receiving the correct diagnosis and treatment for his condition, a genetic disorder known as Osteogenesis Imperfecta (OI), characterised by bones that break easily. The problems associated with obtaining a correct diagnosis further highlighted the disadvantages which stemmed from my early separation from family; I had no knowledge of family medical history. There was no indication of osteogenesis on Dad's side, and Mum's diminished cognisance meant she was unable to provide any information.

We concentrated our energies on ensuring Matthew was able to enjoy a quality standard of life despite his impediment. We considered it just another challenge to be surmounted, which galvanised our family. When Father Cassian told us that the name 'Matthew' signified 'gift from God', we strengthened our resolve.

'Adversity is like fruit. God does not let it grow on trees too weak to bear it,' he said.

Rallying around Matthew's condition was the making of our family, a clear reminder about the important things in life. Though it was a case of history repeating itself when Matthew's fourth child and youngest daughter, Ebony, was also diagnosed with OI. Because she too had 'Mongolian spots', the family were subjected to the same sort of inquisition we had experienced so many years earlier. Thankfully, that experience enabled me to educate local medical staff and child safety officers about the condition.

Having weathered these misfortunes, Terry gave me the nickname of 'The Admiral' in recognition of my leadership and stoicism. It seems I was born to be both a warrior and a worrier. I had no option but to take charge. It was not the first time I had been confronted and overcome a situation of apparently insurmountable odds.

—

In 1976, Terry was promoted to the role of Area Manager with Cummins & Campbell, a subsidiary of Carlton & United Breweries. The position was based in the remote mining town of Mount Isa, some 1200 kilometres inland from Cairns. I was reluctant to move for several reasons:

we were still recovering from the previous family upheaval; I dreaded the thought of starting a new life without supportive family networks; lifestyle considerations, including education prospects for the children, were also a concern. As I had never been further west than Charters Towers, which I already saw as remote and desolate, Mount Isa, by comparison, seemed like a virtual wilderness. With high hopes and heavy hearts, we bundled ourselves, our few possessions and a dog named Gemma into a brown Holden Kingswood wagon and drove west.

The benevolence shown by Carlton & United Breweries allowed for a comfortable transition period, and we received a warm welcome in Mount Isa. The country hospitality and generosity displayed within the local community was the clincher in my decision to stay. It was an eighteen-month transfer. Like most long-term residents, we resolved to go back to the coast. But that was nearly 40 years ago.

In Mount Isa, I reunited with former Palm Islanders Auntie Iris and Uncle Fred Clay and their large family. The Commonwealth Department of Aboriginal Affairs (DAA) employed Uncle Fred as a project officer. Auntie Iris became the first female board member of the then powerful Aboriginal Hostels Limited (AHL) and was also a prominent activist in the national Aboriginal Affairs movement. Receiving both national and international recognition for her achievements, she was held in high esteem by people from all walks of life. Moreover, she was a revered figure and role model within her home region of North Queensland. A large hostel in Townsville was later named in her honour.

Terry began to build a community profile in Mount Isa through his work as a volunteer presenter and host for a popular weekly television program, *Sports Time*, aired on television network ITQ8. He began reporting on the Mount Isa rugby league fixture before being offered his own television program with a half-hour slot on Friday nights. *Sports Time* ran for seven years and 379 episodes. Becoming a well-known local identity, he was also actively involved in the local Mount Isa Rodeo and Rotary International, where he eventually became a District Governor. Terry's television career also served as an entry point for a thirteen-year role as General Manager of the local radio station 4LM.

—

With daughters Nyree and Cassie enrolled in school, in April 1977 I made my first return visit to Palm Island. Auntie Mona Wyles and Auntie Ivy Sam sent word for me to visit. As much as I was happy to rekindle old friendships and renew acquaintances, my trip was overshadowed by the all-round changes on Palm Island. Things had deteriorated significantly in the decade since my departure. I noticed the same impoverished conditions but people's sense of pride and spirit also seemed diminished. The once immaculately maintained houses, streets and public areas were dilapidated. Alcohol restrictions had been eased on the island in 1971, resulting in a sharp rise in alcohol-related offences. Sexual assaults and domestic violence incidents also surged. Public drunkenness and gambling was all-pervasive.

Palm Island experienced a major influx of new residents when the permit and access restrictions to the island were lifted in the early 1970s. The infrastructure, including the town water supply that was built to sustain a population of 1300 residents, struggled to keep pace with a near doubling of the population. Houses became overcrowded. With an absence of any sustainable livelihoods or business opportunities, unemployment and welfare dependency became chronic, killing any drive and initiative among the residents. The only benefit derived from being spoon-fed is that one learns the shape of the spoon.

Palm Island's 'liberation', wrought by the new freedoms and greater Commonwealth Government intervention following the 1967 Referendum, came with a heavy price. The power plays and tussles between the Queensland and Commonwealth Governments led to the Federal Government passing the *Aboriginal and Torres Strait Islander (Queensland Reserves and Communities Self-Management) Act (1978)*, which was designed to prevent the State assuming control of Aboriginal Settlements in favour of steps toward self-management.[106]

The rapid shift from a controlled environment to a *laissez-faire* situation proved disastrous. The State Government had controlled every aspect of the residents' lives for the greater part of the twentieth century. Now, suddenly, the islanders were free to manage their own affairs but lacked the skills, capacity and experience to govern effectively. There was no transition plan. The State's gradual disengagement and 'decolonisation' created a power vacuum. Many of the white staff disappeared when the Settlement management structure was abolished. The Palm Island Aboriginal Council was wracked with instability, divisive infighting and poor financial practices.

Since then, Palm Island has been catapulted into the national and global media spotlight following its entry into the 1999 *Guinness Book of World Records* as the most dangerous place on the planet outside of a combat zone.

30

HEAVEN'S CLOAKROOM

Within weeks of my return to Mount Isa, Uncle Hans telephoned to tell me that Mum had been hospitalised in Mossman for several days. He did not know the exact nature of her illness, but said that after her discharge from hospital he would not be able to provide the constant care she required. He was at a loss as to what was best for both of them, but needed to keep working.

Mum, in her lucid moments, was resistant to leaving Uncle Hans. She wanted to stay on the coast rather than resettle in an unfamiliar environment. Having never ventured inland and living by the coast or on an island all her life, she envisaged Mount Isa as some horse-and-buggy town with dusty roads. There was also her aversion to flying, having never travelled by plane. If all that was not enough disincentive, she also knew I was not too keen on her drinking, being a teetotaller myself, and a boring one at that. Mum much preferred to be around her drinking buddies, and staying with me represented a vastly restricted lifestyle. It was a cruel dilemma, one that pitted quality of life considerations against prolonging her life but with the imposition of limitations and the curtailing of her freedoms.

Eileen offered to care for Mum at her home. It seemed that a love for Dad was not the only thing Eileen and Mum had in common. Mum cheered up immeasurably when Eileen spoke about plans to take her fishing and crabbing once she settled. I was happy that Mum wanted to be with Eileen; I believed she'd be happier in the company of someone with whom she shared many memories, their shenanigans with Dad foremost among them.

The arrangement lasted several months. A combination of factors caused Eileen to make the painstakingly emotional decision to surrender Mum to my care. Her husband, Peter, became ill, and Eileen also had her own medical issues that required careful self-management. Caring for two sick people as well as herself took its toll.

Glenda told me that Eileen wept uncontrollably when she said her final farewell to Mum, although at the time, Mum did not have the clarity of thought to realise what was happening. She smiled blankly as Eileen left her with Glenda. Uncle Hans had already said his final farewells to Mum when she was relinquished to Eileen's care. And although Dad knew of Mum's illness through Glenda, there was no communication from him.

I arrived in Cairns in May 1977 to prepare for Mum to accompany me home to Mount Isa. Mum offered little resistance to staying with me. It did not seem to matter any longer about unfamiliar territory and travel by plane. Her previous protestations were diluted by the sudden onset of an undiagnosed illness. It was as though she was physically present, yet her frailty and vagueness were such it seems she was retreating to a place beyond reach. I readied myself by adopting my 'Little Big Girl' persona, resolving to nurse and care for her and surround her with all the love she grew in me so long ago.

I was grateful for Glenda's company and kindness when Mum and

I checked into Tuna Lodge in Cairns to rest before flying to Mount Isa the next day. Glenda had taken Mum to the doctor to obtain a travel clearance for her to fly. After feeding and bathing Mum with Glenda's help, we tucked her into bed. She looked so weak as I cuddled in beside her.

Stroking her reassuringly, I whispered, 'Don't worry, Mum; it's going to be all right. I am here with you. I love you dearly.'

When I awoke the next morning, I was sucking my thumb.

Mum travelled to Mount Isa with very little other than two beige suitcases full of clothes, some personal papers and an old grey Commonwealth Bank book with a $1 bank balance.

'Grandma Aggie', as my four children lovingly called her, occupied one of the rooms in our three-bedroom rented house in Buna Street. To make space for Mum, the children bedded down in two bunks in another room.

In Mum's room was a lounge chair, where I would sit, and a beanbag for our now pregnant bitch, Gemma. In her lucid moments, Mum became excited about having Gemma in her room and I can still recall the look of delight beaming through Mum's eyes and across her face. Often I would leave the door ajar so that she could hear the kids running through the house or playing outside. Sometimes the children took in her meals.

Gemma brought Mum a tremendous amount of joy and companionship during the long, listless days when she was too weak to move. She was so happy when Gemma's pups came into the world. Meanwhile, we made Mum as comfortable as possible, providing home-based full-time care as she increasingly struggled to walk and eat.

Uncertain about the exact nature of Mum's illness, Terry and I took her to the Mount Isa Base Hospital for a health assessment and medical diagnosis. We also wanted to ensure there was nothing lacking in our provision of care for her. Mum suffered from hypertension for which she was already medicated. A young, officious doctor referred to his notes and told Terry and me that Mum was an alcoholic. He immediately concluded from her symptoms that this was the cause of her illness and general state of health. He conducted a few routine baseline assessments including blood pressure, ear, nose and throat examination, and a pulse check.

'She is clearly suffering from years of neglect and alcohol abuse. Take her home and try to have her look after herself as much as possible. Don't do too much for her. She needs to do things for herself,' he advised.

Unfortunately, in those days, patients and their families were not confident enough to challenge a doctor's medical advice or seek a second opinion.

Doctors' diagnoses were always considered to be correct. There was no recognition that Mum, on account of her failing health, was in the best state of sobriety she had been in for almost 30 years. Terry and I walked out with little more than a pack of aspirin and some Coloxyl tablets to relieve her constipation.

It was a constant challenge caring for Mum, a round-the-clock family effort. On one occasion she went missing from home late evening during heavy rain and torrential flooding. In her delirium, she just disappeared. Wading semi-naked through gushing waist-high water, she wandered several kilometres across the Leichhardt River to Elveena and Laurie Munn's place: Elveena is the sister of my lifelong friend and fellow Girls' Dormitory resident Theresa Anderson.

In yet another miracle, Elveena took Mum around to former Palm Island resident Eric Kyle's house in the hope of establishing Mum's identity. We were gratefully reunited with her in the early hours of the morning when Eric recalled meeting her through me.

My brother Keron (Kingy) also visited Mum in her final weeks; he was running an insurance assessment business in Mount Isa at the time. Kingy was shocked to see her in such an incoherent state.

—

Shortly after Christmas 1977, Mum was admitted to the Mount Isa Base Hospital after experiencing breathing difficulties. She remained undiagnosed. Terry and the children visited her nightly. I maintained a constant vigil as she slowly succumbed to her illness. Moments before her passing, Mum opened her eyes, tried to raise her head from the pillow and stared expectantly towards the door as if a visitor had arrived.

'Is that you, KP?' she asked, before lapsing into unconsciousness.

KP was one of Dad's nicknames, short for Keron Patrick. Even in her final moments, Mum carried a flame for Dad, perhaps believing that he had come to visit her on her deathbed. While I was the only one by her side when she passed, I cannot discount that she did have a vision.

Mum died on New Year's Eve 1977 although her death certificate states she died on 1 January 1978, aged 57. Mum's death was a painful and difficult chapter in my life. Although I came to terms with her passing, I mourned the circumstances under which she died. If it can be so said, she deserved a better death.

Following Mum's death, I had a physical confrontation with the young, officious doctor. The autopsy showed Mum was riddled with cancer that had spread from the carcinoma on her lip to her brain and throughout her body. The fact the doctor told us she was dying as result of years of alcohol abuse, and our acting in good faith by trusting his assessment, made me angry. Seemingly his 'diagnosis' was based purely on racial stereotype and apathy. It became apparent that his treatment of many local homeless, alcohol-addicted Aboriginals known as 'riverbed people' (similar in profile to the 'long-grass' people of the Northern Territory) had influenced his judgment; in providing a blanket diagnosis, he took one look at Mum and claimed her illness to be alcohol-related.

Although Mum was terminally ill, the correct diagnosis would have preserved her dignity, provided our family with a better understanding of her behaviour and allowed for better palliative care so she was in less physical pain during her final stages: aspirin and Coloxyl drops did nothing. The misdiagnosis resulted in her not being given the right pain management and medication. At times her suffering was so distressing I gave serious thought to suffocating her with a pillow to put an end to it.

It is often said 'the candle that burns twice as bright burns half as long'. The tragedy of Mum's life was such. She was a brilliant and talented woman but few of her dreams were fully realised. I equate the circumstances of Mum's life with the lives of Hollywood's reclusive starlets Rita Hayworth, Judy Garland and Ava Gardner, each of whom died all used up. Like Mum, they too deserved a gentler passing. There is much to be said about the dual face of joy and sorrow, wherein our greatest joy corresponds with our greatest sorrow. In my case, the grief of being separated from Mum at a young age, finding her ten years before in 1967, then to have her taken so prematurely seem unjustifiably cruel.

Mum's death was not a simple matter of 'Rest in Peace'. I was left to deal with angry sons who never forgave her for their perceived abandonment. They blamed her for being a bad mother and for their misfortunes in life. At a time when compassion and respect should have been exercised, their judgmental pronunciations came to the fore. For me, this cast another cloud over her death.

Mum's funeral was a quiet affair with no more than eight people in attendance. Uncle Hans did not travel out from Cairns to attend, having already said his final farewells when she left Cairns. Brother Terry, his wife, Dalveen, and infant son, Brock; Johanne and her new husband, Eddie; and Michael all travelled to Mount Isa from Brisbane.

Michael said, 'My mate Joe said the worst thing that could ever happen to any woman, black or white, was to have her children taken from her. I wept silent, bitter tears at my mother's funeral. I wept for us five children. I wept for the mother I never knew. I wept for the question that I never had the courage to ask her when she was alive: "Did you ever love me, even just a little in the short time we had together?" I'll never know.'

I found it hard to understand why, knowing that Mum was dying for six months, they travelled at great expense from all around the state to attend her funeral. I took exception to the fact nobody travelled to see her in her final months when she was alive. But perhaps their presence gave her some peace before she departed from us forever.

'Don't you think it is better to receive one rose when you are alive than a thousand when you are dead?' I asked them.

'We didn't come here to see her; we came to comfort you because we know that you still loved her,' Terry said.

And that I surely did. I was her Little Big Girl.

Being true to form, Dad was a no-show. There was no communication from him whatsoever. I was surprised how little that mattered to me. At the time, I was too tired to be judgmental. Years later I was incensed to learn from Glenda that Dad had claimed to have paid the full costs of Mum's funeral. In fact, I was livid. Terry and I, barely able to afford the burial costs, were obliged to do the honourable thing in ensuring that Mum was laid to rest in a respectful manner. We were still recovering financially, and Terry took holidays and leave loading to pay for funeral expenses. Dad did not contribute one cent.

I received a beautiful letter from Emma expressing her deepest sympathy and describing Mum as a remarkable woman. In her words, 'Aggie saved my life'. Emma closed the letter by expressing her love for Mum. She said she never held any ill will against her because of her relationship with Dad.

A notice was placed in the *Cairns Post* advising of Mum's passing in Mount Isa. It identified Uncle Hans as being Mum's loving companion of almost fifteen years. Dad, outraged, phoned me, quizzing me as to why Hans was mentioned in the newspaper but he was not. Simply put, Uncle Hans loved Mum. His devotion to her continued beyond her death as he wired money from his pension with a request to place flowers on Mum's grave on special occasions such as Mother's Day.

After Mum's death, Terry and I focussed on raising our family although Mum's absence left a huge void in my life. Michael moved to Mount Isa, where he was employed at Mount Isa Mines, doing an assortment of jobs around town. Eric Kyle, through his own activism, enticed me to develop a black consciousness and awareness of Indigenous social injustice. As a consequence, in 1981, I became actively involved with the Aboriginal Legal Service in Mount Isa. In 1983, I became an active member of Injilinji Aboriginal and Torres Strait Islanders Corporation for Children and Youth Services and the Aboriginal and Torres Strait Islanders Corporation for Welfare Services. I think Mum would have been proud of me.

31

DEATH AND DISCOVERY

The year 1984 was one of mixed blessings, hardships and revelations. When Johanne became aware of Aboriginal families being reunited with other members who had become separated at birth or as infants, she began to wonder about Elin. A series of 'what ifs' pervaded her thoughts. What if she were still alive? What if she'd been adopted out? What if she was living somewhere nearby and we didn't know? I admired Johanne's tenacity, yet remained neutral, concerned she would be frustrated by bureaucratic red tape and dredge up the trauma of our childhood separation. I preferred to let sleeping dogs lie.

Several months later, however, Johanne phoned me. Elin was alive! The discovery rocked our worlds. We believed that she had died 26 years ago in 1958, but she was alive and had been living with Mrs Beatrice 'Maud' Peel, a woman of Malay ancestry. Mrs Peel was 66 years old at the time of Elin's foster placement and suffered from consistently poor health until her passing in 1975. In a strange coincidence, Elin lived in the same house as a young woman whom Terry briefly dated. Terry still marvels at the missed opportunity. Over Christmas 1984, Terry and Johanne reunited with Elin, 26 years after our separation. Johanne recollects finding Elin:

> *I wrote a letter and decided to see if I could get some help. I wrote to a lady named Mary Graham who helped families reunite with adopted and fostered relatives. She was the one who contacted me through the Queensland Department of Community Services. She said they had located Elin who had been fostered by Mrs Peel and her name had been changed to Susie. We had a phone call. She lived in Sydney at that time. They gave me a run down of what had happened to her. She was brought up in Innisfail and would have been up there the same time as Terry, Pattie and Michael. Terry was dating one of her stepsisters Priscilla. Terry used to see Elin and did not connect that is was her because she looks so different from all of us. We were so close and yet so far. I spoke to her on the phone. She came up to Brisbane and we reunited. She visited twice and we spent time together.*[107]

I was reunited with Elin the following year, in 1985. It was 27 years since I'd last seen her. When Michael and Elin finally reunited in 1997, 35 years had passed since our baby sister was taken to the hospital and we'd been admitted to the Children's Depot. How sad it was that day back in October 1958 when Mum cradled Elin in her arms on the platform at the Cairns Central Station, not knowing that it would be the last time they'd be together. Unlike John, Terry, Michael, Johanne and I, Elin never had the chance to know her mother.

Our joy upon being reunited with Elin was tinged with great sorrow upon hearing the news of Emma's death in August 1984. Then Granddad Victor also passed away, in November 1984 in Katherine, Northern Territory, aged 83 years. I learned of his passing through Mrs Vi Dowman, a Torres Strait Islander who lived in Mount Isa.

Vi's late husband served with Granddad Victor during the War. I was bewildered by the news, having assumed he died many years before. Granddad Victor's passing was another raw reminder of our separation: I had passed through Katherine on a road trip less than two years earlier. Now Granddad made his final return to Queensland and to our ancestral land when he was repatriated from the Northern Territory and interred at Old Injinoo.

—

That same year, Uncle Hans was diagnosed with an incurable type of bowel cancer. Offloading his few worldly possessions in Port Douglas, including his yacht the *Miss Pat*, Uncle Hans shifted to Mount Isa to be with me. It was his wish to be among family during his final days. We were able to care for Uncle Hans at home due to the compassionate palliative support and tremendous care provided by the Mount Isa Blue Nurses (Blue Care) during their weekly visits.

Uncle Hans's health deteriorated steadily over his last eight months. Despite his discomfort and pain, he never complained once, often sitting silently at the dining table in his green plaid breakfast coat and moccasins, completing crossword puzzles and reading the newspapers. Being a yachtie, he enjoyed watching the Sydney to Hobart Yacht Race on the TV. Sometimes Uncle Hans reminisced, becoming sentimental about the old days with Mum, his adventures at sea and stories of his early life in Denmark. Unbeknown to us, Uncle Hans often invited members of the Seventh Day Adventist Church (SDA) and the Church of Latter Day Saints (LDS) into our home while we were out. He cheerfully granted them an audience over cups of tea and biscuits as they proselytised. But Uncle Hans, a devout agnostic, was not easily swayed.

During the last week of his life, Uncle Hans was hospitalised for palliative care. In stark contrast with Mum's situation, he received a high standard of care and pain management. During his final days, Michael, Terry, Glenda and a family friend, Val McGill, were also by his bedside. By coincidence, Michael met a Danish father and his son one night while drinking at a local pub. We accepted their generous offer to visit Uncle Hans in hospital after they learned of his illness. Although Uncle Hans was too ill to drink the beer Michael had secretly stashed, he clearly appreciated the gesture and the opportunity to reminisce with some fellow Danes. In circumstances similar to Mum's final moments, on his last afternoon he experienced a vision, perhaps morphine-induced, as I entered his room.

'Is that you, Aggie?' he whispered, looking up at me.

He became emotional, believing Mum was present in the room. I reached out, held his hands, comforted him and sat by his side until he drew his final breath. He died on 31 July 1985, leaving behind our loving family, the only family he claimed since migrating to Australia in 1951. He was 63. It was a solemn moment when I reflected upon the bizarre love triangle that had played out on Mum's and Uncle Hans's deathbeds. Mum loved Dad, Uncle Hans loved Mum, and Dad was too much in love with himself to love anybody else.

Although Uncle Hans had made arrangements for his burial, there was a shortfall in funds for the funeral costs. Terry and I made a decision to bury Uncle Hans in the same plot as Mum at the Mount Isa cemetery. Being agnostic, Uncle Hans had requested a simple graveside ceremony without a priest or prayers. Terry delivered a carefully chosen reading from Shakespeare's *Julius Caesar* (Act V, Scene V) that summed up the true gentleman Uncle Hans was: 'Only he acted from honesty and for the general good. His life was gentle, and the elements mixed so well in him that Nature might stand up and say to all the world, "This was a man."'

As the coffin was lowered, I could not restrain from smiling as I recalled Mum's wicked wit from a conversation at Port Douglas many years before.

'I hope my boyfriends die before me,' she quipped. 'They've been on top of me most of my life; I want to be on top of them for a change.'

Sorry, Mum!

Not long after Uncle Hans's funeral, Dad's Irish temper resurfaced. Once again it was ironic that while he never offered one cent of support for Mum's funeral, he now offered to pay the costs of exhuming Uncle Hans's coffin and having him placed in a separate plot: the gall of the 84-year-old bastard! I respectfully declined his offer.

—

Father Cassian continued to play an active part in my life. He visited Mount Isa on several occasions even though he lived a considerable distance away, at the Franciscan friary in Townsville's West End, where he served as the Catholic chaplain at the General Hospital. He eventually became the chaplain at the Mater Hospital in Brisbane.

Dad was the next to move to Mount Isa when he 'jumped ship' in 1986. At the time, he was living with Glenda and her partner, Mick Kelly, in Derby, Western Australia. Glenda was the owner-operator of a thriving TAB franchise. Juggling her new relationship with Mick, managing a booming small business and taking care of Dad had become too burdensome for her. We'd arranged for Dad to move to the Good Samaritan Nursing Home in Cairns. En route to Cairns, Dad and Glenda had a brief stopover in Mount Isa during the long drive from Derby as Glenda's daughter, Jeannie, her husband, Rod, and four children were also living in Mount Isa at the time. Now 85, Dad had limited mobility and sometimes required the use of a wheelchair.

Initially, Dad had no desire to stay in Mount Isa, and nor did he have plans to go into a nursing home. Being a selfish, manipulative old codger, he attempted to divide Glenda's loyalties by having her choose between him and Mick Kelly. When his tactics failed, he decided to stay with us.

Irrespective of Dad's conduct, we welcomed him into our home. We modified the bathroom by installing rails and put a bench in the shower cubicle so he could sit while showering. My family became Dad's private army of personal carers. He was pampered to say the least, being well fed, having his laundry done and also being served his daily bottle of chilled Guinness Stout.

'Guinness Stout prevents gout,' he often said.

On occasions, Dad refused to shower himself. He coaxed Adam to wash him twice a day, dabbing his body with methylated spirits to ward off skin sores, and brushing the mashed Weet-Bix out of his false teeth after breakfast. In contrast with Uncle Hans's placid, unassuming nature, Dad was a demanding guest. No matter what, he was impossible to please. And, although living with us, he fretted constantly for Glenda. The situation became untenable when Glenda phoned one evening and told us that Dad had been writing and calling her to complain about the family mistreating him. Luckily, an amicable solution presented itself, courtesy of Mum and Uncle Hans.

Over the years, the large shed adjoining our house had innocently morphed into being called 'Heaven's Cloakroom' on account of Uncle Hans and Mum both having checked in their bags before moving on. The shed contained an assortment of baggage, ports and personal items that belonged to Mum and Uncle Hans, in addition to other small boxes and folders containing personal letters and cards. It was a hoarder's paradise. Still is! Occasionally, I look through the bags, touching one of Mum's treasured garments, or reading through some letters and cards, and amid the musty smell of memories, I have a sentimental little cry.

It was not long after Glenda called that Dad asked if we could store some of his surplus belongings in our 'cloakroom'.

'Are you sure about that?' I asked, laughing. 'It's where Mum's and Uncle Hans's luggage is stored. It's like a great cloakroom to the sky, the place where departing family check-in their bags before moving on to see God or wherever they go.'

Dad was reluctant to complete the trifecta. Mulling over his own mortality and fearing he would be the next to die if he stayed with us, he promptly decided to return to Cairns. Not long after, his declining health and diminished capacity to live independently led to him being placed into full-time nursing home care. He passed away two days after my birthday on 23 August 1994. He was 92.

Despite Dad's imperfections and selfishness, and the anger I harboured against him, I made peace with him a long time ago. I was grateful to get to know and love him unconditionally prior to his death. With growing maturity and the passage of time, I have learnt to accept other people's failings, as well as my own, although it's not always been easy to restrain the bitterness in my heart. With Dad, I was able to overcome my feelings of resentment, allowing me to love the unlovable and separate the sinner from the sin.

32

LETTERS FROM MUM

In 1996, I submitted a Freedom of Information (FOI) application to the Queensland Department of Families and Community Services for copies of the government files relating to the institutionalisation of my siblings and me in Townsville and on Palm Island. I requested the files to help the five of us to prepare for our appearance before the National Inquiry into the Separation of Aboriginal & Torres Strait Islander Families in Cairns later that year. This inquiry resulted in the *Bringing Them Home Report (1997)*, in which our story is partly told.

At the time of lodging the information request, I expected to receive a small dossier – not the 300 pages of combined family files that arrived by post. The files contained official correspondence, our removal and committal orders, school reports and internal memos spanning two decades. Turning the pages and reading the files was like reopening old wounds as pieces of the puzzle of our lives began to fall into place. I still become distressed when I refer to the files and read the judgmental, racist, incorrect and hypocritical comments made by officials in those times.

As I flicked further through the pages of our files, I paused intermittently to have a cry, then composed myself while restraining waves of fresh anger and disbelief. What I saw at length took me by complete surprise. Lying among the bureaucratic papers were two letters Mum had written to us more than 38 years before, on 15 October 1958, within four days of our being removed from her care in Cairns. We never received those letters. The State Children's Department had destroyed the original handwritten letters but transcribed and typed the content and placed them on file, along with the official departmental responses.

My Darlings,

How are you and do you like your new home? I miss you all very much and I am coming to Townsville, Patsy. Tell Johanne, that we are to live there, soon as we can get a place suitable. Uncle Kai is working on the wharf at Townsville now, and I am living with Dad and Aunty Eil.

Lorraine has got Bjørn now and he will get looked after. Dad is selling the house at White Rock as I don't want to live here anymore. If they allow visitors Uncle Kai will go to see you.

Dad and Aunty Eil will take Mum by car, when he can get a house or a flat.

I know it's a nice place you're at and Baby Elin, do they let you see her? How is she? Is she putting on weight? I don't think I will know her when I see her again. Johanne, you sing all those songs you used to sing to her.

Write and tell Mum all about yourself and the home, as I like to know if you have any new playmates. Uncle Frank was here yesterday and he said he will be down to see you when he passes through one weekend.

Well darlings, I can't think what else as I haven't been out. So until I see you all again, May God bless you and watch over you for me. All my love XXXXXX

Your fond mother

A. Eggertsen

X (Special) for Elin

—

Hello Terry & Michael,

How are you? Do you like it down there? It won't be long be long before Mum will be coming down to see you all. I miss you all very much but I know it's a nice place there, as Aunty Etta lives in Townsville and she told me.

Have you any new friends and Michael, I bet they can't beat you in boxing. Uncle Hans is coming on Thursday to take the boat back to Bloomfield. I know he will be very mad at Mum and Uncle Kai. I am living with Dad and Aunty Eileen at Scott St. Dad is selling the house at White Rock. Michael, Bjørn is with Lorraine and is well looked after.

Well, Terry and Jumbo, I will let you know by next mail what day I'll be down as Dad and Aunty Eil are taking me down by car.

Felix, Tom and Jerry are all right. Do they let you see the baby sometimes? Has she any teeth yet? Do you see Patsy and Johanne?

Yes you will get a surprise on Sunday so be good boys and watch out for visitors. Well, all my love to you all.

May God bless you and watch over you.

XX Your loving Mum,

Agnes Eggertsen.

Tell Mum if you are allowed anything to be sent to you.

—

15th October, 58

Mrs A.P. Eggertsen
Scott Street
CAIRNS

Dear Mrs Eggertsen

Your letters, which arrived today, for your children are being handed on to them at the State Receiving Home, 42 Warburton Street, North Ward, Townsville. You may write to them at that address and they will reply.

However, I must ask you to not include in your letters any subject which may tend to unsettle them.

They have settled down quite well here, and are attending school. All in good health with the exception of the baby who had a heavy cold when she arrived. After medical examination she was admitted to hospital and the latest information is that her condition is good and there is not the slightest need of alarm.

Visitation to the children is only once every four weeks and there is no point in your coming to Townsville this coming weekend. A permit should first be obtained from this office.

If you would supply the name and address of the relatives in Townsville, perhaps we could arrange for them to see the children. We would also like to see Mr Eggertsen who apparently is working here.

We have already written to the Police asking them to ascertain from you what immunisations the children have received in respect of diphtheria, whooping cough, tetanus and poliomyelitis. Any immunisation cards in your possession you might set aside for the information of the Police Officer.

Yours faithfully
District Officer

Handwritten note on file: K Eggertsen says her Father in Darwin – Filipino. Her mother dec'd – Torres Strait Islander. Glendon (Irishman) father of 3 eldest. He does not know who is Johanne's father.

—

It took some time for me to fully absorb these letters and what they signified. Eventually, the sadness which accompanied their discovery was replaced with joy born of a renewed understanding and confirmation of Mum's love for us. Her words had some healing effect for Terry and Michael, both of whom still harboured deep resentment toward her even long after her death. The fact Mum had written so soon after our separation and made numerous attempts to visit us was indicative of the depths of her love.

No records existed to support Dad's ongoing assurances that he had hired 'the best lawyers in town' to represent us. Similarly, there is no record of his ever contacting the authorities to enquire about our welfare. The State Children's Department harangued and harassed Uncle Kaj for several years with the threats of legal action and arrest to pressure him to pay maintenance for Elin's upkeep; the threats continued until his death, with Mum remitting one payment to the State after he died. Dad was not required to pay maintenance for Terry, Michael, Johanne and me.

The State officials were unjustifiably cruel in some of their statements. In one instance, a caseworker bemoans the potential difficulties in fostering one of my siblings to a new home on account of being 'coloured and by no means an attractive child'. In another letter, the Department expresses its disapproval of one potential foster parent because her house was frequented by a number of Aboriginal families who were 'militant Black Power advocates and likely to be most uncooperative'. Mum would have felt smug, however, if she knew the bureaucrats described her as a 'superior type for a coloured woman'. She would have attributed this to her convent education.

In August 1996, Terry, Johanne, Michael, Elin and I, along with my eldest daughter, Nyree, and other family members, attended a hearing before the *National Inquiry into the Separation of Aboriginal & Torres Strait Islander Families* to present our story. Our session was held at the Holiday Inn, Cairns, before Mick Dodson and other representatives from the Human Rights and Equal Opportunity Commission (HREOC).

'I don't know what category our family fits into; however, I know we must fit somewhere,' I said in my opening address.

Unlike many of the accounts and case studies presented before the commission in which people maintained they were separated from their families on the basis of colour and race, our story offered another scenario. We were removed on the grounds of neglect from an already 'assimilated' family environment. Our perceived 'Aboriginality' later became the deciding factor in our welfare, placement and subsequent maltreatment by the State.

I often wonder about the extent to which the Edmonton police targeted Mum in the week prior to our removal. At our hearing on 9 October 1958, Constable Stan Whyte advised Magistrate Hickey that Mum was arrested on two days, 2 and 7 October, for being drunk and disorderly. It seems curious that she was charged with two public drunkenness offences in the same week. With the exception of one obscene language charge in March 1945, no evidentiary documentation has been found to support the allegations that Mum had been charged with similar offences in the past.

Did the punishment fit Mum's supposed crime? As children we paid a heavy price because Terry and Michael stole £1's worth of firecrackers from our neighbour, Mrs Felingham, and made some unauthorised phone calls from her landline. Apart from Mum having no legal representation, what judicial consideration was given to allowing Terry's confession as a minor to form part of Constable Whyte's deposition?

The neglect charges were based on the number of meals we received, the type of clothes we wore and the conditions in which we lived. Although the legal definitions of 'neglect' are contained in Section 1, Part 4 of the *Queensland State Children Act (1911)*, no law could measure the strength of our family's emotional bond, our togetherness or the depth of Mum's love for her children despite her imperfections. We were simply caught in the scrutiny that befell our domestic situation.

Attempts by Adam during the research for this book to contact Constable Whyte were unsuccessful, although we'd heard rumours that he was still alive and living in Normanton, Queensland. Adam eventually discovered that Constable Whyte died many years ago after serving his final stint with the Queensland Police Service in Mossman. Former colleagues, now members of the Queensland Retired Police Association, recall him as a likeable man who was 'a bit rough around the edges but his heart was in the right place'. They added, 'We also remember the accepted way of doing things back in those days varies greatly to what we expect today.'[108] Constable Whyte, believing he was making the right professional decision at the time, acted accordingly. I never judged him.

Likening my experience to that of a 'wounded healer', I went on to support other individuals through my short-term employment as a Stolen Generations Counsellor with the Townsville Aboriginal and Islander Health Service in 2009. Perhaps not surprisingly, many Palm Islanders were among my clients.

I occasionally meet people who believe I should, somehow, be thankful for my separation. 'You wouldn't have received an education!' they say. 'You would not be the successful person you are today if you hadn't been removed.' The most common is, 'It's time to move on and stop living in the past.' Unfortunately, it is often not so much a case of our living in the past but, through traumatic circumstances, the past living in us. There seems no point speculating about what could or might have been. The reality is my siblings and I suffered terribly as a result of the paternalistic policies and practices of our time. The abuse and trauma we endured under the State's 'care and protection' was far, far worse than anything Mum could have done to us.

For whatever reasons, some members the Aboriginal and Torres Strait Islander community have been the least accepting of my indigeneity. Innumerable times, I have been branded a 'coconut' (pejorative term used to describe someone who is brown on the outside and white on the inside), an 'uptown nigger' (a slur to define someone who thinks they are a cut above other Aboriginal people) and an 'Uncle Tom' (a slur to define someone considered excessively obedient or servile to white people) by my detractors. As I matured, became more certain of my place in the world and gained self-acceptance, the potency of such words and judgment dissipated.

In 2014, Nobel Peace Prize winner and prominent peace activist Archbishop Desmond Tutu supported calls for Australia to hold its own version of South Africa's Truth and Reconciliation process to 'lay bare the horrors of the past' suffered by Aboriginal people and Torres Strait Islanders followed by a national healing process for all Australians.[109]

I support this approach, believing – as I have said earlier – sunlight to be the best form of disinfectant.

The journey towards forgiveness and reconciliation has often been thwarted, as far as I can see, by the intolerance of some of my own people through their judgmental rejection of people's identity. Not only do I, as a fair-skinned Indigenous person, have to deal with the effrontery of conservative social commentators but I must also endure the name-calling and rejection from my 'own'. I have been in the unfortunate position of being 'not black enough to be black' and 'not white enough to be white', forced into the middle ground and having to explain myself to both sides.

'I haven't had a perfect life but I have had a perfectly good life!' has become my preferred quip when responding to questions about my separation and life experiences. On the surface, my siblings and I appear to have lived successful lives; we own our homes, are gainfully employed, and are law-abiding and tax-paying citizens. But the personal cost for us remains deeply concealed. Terry has been diagnosed with paranoid schizophrenia and has attempted suicide on numerous occasions; Michael battled with alcoholism for more than fifteen years although remained sober for decades; Johanne required professional psychological and psychiatric care in her earlier days.

The State Government files have been useful over the years to help my siblings and I right some of the injustices we endured while under State care. In 2006, Terry, Michael and I were among the 5,779 Aboriginal and Torres Strait Islander residents in Queensland to receive a formal apology and nominal reimbursement from the Queensland State Government in lieu of our 'Stolen Wages'. I recall the bitter irony of the Queensland Government hounding me to repay a 20-cent debt between 1971 and 1972. I still consider this a debt that I did not owe.

33

REMEMBERING ROY HENRY BARTLAM

In the words of an unknown sage, 'History depends on who writes it.'

Former Palm Island Superintendent, Mr Roy Henry Bartlam, has been a soft target for condemnation following his death in 1982 and Mrs Bartlam's in 1986. Much of the negative sentiment toward Mr Bartlam emanates from his role in the well-referenced Palm Island strike of 1957. Regrettably, little has been written of his legacy and achievement beyond that event.

Mr Bartlam was Palm Island Superintendent from 1953 to 1967, and he remains a much maligned and controversial figure in Aboriginal and Torres Strait Islander history. In some recent accounts of Palm Island's history, Mr Bartlam is portrayed as despotic, brutal and controlling. He has been branded 'heartless', 'a bastard', 'the Red Emperor' and 'Tomato Face'. Other critics compared him to Hitler, running a Gestapo-style prison camp while obsessed with order and cleanliness.[110] Such unflattering descriptions grew legs and walked into the pages of online articles, journals and books, as well as, in 2007, the Australian Parliamentary Hansard in which 'Mr Bartlam was said to be notorious for his sadistic punishments.'[111]

At the risk of being labelled Mr Bartlam's apologist or as suffering from Stockholm Syndrome, and not wanting to idealise him in death beyond what he was in life, these accounts are at odds with the dedicated man I grew to know, love, respect and regard as a father figure. His scorecard as Palm Island Superintendent is not without blemish, and nor was he without personal flaws and faults.

But I wonder how many prejudices are born of hearsay? I write purely from the prism of my own experience and continued personal association with the Bartlam family, with whom I formed an enduring, lifelong bond after leaving Palm Island in 1966. Mr and Mrs Bartlam's affirming guidance nurtured me in all those terrible years during Mum's absence.

Much like a student forging a long-term friendship with their school principal, my being a Ward of the State under Mr Bartlam's care created a permanent chasm in our relationship born of his authority. As an adult, I was uncomfortable when he encouraged me to call him Roy and not Mr Bartlam. I was able to forge a deeper, somewhat warmer bond with Mrs Bartlam on account of us both being women, mothers and wives. But nevertheless, I appreciated them both for their firm guidance and tutelage.

Terry and I shared part of our honeymoon period with the Bartlams in Townsville following our marriage in 1969. Previous to this, my brothers Terry and Michael and I were welcome visitors to their family home at Mermaid Beach, where they settled upon their retirement. My children knew Mr and Mrs Bartlam as Pop and Nanna. I corresponded with Mrs Bartlam for many years, and learnt of Mr Bartlam's passing in 1982 when Mrs Bartlam wrote an account of his death from a massive heart attack. She expressed her feelings of loneliness and grief at having lost her lifelong companion; they'd been married for 44 years.

I shared Mrs Bartlam's sorrow. I have fond memories of hosting the Bartlams in Canberra and remember Mrs Bartlam sitting on my couch crocheting warm clothes for my children. She helped out with the children, not only changing nappies but also showing me different folding and pinning styles. She shared her treasured family recipes with me.

On occasion, we also indulged Mr Bartlam's love of fly-fishing along the Molonglo River, where we picnicked. Funnily, the only time I saw Mr Bartlam's temper was on a golf course in 1969 when we co-partnered using a Stableford style of scoring; my inexperience was the only handicap that day, much to his frustration and annoyance.

For some, Mr Bartlam was intimidating in the extreme, the devil incarnate; for others, he was a softly spoken, gentle giant. For me, Mr Bartlam was a true visionary, standing firmly at the helm of Palm Island's thriving community during its most productive period in the 1960s.

Mr Bartlam developed a pipeline to further training and employment from the island that was connected to attendance at elite boarding schools in Charters Towers. Scholarships were established. Matriculation to universities and other formal education was provided. Work placements and training opportunities were available to all residents, especially women, in Brisbane, further south and on cattle stations throughout Queensland.

Mr Bartlam remains the common denominator in many of Palm Island's success stories from the 1950s to early 1970s. Some of Australia's finest Aboriginal leaders and role models emerged during Mr Bartlam's time, Australia's first Aboriginal Senator and Member of Parliament, Neville Bonner, among them. When I served with Neville on the Queensland Indigenous Advisory Council from 1996 to 1998, we had many discussions about the Palm Island days and socio-political developments at the time. Neville said he understood and appreciated the progressive contribution Mr Bartlam had made to the island, even if they did not always agree.

In 1959, another Palm Islander, Mick Miller, became one of the first Aboriginal teachers to graduate in Queensland. Considered an Aboriginal statesman, Mick went on to assume a number of leadership roles including being a commissioner with the former Aboriginal Development Commission (ADC). Phillip Stewart mirrored Mick Miller's success in graduating as another of the first Indigenous teachers in the State of Queensland.

In 1974, Iris Clay became the first female board member of Aboriginal Hostels Limited, a highly significant achievement at the time. Mr Flynn Wallace was among the first Aboriginal recruits, if not the first, to the Royal Australian Navy. Palm Islanders Muriel Morgan, Marie Saylor, Sylvia Conway, Pamela Bligh, Ellen Johnston and Dawn Johnston were in the first generation of Aboriginal nurses in the state, the majority of whom went to Brisbane for training.

When I was employed as a Stolen Generations counsellor at the Townsville Aboriginal and Islander Health Service, on several occasions I visited Palm Island to assist clients with family history research. Many of these were former dormitory girls and they usually lamented the deterioration of the island's social standards and often commented how much better conditions were in the old days. I recall a scheme introduced by the Department of Native Affairs that enabled several responsible families to pursue their education and employment opportunities on the mainland. Those families who encountered difficulties during the transition requested a return to Palm Island, which Mr Bartlam accepted.

Irene remembers the Bartlam's well too:

A lot of people had bad experiences with Mr Bartlam, but our family wasn't one of them. Both Mr and Mrs Bartlam couldn't do enough for my family. They had a very human side to them, in spite of what others may think.

Matron Bartlam was a good old stick. I think most of the dormitory girls liked her. She was especially close to Janke. I think she understood Janke's plight. And, although it hadn't happened before, the higher-grade girls started to go to the Bartlam's home to do their homework. The rest of us felt a bit awkward and could hardly settle down to do homework but Janke was in her element. She socialised with Matron and her daughter Alison, sharing family histories, with Janke talking about the white side of her family. We felt Janke was favoured and we secretly resented her for that.[112]

Olive also has positive memories of the Bartlams:

They were like a second mother and father. They looked after us. They used to pick us up and take us driving. They were pretty good. He was the Superintendent for the whole community. Mrs Bartlam looked after the dormitory girls. She used to get upset if anything happened to us. They were there for years.[113]

Alison Bendall (née Bartlam), Mr and Mrs Bartlam's youngest daughter, has her own memories of Palm Island and her own thoughts on her father's legacy:

I lived with Mum and Dad on Palm Island from when I was three years old until they left, approximately fourteen years later, and then with them in Pallarenda, Townsville until I married in 1970.

The main focus of my father's tenure as Superintendent of Palm Island was to help the Aboriginal and Islander people acquire the necessary skills through education to enable them to get a job on the mainland. By acquiring skills they would create self-respect and receive respect from others, both on the Island and in the wider Australian community.

Formal education at that time, while encouraged, was not always successful, so he organised training enterprises which served a number of purposes: a more healthy lifestyle, cooperation with people from differing heritages, the training of people in the various skills required by employers and general life-skills.

These enterprises included a joinery where all manner of furniture and building was carried out, a bakery, an agricultural farm & piggery which grew produce, a timber yard, a dam project with a cattle farm built in the hills behind the settlement, a maternity and nursery unit, a boat-building yard, a sewing centre and a home-training centre. People were encouraged to make traditional craft items for display and for use. These enterprises taught many of the necessary skills to enable people to get jobs; they also provided a higher standard of living, a work ethic and a healthier life. Palm Island through the 1960s was almost self-sufficient.

My father was not a political person. He firmly believed that a person had to work to get on in life; that work provided self-respect and opportunities for advancement – things that Palm Islanders desperately needed. His own life mirrored that belief. Together with my mother, who worked as a 'Matron' in co-charge of the Girls' house, or Girls' Dormitory as it was called, the Boys' Dormitory and the Women's Dormitory with nursery attached, they worked compassionately for the better welfare and advancement of the Palm Island people.[114]

I respectfully acknowledge that some former residents, including my dormitory family, may not hold Mr Bartlam in high regard on account of their own experiences. Still, I honour him as being among the most inspirational, compassionate and caring individuals I have ever met. He influenced my life for the better. May he and Mrs Bartlam rest in peace.

GOODNIGHT OUR SUPERINTENDENT

Palm Island Women's Dormitory nightly song
With thanks to Theresa Anderson

Goodnight our Superintendent
And whites and natives too
We are here to entertain you
And do our best for you

We've songs and dance and patter
So what can be the matter?
If we help to entertain you
Then we'll be happy too

34

WE ARE GOING

My separation from Mum occurred over 60 years ago but the impact of that traumatic upheaval remains etched inside me today. Many of those who shared my life's journey have since passed away, including my younger brother Michael, who died in Cairns from cancer on 31 July 2019.

Michael battled alcoholism during the darkest years of his life, as he searched for what was taken from him, denied him and lost.

'I wasted a lifetime drinking and drifting from place to place, an aimless and purposeless life,' he once said.

Around 1993, Michael's life was upended when he suffered renal failure. His drinking came to an abrupt halt. He sought professional help and began a process of turning his life around. Michael graduated from James Cook University in 2001 with a Bachelor of Community Welfare. Mrs Hogbin proudly attended the ceremony. Michael worked for the Queensland Department of Corrective Services, counselling Aboriginal prisoners at Lotus Glen Prison situated in Far North Queensland. He later worked for the international mining company Rio Tinto in Weipa, Cape York, where he was employed as a Community Liaison Officer. Health complications eventually forced Michael into an early retirement; his golden years comprised medical appointments and attending four-hour long haemodialysis sessions three times a week at the Cairns Base Hospital.

Michael's health deteriorated rapidly in the days before his death, having been diagnosed with metastatic malignancy only a few weeks before. I flew from Mount Isa to Cairns to be by his side during his final hours. I spent the morning holding his hand and talking to him even when he couldn't respond. The treating doctor said it was if Michael was waiting for me to arrive before letting go. He died peacefully while sleeping. He was 68.

'Before we part company to continue our separate journeys through life, I want you to know that I did find something. Perhaps I did not lose it at all, that it laid buried under a lifetime of bad memories. What I found was forgiveness and a love for a mother they took away from me. Peace of mind, will I ever find it?' Michael once wrote.

Having been present with other loved ones during Michael's final hours, I can say it is my sacred belief that he did find peace of mind and heart.

Michael was cremated at his request and he did not want a funeral notice placed in the local newspaper. We honoured his wishes. A simple, non-religious service was held in the chapel of a Cairns funeral home. In observance of Torres Strait Islander custom, my sons Adam and Matthew dressed Michael in his favourite clothes and cut locks of his hair the day before the funeral. About fifty of Michael's family, closest friends and acquaintances attended his final farewell before gathering at his wake to share stories and celebrate his life. It was a simple but beautiful occasion.

The rest of Mum's brood – including my brothers John, Terry and my sisters Johanne and Elin – are all still alive and reside in various towns and cities across Australia. Our family continues to enjoy close and loving bonds, and I am in regular contact with the Glendon side of the family.

In 1993, I was reunited with Aunt Tina's daughter, my cousin Aggie Dan, her partner, Robert, and her daughter, Leytricia. I had last seen Aggie 35 years before when she farewelled us at Cairns Central Station. Aggie passed through Mount Isa on a road trip to the Gulf of Carpentaria and the Torres Strait, and we remained in intermittent contact until her recent passing in NSW.

My naval colleague and lifelong friend, Fran Loban, succumbed to bowel cancer in 2008. It was only in her final months that Fran and I discovered that Granddad Victor and her father, Ted Loban, were close mates and had enlisted in the Second World War together from Thursday Island. Mr Loban performed the eulogy at Granddad Victor's funeral in 1984. In many respects, our friendship was fated. I remain in contact with Fran's family.

Father Cassian died in September 2009, aged 84, after losing his battle with cancer. He served in the Franciscan Order for 53 years. It was difficult to farewell the man who was more of a father to me than my own biological father. Father Cassian was a permanent presence in my life for almost 50 years. His legacy endures through the life lessons of love, compassion, forgiveness and understanding, which he instilled by his lived example in myself and many others. In turn, I hope I have passed on those qualities to my own children, grandchildren, family and friends.

Bowel cancer claimed my beloved sister Glenda in December 2010, and I considered it a privilege to have been her full-time carer. My caring for Glenda was a way of returning the kindness and generosity she had shown our family when we were most in need; I only wish my gratitude could have been repaid under happier circumstances. My sister Megsy passed away in January 2010, aged 78.

Palm Island schoolteacher Mrs Beryl Hogbin passed away in October 2014. Michael, my dormitory friend Theresa Anderson and I attended her memorial service to say our final farewells and to honour her contribution in our lives.

Mum's former Sacred Heart Convent fellow pupil, Ina Titasey, passed away in November 2014, five months after completing a telephone interview for this book.

My string of bad luck with boats continued. By recent accounts, Uncle Hans's boat, the *Miss Pat* (a different vessel from the former, defaced *Piss Pot* of Palm Island), ran aground on a sandbar at Magazine Island near Port Douglas several years ago, where she gradually deteriorated.

Many dormitory girls and other Palm Islanders have died over the years. Marie Saylor died not long after my draft manuscript was listed as a finalist in the Queensland Literary Awards in 2015. So few of us remain to share the 'remember whens'.

At the time of writing, Oriel Wilson, one of the beautiful hula artistes on Palms in my time, was buried in Ayr, North Queensland. I still see some former Palm Islanders at various locations throughout the country. In January 2015, I had a chance encounter with a former dormitory resident, Bonny Noble. As she passed by, I called out her name. She looked about but continued walking. I called her name again. She responded by coming over to me. I gave her a friendly greeting and asked how she was.

'Excuse me, do I know you?' she asked quizzically.

'Hey, it's me, Patsy Janke!' I said.

'Ohhhhh, I didn't recognise you! You look like a white lady, a *migloo*,' she added, bursting out laughing.

The questions of colour still continue so many years later. Once she knew who I was, she gave me a big hug and told me how good it was to see me again after so many years.

I am still in regular contact with my Palm Island dormitory friends including Irene, Theresa, and Olive. We've been a part of each other's lives since leaving Palm Island in the 1960s.

My generation was among the last of Palm Island's Girls' Dormitory residents. A larger girls' home opened in 1965, resulting in 71 children being housed in dormitories in 1967, the year after my departure from the island. The Women's and the Girls' Dormitory structures from my era were closed in 1967 and demolished in 1969. Due to changing ideas about the care of young people, by 1975 only 27 children were housed in dormitory-style accommodation on Palm Island. All dormitories officially closed on 5 December 1975.[115]

The mainly white Palm Island Provisional School closed its doors in 1971.[116] The Townsville Receiving Depot in Townsville became known as Carramar Children's Home between 1964 and 1967, then as Carramar Receiving and Assessment Centre until it ceased operating as a State-funded institution in 1995.

Although State- and church-run Aboriginal Settlements and Missions like Palm Island no longer exist, other forms of institutionalisation have taken their place. Prisons have become something of a substitute for Boys' Dormitories. As of 30 September 2019, Aboriginal and Torres Strait Islander people comprised 28 per cent of the total adult Australian prison population, despite being only 2.5–3.0 per cent of the Australian population.[117] Women's domestic violence shelters have become the modern-day safe havens and refuges for women and their families in place of the old-style Girls' and Women's Dormitories. 'Neglected' Aboriginal and Torres Strait Islander children are still being removed from their families. One-third of Australia's Indigenous children are reportedly fostered out and living with other families. Institionalisation in State-run facilities and on Aboriginal missions has now been traded for 'out of home' care arrangements. According to the Federal Government's *Bringing Them Home Report (1997)*, 2,785 Indigenous children were removed from their families in 1997. As of 30 June 2018, 17,787 Aboriginal or Torres Strait Islander children were placed into out of home care arrangements across Australia – this is 11 times the rate of non-Indigenous children.[118]

Now a grandmother of twelve and a great-grandmother to one, I still reside in Mount Isa, where I am the Chief Executive Officer of an Indigenous Corporation that offers support services for youth and elders. My husband, Terry, is semi-retired and actively involved with the Catholic Church. He enjoys spiritual journalism and is an occasional contributor to the nation-wide *Catholic Leader* newspaper. We both received Australia Day honours in January 2017 for our significant contributions to the Mount Isa community. I was also awarded the NAIDOC Mount Isa Elder of the Year in 2018.

My children, Nyree, Cassie, Adam and Matthew, have enjoyed measures of success in their own personal and professional lives. My eldest daughter, Nyree, lives in Townsville with her husband of 30 years, Dale – they have three children and a granddaughter. Cassie lives near Byron Bay with husband, Scott, and two children. She works in the Child Protection area for the New South Wales Government. Cassie's eldest son, Brendan, lives in Melbourne and has been a drummer for renowned musicians Pete Murray and Toni Childs. My youngest son,

Matthew, is now a father of six; he still lives in Mount Isa and recently became a father to my newest grandson, Percy. Adam lives in Perth but has spent a significant part of his career living and working overseas.

I have dedicated much of my personal and professional life to addressing Aboriginal and Torres Strait Islander social and economic disadvantage. For seventeen years, I was the CEO of the West Queensland Aboriginal and Torres Strait Islanders Corporation for Legal Services. I also served for six years as a Regional Councillor for the now defunct Aboriginal and Torres Strait Islander Commission (ATSIC), from 1993 to 1999.

The highlight of my professional life remains representing the National Aboriginal and Islander Legal Services Secretariat (NAILSS) at the United Nations (UN) Commission of Human Rights, Draft Declaration on the Rights of Indigenous Peoples (Geneva, 1996), the UN Commission on the Status of Women Beijing +5 Prepcom (New York, 2000), and the United Nations General Assembly Special Session, Women (New York, 2000). I was also a delegate and presenter at the World Indigenous Women's Conference (New York, 2000).

—

I identify as an Australian of mixed-race ancestry. My identity might have evolved over the years but it remains multi-faceted. In my earlier life, I identified as Aboriginal because of my upbringing and because of my formative years spent among the dominant Aboriginal people and cultures on Palm Island. In my view, identity is shaped by our need, desire and even necessity to belong. Identity can also reflect our process of socialisation and our immediate surrounds.

My brother Terry identifies as both Torres Strait Islander and Aboriginal, while Michael identified for most of his adult life as a Murri

(Aboriginal). In an article he wrote, 'Stories for Sharing', published in *Aboriginal and Islander Health Worker Journal* in November 1995, Michael said:

> *I call myself a man of mixed descent and rightfully so. A coloured man, a dark man. Not an Aboriginal, not a Murray Islander, definitely not a white man. Neither one or the other. My dark blood, I got from my mother's side. My great grandfather Filipino, my great grandmother Aboriginal, their son, my grandfather married a Murray Island woman – grandmother. Their daughter – my mother. My father was a white man. So, my dark blood is thus Filipino, Aboriginal, Murray Island. I'm there in no-man's land what I call the middle ground. I was forced out there – I had nowhere to go.*

Like me, my son Adam identifies as an Australian and acknowledges all aspects of his ancestry. He travelled to the Philippines for three months in early 2014, actively researching our Filipino forefather Juan Blanco's family history. His adventures took him all around Panay Island in the Western Visayas region, in addition to weeks at the National Archives of the Philippines in Manila.

While researching this book, Adam unexpectedly solved a 60-year-old mystery about Uncle Kaj's first-born child, Judy Nielsen. Now living in Viby, Denmark, Judy contacted Adam in March 2014, after he uploaded Uncle Kaj's biographical information on the popular family history research site, ancestry.com. Judy had last seen her father in 1949 when she was hospitalised as a five-year-old. Uncle Kaj walked out on his life in Denmark, severing all ties and leaving no clues as to his whereabouts. As one door closes, another opens, and so he became a part of our lives in Australia.

Judy, by her own admission, has shed many tears at the bittersweet discovery. Although her father died in 1961, she was overjoyed to discover she has a sister, Elin, in addition to our large extended step-family in Australia. Although separated by distance, we remain bound by both circumstance and fate. As Judy writes:

I had not expected to find my father alive. Not at all, yet the hope of finding a family has been with me since I was very young. Only ten years ago, there was a knock on our door one Christmas Eve. Outside was an old man. My first thought was it must be my Dad, but it wasn't. It was the neighbour's Dad and he couldn't remember where his daughter lived. So the thought of finding him was never far away.

I have had a good life. I grew up with my maternal grandmother who brought me up lovingly. She also looked after my mother's first child, a girl, but she was adopted at the age of two. I have two siblings who are still alive, so in all we were four children, all with different fathers.

In 1985, I discovered the name of my older sister, but unfortunately she was no longer alive. What was worse was that she had lived in an apartment one door down from my mother for fifteen years, without either of them knowing who each other was. That also touched me deeply at the time.

Of course, my father disappeared but he didn't harm me. He and my mother didn't get on because of the drinking, and when he wasn't allowed to see me (yes, that's another story) he chose to disappear. It just happened so suddenly and without telling anybody he was suddenly gone. The story also goes – well there are many stories. One of them is that he worked for the Germans during the war, another that he worked against the Germans during the war; a third that he was wanted by the police because of cheque fraud and failure to pay child maintenance, among other things.

> *According to one story he got someone to contact his father and mother. He needed some papers because he was getting married. It is quite possible that would have been to Agnes. The person in question might have been Hans.*
>
> *I know that my father loved me dearly, and I'm therefore pleased he told his Australian family about me.*[119]

Judy and I correspond via email. I have shared my memories of Uncle Kaj with her, in addition to exchanging family history documents, including his naturalisation papers, his inquest file and other personal records about his life and migration to Australia.

Elin was also overjoyed to discover she has a sister in Denmark. She recalls her feelings about discovering her Danish family:

> *I was excited and didn't believe I had a real family somewhere … when I got a phone call from Johanne I was counting down the hours to speak to her on the phone … and when I had my holidays to go up to Brisbane I was counting the months … and to find out I have a sister Judy from Denmark it was unbelievable and surreal.*[120]

—

Mum's deep yearning to return to Murray Island never eventuated. But while in Cairns in March 2014, Adam and I made a spontaneous decision to fly to Cape York and Murray Island via Thursday Island. Recalling Mum's words about her birthplace, I decided to take the trip for her and to bring her home in spirit.

We stopped by Granddad Victor's grave at the Old Injinoo Cemetery, where we paid our respects by laying flowers and reflecting on his legacy. We continued on to the community of Bamaga, where we met 'Rusty' Williams, now 93, and his children Reg, Roger (Bolly), Fannie, Fred, Ronnie and Michael and their families. Rusty is related to me through Annie Blanco, who was his grandmother and my great-grandmother. There was an immediate bond, a wonderful sense of familiarity and deep comfort. We passed the time talking about family history, exchanging photos and old yarns about family members, completing missing branches and leaves from one another's family trees.

I was immediately drawn to Rusty, feeling a paternal, father–daughter connection. Rusty recounted his memories of Granddad Victor, Great-grandmother Annie and Mum. He told us about the time he visited Mum in Cairns in the early 1950s. Rusty and Mum were both fired upon by an overly protective private property owner as they trespassed carrying a carton of beer. We eventually met Rusty's sisters, Reenie and Fannie, who also had many memories of Mum.

The trip north provided another opportunity for us to re-connect with my niece Samara and her daughter Tatsiana on Thursday Island. We also met family members Jenny, Henrietta and Nicholas Thompson, descendants of Granddad Victor's sister, Maria Trinidad Blanco, and Mum's cousin and companion Auntie Theresa Zitha (with thanks to Ted Wymarra).

The journey to Mer took an ominous turn as Adam and I boarded the small, single engine, single pilot Cessna Caravan at Horn Island airport. Cyclone Ita was brewing, resulting in heavy torrential downpours and inclement weather. Surprisingly, the flight was not cancelled. I smiled to myself, discreetly nudging Adam after noticing a Meriam woman sitting at the table opposite. I could see glimmers of Mum in her facial features, particularly in the way she styled her hair.

I felt at ease regardless of the bumpy take-off. The Cessna pushed through the turbulent weather as heavy rain pounded the windscreen and eventually levelled out above the storm. I nodded off for a while as a result of the 4am wake-up call. It was a relief as the plane commenced its gradual descent. Mother Nature laid out a magnificent welcome mat as expansive tracts of the Great Barrier Reef revealed themselves through a break in the clouds. The sheer beauty of the Murray Islands struck me as Waier, Mer and Dauar came into full view on our final approach.

Uncle George's youngest daughter, my cousin Annie Zaro, and her husband, Burnie, met us on arrival. With feet placed firmly on hallowed ground and overwhelmed by the emotions, I hugged her tightly. This was an important personal journey.

It was a beautiful homecoming. We met our Meriam family for the first time and were warmly received by cousins Alice Kudub and John Tabo and their families. Again, we spent hours talking about family history, exchanging information, photos and discoveries. We had never seen a photo of Uncle George before.

It was unusual to hear of physical comparisons to other relatives. Until this trip I had underestimated the importance of those little likenesses in attaining a sense of family and belonging. Annie or some another relative would comment: 'You look like this relative'; 'Adam is tall like our brother Victor'; 'He has the same big build as other boys in the clan'; or 'Michael and Simeon look alike.'

It was profoundly moving to walk through Gigrid and Deau villages, where Mum and Aunt Tina were born many years before. Annie escorted us to Uncle George's plot at the Mer cemetery, where we laid flowers and paid our respects. We later visited the grave of native title champion and rights activist Eddie Koiki Mabo, interred at Las, his ancestral village.

On our final day, the clan united to prepare a bountiful farewell feast, including turtle baked in an earth oven (*kup mauri*), freshly netted Murray Island sardines and other barbecue meats, fried scones, salads and desserts.

I quietly immersed myself in the saltwater while lunch was being prepared. Children splashed and paddled about, oblivious to the tawny nurse sharks circling the dense sardine shoals nearby. Darnley Island (*Erub*), Granddad Victor's birthplace, was visible on the horizon. It was a solemn occasion, akin to a baptism in holy waters.

In a quiet moment of reflection, I imagined Mum as a young girl, splashing about, carefree, laughing and swimming near the same patch of beach where I now sat partly submerged. Glancing back to shore, I could see the family industriously chopping, cooking and arranging the banquet. I was strengthened by the acceptance and oneness in family we'd been shown. The Meriam speak of the importance of family roots (*giz)* and the place of one's origin (*giz ged*). It was heartening to know I had returned to the place where a significant part of my story began.

Mum's spirit was finally free to rest among the wind, the sea and the stars. I had fulfilled my duty to bring her back to Mer. She had finally come home through me, and I had come home through her. My journey to belonging was complete. Rising from the water, I felt an inner peace, a sense of abiding contentment.

My final task as Little Big Girl was done.

REFERENCES

1 Lawrie, Margaret Elizabeth (1970). *Myths and legends of Torres Strait.* St. Lucia, Qld: University of Queensland Press, p.301

2 Shnukal, Anna (2001). *Torres Strait Islanders.* Retrieved from http://www.multiculturalaustralia.edu.au/doc./shnukal_torres_strait.pdf, accessed June 2014

3 *ibid.*

4 State Library of Queensland (nd). *Information Awareness Torres Strait Islands.* Via content/uploads/2013/03/000210_informationawareness_tis.pdf, accessed September 2014

5 *ibid.*

6 Beckett, Jeremy (1987). *Torres Strait Islanders – Custom and Colonialism.* Cambridge University Press, p. 44

7 National Archives of Australia, *Immigration – A legacy of White Australia: Records about Chinese Australians in the National Archives,* retrieved 1 January 2015, from http://www.naa.gov.au/collection/publications/papers-and-podcasts/immigration/white-australia.aspx, accessed November 2014

8 Shunkal, Anna (2004). 'Language Diversity and Torres Strait national

identity' in *Woven histories, dancing lives: Torres Strait islander identity, culture and history* edited by Richard Davis, Acton, ACT: Aboriginal Studies Press, pp.107–123

9 Loos, Noel & Mabo, Edward (2013). *Edward Koiki Mabo: his life and struggle for land rights*. St Lucia, Queensland: University of Queensland Press, p.96

10 Lamb, Barry (2012). *History of Our Lady of the Sacred Heart School, Thursday Island 1887–2012*. Cairns, Queensland: Catholic Diocese, pp. 129–131

Gould, Monica cited in Shnukal, Anna & Ramsay, Guy & Nagata, Yuriko (2004). *Navigating boundaries: the Asian diaspora in Torres Strait*. Canberra: Pandanus Books

Titasey, Catherine (2012). *Ina's story: the memoir of a Torres Strait Islander woman*. Thursday Island, Qld: Catherine Titasey

11 QS787/1/3: 12/1/1931: Azey Blanco wife of Victoriano Blanco vs Victoriano Blanco for Leaving wife without means of support. No appearance. Case heard *ex parte*. Defendant ordered to pay maintenance [torn]. QS787/1/3: 12/1/1931: Azey Blanco vs Victoriana Blanco – leaving children Agnes (9) and Celestina (6) without means of support. Ordered to pay the sum of four shillings and sixpence weekly and every week in respect of the maintenance and support of each child

12 Sacred Heart Mission (2012). *Our First One Hundred Years – Sacred Heart Mission Thursday Island 1884–1984*. Sacred Heart Mission Thursday Island, Qld (local newsletter)

13 personal communication, 1 February 2014

14 Anna Shnukal cited in Brandle, M. & Queensland. Multicultural Affairs Queensland (2001). *Multicultural Queensland 2001: 100 years, 100 communities, a century of contributions*. Brisbane: Multicultural Affairs Queensland, Department of the Premier and the Cabinet

15 *ibid.*

16 personal communication, 1 February 2014

17 personal communication, 14 September 1996

18 personal communication, 13 June 2014

19 Haddon, Alfred Cort et al (1898). *Reports of the Cambridge Anthropological Expedition to Torres Straits.* Volume VI Sociology, Magic and Religion of the Eastern Islanders, Cambridge: University Press, p.233

20 Dan, Henry & Neuenfeldt, Karl William et al. (2013). *Steady steady: the life and music of Seaman Dan.* Canberra, ACT: Aboriginal Studies Press

21 National Archives of Australia NAA: A1, 1925/18737 – Janke, Johann Ludwig – Application, Naturalisation Certificate

22 *ibid.*

23 Queensland State Archives SRS 505/1 Box 259 1D/49 [also QS 505/1 1D/49]: *Particulars of coloured Thursday Island Evacuees in the Babinda District* [4/1942]

24 *Townsville Daily Bulletin* (1949). 'Two Divorce Pleas Succeed'. Saturday, 16 July 1949, p. 3

25 *Brisbane Courier Mail* (1882). 'Shipping Information'. Friday, 14 July, p.2 via http://trove.nla.gov.au

26 *Cairns Post* (1944). 'Liquor Forfeiture Cases'. Thursday, 21 December, p.4

27 *Cairns Post* (1944). 'Alleged Sly Grog. Cairns Prosecution'. 13 September, p.4

Cairns Post (1944). 'Alleged Sly Grog. Evidence for Defence'. Saturday, 23 September, p.4

Cairns Post (1943). 'Woman Charged. Alleged Illicit Sale of Liquor'. Wednesday, 13 October, p.2

Cairns Post (1943). 'Alleged Sly Grogging'. Saturday, 11 September, p.4

Cairns Post (1943). 'Alleged Sly Grog'. Friday, 24 September, p.4

Cairns Post (1943). 'Imprisoned for Eight Hours'. 27 October, p. 2

28 *Cairns Post* (1935). 'Fire Enquiry'. Saturday, 16 March, p. 6

29 personal communication, 1 April 2014

30 *Cairns Post* (1937). 'Double Drowning In Mossman River, Father and Daughter Victims'. Tuesday, 12 January, p.6

31 *Cairns Post* (1950). 'Woman Committed For Trial On Charge of Willful Murder. Sequel to Cairns Man's Death'. 12 April, p.5

32 *ibid.*

33 *Brisbane Courier Mail* (1950). 'Not guilty: wept'. Saturday, 29 July, p.3

34 Queensland State Archives Item ID 349791 2, Inquest File No. 97/1951 for Gordon Keith Tooth

35 *ibid.*

36 *ibid.* pp: 28–34, 40–48, 52–54

37 *Cairns Post* (1951). 'Washed Over Tully Falls – Young Man's Death'. 16 January, p. 5

38 *Queensland Times* (1954). 'Body Found at Foot of Tully Falls'. (Ipswich, Qld) July 7, 1954 p.6 Edition: Daily. http://nla.gov.au/nla.news-article118258591, accessed April 16, 2015

Townsville Daily Bulletin (1939). 'Tully Falls Death'. Qld November 27, p.2. Via http://nla.gov.au/nla.news-article62828531, accessed April 16, 2015

39 *Cairns Post* (1951). 'Judgments Nisi Granted'. Monday, 22 October, p.2

40 *Townsville Bulletin* (1952). 'Defendant To Pay Dishonoured Cheque Claim'. Wednesday, 5 March, p.1

Cairns Post (1952). 'Woman Ordered To Pay £150. Dishonoured Cheque Claim. Security in Mine Negotiations'. Wednesday, 5 March, p. 5

41 Queensland Department of Aboriginal, Torres Strait Islander & Multicultural Affairs. *Cultural Diversity in Queensland*, retrieved 2 January 2015, from http://www.qldmigrationheritage.com.au/wp-content/uploads/2012/10/Danes.pdf, accessed June 104

42 National Archives of Australia NAA: BP25/1, EGGERTSEN K A S – DANISH

43 Queensland Parliament (1962). *Queensland Parliamentary Debates (Hansard). Thursday, 1 November 1962.* QGPS: Brisbane, Qld, pp.1245–46

44 *ibid.* p. 1253

45 personal communication, 18 April 2015

46 personal file

47 personal file

48 *Sydney Morning Herald* (1929). 'Palm Island – Abo's Paradise'. 29 June, p.11

49 Galvin, Nick (2012). *Sydney Morning Herald.* 'Paradise Lost'. http://www.smh.com.au/entertainment/theatre/paradise-lost-20121108-28z8c.html, accessed November 2014

50 State Library of Queensland. *Aboriginal & Torres Strait Islander missions and reserves in Queensland*, retrieved from http://www.slq.qld.gov.au/__data/assets/pdf_file/0018/82602/missions_and_reserves.pdf, accessed June 2014

51 personal communication, 30 March 2015

52 Alrc.gov.au (2015). *Changing Policies Towards Aboriginal People | ALRC.* http://www.alrc.gov.au/publications/3.%20Aboriginal%20Societies%3A%20The%20Experience%20of%20Contact/changing-policies-towards-aboriginal, accessed 14 April 2015

Humanrights.gov.au, (2015). *Bringing them Home – Chapter 5 | Australian Human Rights Commission.* https://www.humanrights.gov.au/publications/bringing-them-home-chapter-5, accessed 14 April 2015

53 National Archives of Australia (NAA): A432, 1963/3171 Australian Aborigines – Assimilation. *The Honourable Paul Hasluck, M.P., Assimilation in Action. Statement in the House of Representatives.* Canberra, Wednesday, 14th August 1963, p.4

54 National Archives of Australia (NAA): NAA: A452, 1958/4514. *Government plans for assimilation of the Aborigines of the Northern Territory*, article by KG Kennedy [1cm], pp.7, 21

55 Jones, D. (2009). 'Albert Namatjira: fame but not freedom'. *The Australian*, retrieved from http://www.theaustralian.com.au/news/albert-namatjira-fame-but-not-freedom/story-e6frg6n6-1225753137323, accessed May 2014

56 Australia. Parliament, (1961). *The records of the proceedings and the printed papers Report from the Select Committee on Voting Rights of Aborigines Palm Island Hearing. 9 June. Statement by Roy Henry Bartlam*: pp. 1533–1541

57 *ibid.*

58 cifhs.com. (2014). *Centre for Indigenous Family History Studies (Queensland Removals 1912–1939),* retrieved from http://www.cifhs.com

59 Elder, Bruce (1988). *Blood on the wattle: massacres and maltreatment of Australian Aborigines since 1788*. Frenchs Forest, NSW: Child & Associates, p.176

60 Long, Jeremy Phillip Merrick (1970). cited in Royal Commission into Aboriginal Deaths in Custody & Johnston, Elliott, 1918–2011 (1991). *Report of the Inquiry into the Death of Vincent Roy Ryan National report.* Australian Government Publishing Service, Canberra

61 Queensland State Archives Item ID 716316, The Aboriginal Regulations, 1945

62 National Archives of Australia: NAA: A2354, 1969/264 *Palm Island,* pp.160–161

63 Hughes, R. (1992). *Neville Bonner – Interview Transcript, Australian biography.gov.au*, retrieved from http://www.australianbiography.gov.au/subjects/bonner/interview2.html, accessed August 2014

64 Queensland State Archives Item ID1671219 – ID167123, *Police Charge*

Bench Book (1963–69)

Queensland State Archives Item ID 504903, *Palm Island – Detention – Types of Punishment – Dormitories (1941–1963)*

65 *ibid.*

66 Queensland State Archives Item ID *716316, The Aboriginal Regulations*, 1945

67 Queensland State Government, Palm Island File, *Third Party Extract – Palm Island Wards of the State*. 22 December 1960 8A/19, p. 32

68 Sibley, Jack & Connors, Phillip (1999). *Jack Sibley interviewed by Phillip Connors in the Bringing them home oral history project*. http://nla.gov.au/nla.oh-vn290757, accessed May 2014

69 *Townsville Daily Bulletin* (11 Jan 1955). 'Victim of Axe Attack, Young Woman Alleges'. p.2. http://trove.nla.gov.au/ndp/del/article/62534839, accessed June 2014

70 NAA: A2354, 1969/264, *Palm Island* p.46

71 personal communication, 4 May 2014

72 personal communication, 30 March 2015

73 Michael, Keiran & Connors, Phillip (1999). *Keiran Michael interviewed by Phillip Connors in the Bringing them home oral history project*. http://nla.gov.au/nla.oh-vn229876, accessed June 2014

74 personal communication, 14 May 2014

75 personal communication, 30 March 2015

76 personal communication, 26 February 2015

77 Hooper, Chloe (2008). *The Tall Man*. Camberwell, Vic: Hamish Hamilton, p.53

78 personal communication, 30 March 2015

79 personal communication, 27 June 2014

80 personal communication, 30 March 2015

81 McMahon, P. Searle, C. & J. (2009). *Father Cassian's Eulogy*. 17 September, Church of St Therese and St Anthony: Nudgee, Brisbane

82 personal communication, 30 March 2015

83 personal communication, 4 March 2014

84 personal communication, 30 March 2015

85 National Inquiry into the Separation of Aboriginal and Torres Strait Islander Children from their Families (Australia) & Wilson, Ronald & Australia. Human Rights and Equal Opportunity Commission (1997). *Bringing them home: report of the National Inquiry into the Separation of Aboriginal and Torres Strait Islander Children from their Families*. [Sydney]: Australian Human Rights Commission, p.78

86 Queensland State Archives Item ID 10388, Returns – Schools: Palm Island Settlement State School

87 Queensland State Archives Item ID 390112, Administration File – Palm Island State School

88 personal communication, 30 March 2015

89 Hogbin, Beryl & Somersall, Deborah (1999). *Beryl Hogbin interviewed by Deborah Anne Sommersall in the Bringing them home oral history project*. http://nla.gov.au/nla.oh-vn1808375

90 personal communication, 21 July 2014

91 Brady, D. (1979, January 10). 'Back from Palm Is. Natives are afraid to be free: Pastor'. *Courier Mail* cited in National Archives of Australia: NAA: A2354, 1969/264 *Palm Island*, p.9

92 Kidd, Rosalind (2000). *Black lives, government lies*. Sydney: UNSW Press, p.51

93 Michael, Keiran & Connors, Phillip (1999). *Keiran Michael interviewed by Phillip Connors in the Bringing them home oral history project*. http://nla.gov.au/nla.oh-vn229876, accessed June 2014

94 personal communication, 18 January 2014

95 personal communication, January 2015

96 Queensland State Archives Item 1D3500113, Inquest File No. 106/1962 for Kaj Aron Svend Eggertsen

97 *ibid.*

98 *ibid.*

99 personal communication, 11 April 2015

100 personal communication, 18 April 2015

101 Royal Australian Navy (2015). *HMAS Albatross | Royal Australian Navy. Navy.gov.au*, retrieved from http://www.navy.gov.au/establishments/hmas-albatross, accessed November 2014

102 Armstrong, D. (1983). 'A Study in Racism: Nowra flag still smoulders'. *Sydney Morning Herald,* p.4, retrieved from http://news.google.com/newspapers?nid=1301&dat=19830211&id=h51WAAAAIBAJ&sjid=BucDAAAAIBAJ&pg=1902,2782233, accessed November 2014

103 personal communication, December 2014

104 Double, Cassian & Erskine, Barbara (1999). *Cassian Double interviewed by Barbara Erskine in the Bringing them home oral history project.* http://nla.gov.au/nla.oh-vn332044, accessed May 2014

105 personal communication, 18 January 2015

106 Frankland, Kathy (1994). A brief history of Government Administration of Aboriginal & Torres Strait Islander Peoples in Queensland, cited at http://www.slq.qld.gov.au/__data/assets/pdf_file/0008/93734/Admin_History_Aboriginal_and_Torres_Strait_Islanders.pdf, accessed June 2014

107 personal communication, 18 January 2015

108 personal communication, 31 August 2014

109 Bishop Desmond Tutu prays for the rights of Australian Aboriginal peoples on World Peace Day. (n.d.), retrieved from http://www.anglicancg.org.au/news.php/134/bishop-desmond-tutu-prays-for-the-rights-of-australian-aboriginal-peoples-on-world-peace-day

110 Watson, Joanne (2010). *Palm Island: through a long lens*. Canberra, ACT: Aboriginal Studies Press

111 http://www.lcc.asn.au/UserFiles/File/Hobart%20Airport/Airports%20Amendment%20Bill%20Hansard%2028%20March%202007.pdf, accessed August 2014

112 personal communication, 30 March 2015

113 personal communication, 26 February 2015

114 personal communication, 20 May 2014

115 Queensland Department of Aboriginal, Torres Strait Islander & Multicultural Affairs (2013). *Aboriginal & Torres Strait Islander Community Profiles: a Resource for the Courts. Palm Island*, retrieved from http://www.datsima.qld.gov.au/resources/datsima/publications/justice-resources/palm-island.pdf, accessed October 2014

116 Queensland State Archives Item ID 390112, Administration File – Palm Island State School

117 Queensland Department of Aboriginal, Torres Strait Islander & Multicultural Affairs (2013). *Aboriginal & Torres Strait Islander Community Profiles: A Resource for the Courts. Palm Island*, retrieved from http://www.datsima.qld.gov.au/resources/datsima/publications/justice-resources/palm-island.pdf, accessed October 2014

118 Queensland Department of Aboriginal, Torres Strait Islander & Multicultural Affairs (2013). *Aboriginal & Torres Strait Islander Community Profiles: a Resource for the Courts. Palm Island*, retrieved from http://www.datsima.qld.gov.au/resources/datsima/publications/justice-resources/palm-island.pdf, accessed October 2014

119 personal communication, 21 March 2014

120 personal communication, 2 February 2015